Edward B. Segel

The Ninth

The Ninth

Beethoven
and the World
in 1824

HARVEY SACHS

RANDOM HOUSE / NEW YORK

Published in the United States by Random House,
an imprint of The Random House Publishing Group, a division
of Random House, Inc., New York.

RANDOM HOUSE and colophon are registered
trademarks of Random House, Inc.

An excerpt from "Postlude" was originally published as "Beethoven Visits Cleveland" in
The American Scholar, published by the Phi Beta Kappa Society.

Grateful acknowledgment is made to the following to reprint previously published material:

CAMBRIDGE UNIVERSITY PRESS: Excerpt from *My Life* by Richard Wagner, translated by
Andrew Gray and Mary Whittall (Cambridge, UK: Cambridge University Press, 1983).
Reprinted by permission of Cambridge University Press.

HOUGHTON MIFFLIN HARCOURT PUBLISHING COMPANY: Excerpt from *Cosima Wagner's Diaries,
Volume I: 1869–1877,* copyright © 1976 by R. Piper & Co. Verlag, English translation
copyright © 1978, 1977 by Geoffrey Skelton and Harcourt, Inc.; excerpt from *Cosima Wagner's
Diaries, Volume II: 1878–1883,* copyright © 1977 by R. Piper Verlag Munchen, English
translation copyright © 1980 by Geoffrey Skelton and Harcourt, Inc. Reprinted by
permission of Houghton Mifflin Harcourt Publishing Company.

W. W. NORTON: Excerpt from *Beethoven: The Music and the Life* by Lewis Lockwood (New York:
W. W. Norton & Co., 2003) and "Das Kunstwerk der Zukunft," translated by Oliver Strunk
from *Source Readings in Music History,* edited by Oliver Strunk and Leo Treitler (New York:
W. W. Norton & Co., 1998). Reprinted by permission of W. W. Norton & Co.

PALGRAVE MACMILLAN: Excerpt from *The Letters of Beethoven,* edited by Emily Anderson
(London: Macmillan, 1961). Reprinted by permission of Palgrave Macmillan.

STANFORD UNIVERSITY PRESS: Excerpt from *Distant Pleasures: Alexander Pushkin and the
Writing of Exile* by Stephanie Sandler, copyright © 1989 by the Board of Trustees of the
Leland Stanford, Jr. University. Reprinted by permission of Stanford University Press.

THAMES AND HUDSON LTD. Excerpt from *Beethoven: His Life, Work and World* by H. C. Robbins
Landon, copyright © 1992 by H. C. Robbins Landon. Reprinted by the kind permission of
Thames and Hudson Ltd., London.

UNIVERSITY OF NEBRASKA PRESS: Excerpt from *Letters to Beethoven, Volume 3,* edited by
Theodore Albrecht (Lincoln, NE: University of Nebraska Press, 1996). Reprinted by
permission of University of Nebraska Press.

Title-page image copyright © iStockphoto.com

LIBRARY OF CONGRESS CATALOGING-IN-PUBLICATION DATA

Sachs, Harvey
The Ninth: Beethoven and the world in 1824 / Harvey Sachs.
p.   cm.
ISBN 978-1-4000-6077-1
eBook ISBN 978-1-5883-6981-9
1. Beethoven, Ludwig van, 1770–1827. Symphonies, no. 9, op. 125, D minor.
2. Music—Social aspects—Europe—History—19th century.   3. Music—Political aspects—
Europe—History—19th century.   4. Music—19th century—History and criticism.
5. Romanticism in music.   I. Title.
ML410.B4S117   2010   784.2′184—dc22   2009919716

Printed in the United States of America on acid-free paper

www.atrandom.com

2   4   6   8   9   7   5   3   1

Book design by Victoria Wong

For Julian and Lyuba

Contents

The Ninth

Prelude

Ludwig van Beethoven's Symphony No. 9 in D minor, op. 125, is one of the most precedent-shattering and influential compositions in the history of music. Its word-driven final movement is a declaration in favor of universal brotherhood, which explains why the Ninth is the work most often used to solemnize an important event—the opening of the United Nations, the signing of a peace treaty at the end of a war, the fall of the Berlin Wall, or the consecration of a new concert hall: It is perceived as a vessel for a message that confers a quasi-religious yet nondenominational blessing on all "good" and "just" people, institutions, and enterprises—in short, on "our side," whatever that may be. It has been used as a battle flag by liberals and conservatives, by democrats and autocrats, by Nazis, Communists, and anarchists. Composed during the last and most remarkable phase of Beethoven's artistic trajectory, the Ninth consolidated and elaborated on elements of his earlier creations, and transcended them. It also became a reference point and stimulus for generations of artists throughout Europe and beyond, and it continues to resonate in the parallel worlds of ideas and ideals.

Charging, or cluttering, the Ninth with such ideas and ideals, not to mention feel-good meaning, was and is possible only because the last of its four movements contains words that express aspirations toward peace on earth and goodwill toward all human beings. But the first three extended, dramatic movements of the deaf composer's symphonic masterpiece are not paeans of praise to freedom of the spirit or to all-embracing joy or to anything else. They deal in a variety of ways with intimate and extremely complex emotions and states of being. Thanks to its finale, however, the Ninth has become a paradigm for both freedom and joy, although it made its appearance in the middle of a decade in European history that was characterized by repression and ultraconservative nationalism, as Bourbons, Hapsburgs, Romanovs, and other terrified dynastic rulers strove to spruce up and enforce the concept of divine right in the wake of the French Revolution and the upstart Napoleon's imperialism. Through this single symphonic movement, Beethoven was, in effect, serving up a one-of-a-kind counterargument to the retrograde tendencies of the day; consequently, an understanding of the circumstances under which it was created reveals as much about the politics, aesthetics, and spirit of its time as it does about its composer's musical development.

Like many of the Revolution's other spiritual heirs, Beethoven had to camouflage his libertarian aspirations and pay lip service to the rulers on whose patronage he depended and for whom expressions about universal brotherhood were only too reminiscent of the ideals bandied about by the French Revolution—ideals that these rulers had only recently managed to smother. And yet, Beethoven required the singers and instrumentalists who gathered in Vienna on a spring day in 1824 for the world premiere of his new symphony to proclaim, repeatedly and insistently, the potentially subversive goal of universal brotherhood. "Alle Menschen werden Brüder" ("All men become brothers") and "Seid umschlungen, Millionen" ("Be embraced, ye millions") were the key phrases in the excerpts from an ode by Friedrich von Schiller that Beethoven set to music in the symphony's finale. The poem was called "An die Freude" ("To Joy"), but in Beethoven's transforming hands it became a subtle yet robust, unmistakable ode to and prayer for suffering humanity.

From today's perspective, the premiere of Beethoven's last symphony was the most significant artistic event in 1824, but other works and deeds by other artists expressed, in many different ways, discontent over the return of antiliberalism as a guiding principle and over the restoration of regimes that rejected the gains made not only by the Revolution but even by its predecessor, the Enlightenment. Byron, Pushkin, Delacroix, Stendhal, and Heine, among others, all played important parts in the year's cultural history. And then there were the political figures in the "real," everyday world: a fanatically religious tsar and a pope with an eye fixed on secular matters, two French kings and a South American liberator, Prince Metternich and President Monroe.

"Beethoven is the quintessential genius of Western culture," wrote Tia DeNora in her 1995 study, *Beethoven and the Construction of Genius,* which deals with the composer's first decade in Vienna. The statement sounds nice, but it is too sweeping. It would be more accurate to say that Beethoven is, among other things, an iconic figure to worshippers of a certain type of genius, whereas Michelangelo serves that purpose for others, and Mozart or Dante or Goethe or Shakespeare or Picasso or Stravinsky for still others. Many human beings need to worship someone or something, but the object of a worshipful person's worship says more about that person than about the worshipped object. Yet Beethoven and his works, and the Romantic cult of genius that his example and his legend certainly did help to foster, exerted a powerful influence on later generations of musicians, artists, and thinkers, and the Ninth Symphony in particular became a symbol of Beethoven's protean status and predominant stature. After Mikhail Bakunin, the Russian revolutionary and sometime anarchist, had heard the work for the first time, in Dresden in 1849, he told the conductor, Richard Wagner, that "if all the music that has ever been written were lost in the expected world-wide conflagration, we must pledge ourselves to rescue this symphony, even at the peril of our lives."

Many books and essays examine in great detail Beethoven's life (all or part of it), works (many or a few or only one of them), or influence (musical, cultural, or political), and I have referred to them in my notes and occasionally even in my text. But I must make a confession. I am not an authentic musicologist. I state this fact neither ashamedly nor proudly, but simply to give you an inkling of what lies ahead. My post-high-school formal education was too brief and too erratic to allow me to claim titles that others earned by doing what I was too undisciplined to do. On the other hand, by the time I made up my mind to become a full-time writer—mainly about music—I was thirty-eight years old and had a dozen years' experience as a conductor behind me, in addition to three published books on musical subjects. Whatever I know about music, I know from both the inside and the outside. When asked what my profession is, I usually say, for the sake of expedience, "writer and music historian," but "daydreamer, appreciator, and curiosity addict" would be a more accurate definition. I will try to wear all five of these hats now, as I approach Beethoven and the world in which he created his Ninth Symphony. And since part of the historian's task is to sift through the refuse of the past, what could be a better place to begin this tale than amid some trash bins in the city that Beethoven called home for most of his life?

PART ONE

A Grand Symphony with Many Voices

Reeking, rotting garbage, overflowing from bins: That is what I found when, in November 2004, I pushed open the main door of a massive but anonymous gray stone apartment building in Vienna's third *Bezirk* (district) and made my way through a hallway to an internal courtyard. The rectangular four-story building's façade bears a commemorative plaque put up by the Vienna Schubert Society on May 7, 1924—the hundredth anniversary of the premiere of Beethoven's Ninth Symphony—as well as another, more recent plaque bedecked with banners dirtied by automobile exhaust, which proclaims that the symphony's "Ode to Joy" theme has been the European anthem since 1972, when the Council of Ministers in Strasbourg officially adopted it as such. There is no museum in the building at Ungargasse 5, on the northwest corner of a busy intersection; in fact, by going through the entrance door I was trespassing on private property.

In the composer's day the address was Landstrasse 323, and the building was called the house Zur schönen Sklavin (By the Beautiful Slave Girl); Beethoven lived in it throughout the final months of the symphony's creation and until shortly after its first performance. His apartment was situated on the top floor—the cheapest one, in pre-elevator days—but he usually received friends and acquaintances at a nearby, no longer extant coffeehouse, Zur goldenen Birne (By the Golden Pear), where he spent many an afternoon. As one contemporary writer put it, "If you have something important to tell a Viennese man, you can go ten times to his apartment without finding him in, but if you know which coffeehouse he frequents you'll meet him there for sure."

Occasionally, however, people would visit Beethoven at home. Once, during the composition of the Ninth, he invited the poet Franz Grillparzer to the Landstrasse apartment to discuss an opera project; Grillparzer found Beethoven, who was ill at the time,

> lying on a disordered bed in dirty night attire, a book in his hand. At the head of the bed there was a small door which, as I discovered later, communicated with the larder and which Beethoven was, in a way, guarding. For when subsequently a maid emerged from it with butter and eggs he could not restrain himself, though in the middle of a spirited conversation, from casting an appraising glance at the quantity of the food that was being carried away—and this gave me a painful picture of his disordered household. The opera project never came to fruition, and we don't know what happened to the butter and eggs.

The composer Carl Maria von Weber visited Beethoven during the same period, and his son later recounted the father's impressions of "the dreary, almost sordid room inhabited by the great Ludwig." It was "in the greatest disorder: music, money, clothes, lay on the floor, linen in a heap on the unclean bed, the open grand piano was covered in thick dust, and broken coffee-cups lay on the table." Beethoven tossed all the

The building in which Beethoven composed the Ninth Symphony.

music off the sofa "and then proceeded to dress for the street, not in the least embarrassed by the presence of his guests." Another man present on that occasion described Beethoven's appearance:

> His hair dense, grey, standing up, quite white in places, forehead and skull extraordinarily wide and rounded, . . . the nose square, like a lion's, the mouth nobly formed and soft, the chin broad and with those marvelous dimples which all his portraits show, formed by two jaw-bones which seemed capable of cracking the hardest nuts. A dark ruddiness colored his broad, pockmarked face; beneath the bushy and sullenly contracted eyebrows, small, shining eyes were fixed benevolently upon the visitors.

Of another visit to Beethoven, presumably a few weeks later, Weber wrote to his wife that the day would "always remain a most memorable one for me" and that it was "curiously exalting to be overwhelmed with such affectionate attentions by this great man."

The Vienna of today feels like a museum, or museum-sepulchre, although, thanks in part to the arrival of so many Asian and African immigrants, it does seem a little livelier in the early twenty-first century than it did during the years of grave East-West tension. Even on sunny days a layer of sadness seems to pervade its atmosphere, as if a long winter had passed but no spring had followed. Perhaps a mild form of depression has been and continues to be transmitted from generation to generation—a result of the grayness that followed Vienna's brilliance, of the sharp cultural decline that followed its long period of splendor—notwithstanding the fact that virtually no one under the age of ninety has adult memories of the city as it was before its Jewish and leftist artists and intellectuals were kicked out or liquidated, and no one at all has adult memories of Franz Josef's pre–World War I imperial capital. Or perhaps the feeling is now bred in the bone that a city that once counted no longer counts, except as a magnificent repository of memory, and for most people, in Vienna as elsewhere, historical memory is of little importance. What matters is today's business, and in that sense Vienna seems more humdrum than brilliant.

As for music: Today's Vienna honors, and profits hugely from, the composers it barely noticed or even rejected when they were alive. Haydn, Mozart, Beethoven, Schubert, Bruckner, Brahms, Schoenberg—

the list goes on and on—have monuments, memorial sites, or full-fledged museums dedicated to them, and one can buy chocolates, T-shirts, and souvenirs of every sort with the faces and names of these and other iconic figures emblazoned on them. Tourists who couldn't distinguish Mozart's *Eine kleine Nachtmusik* from Schoenberg's *Verklärte Nacht* buy the gewgaws and feel, or so one presumes, that they will be taking something quintessentially Viennese back home with them.

Yet some of the sites of cultural tourism can arouse authentic emotions. Take, for instance, the circumspect little museum dedicated to Beethoven in the Pasqualati House on the Mölker Bastei, a pretty part of town directly opposite the monumental main buildings of the University of Vienna. The composer lived in this apartment house—which has an empty, cold feeling, like much of the rest of the city—at the height of his career, from 1804 to 1808 and from 1810 to 1814, but his fourth-floor walk-up flat contains items from various periods in his lifetime. The rooms no doubt look and smell much better today than they did when they were stuffed with his disorder and filth, and I wondered, when I visited them, whether Beethoven would have laughed had he known that people from all over the world would someday pay good money just to have a peek at the place. Or would he have been astonished, maybe even grateful, to think that people would want to see, and would perhaps even be moved by, some fairly paltry relics of his life?

In any case, if you are interested in Beethoven and are planning a trip to Vienna, by all means visit the Pasqualati House and other sites that contain Beethoven memorabilia, but don't feel obliged to visit the house on the Ungargasse in which the Ninth Symphony was completed—unless you want to spy on some twenty-first-century garbage bins. More important, don't expect to be able to visit the Kärntnertor Theater (Theater by the Carinthian Gate), where the symphony's first performance took place: It was torn down less than half a century after that momentous event. Yet as I stood near the garbage cans of the house Zur schönen Sklavin, I could easily imagine Beethoven—together, presumably, with his sometime amanuensis, Anton Schindler, and with his restless nephew, Karl van Beethoven, who was also his adoptive son—walking past this very spot, then out to the Landstrasse and over to the Kärntnertor Theater, an hour or two before the premiere. At a moderate pace the trip would not have taken more than fifteen minutes, and, depending on which route was chosen, the little group could have passed within a few yards of what is now the Beethovenplatz—Beethoven Square—a quiet, grassy spot dominated by a late-nineteenth-century statue of the scowling master seated on a pedestal and surrounded by bored-looking cherubs and twisting, heroic, winged Michelangelesque figures. Once Beethoven had reached his destination, he would have found himself caught up in the noise and bustle that precede all concerts involving substantial numbers of participants. And he would have been greeted at the stage entrance with much applause and respectful bowing: Although his works were not as popular as those of Gioacchino Rossini—the musical hero of the hour in Vienna as in many other European cities—Beethoven, at fifty-three, was the most revered living European composer. Rossini, who was then thirty-two years old, owed his enormous success to his wonderfully attractive operas and to the sheer beauty of his vocal writing; his music was brilliant but just as accessible in its day as in ours, whereas Beethoven's was brilliant but difficult—big-caliber artillery aimed at the future. Still, a concert dominated by the premieres of major new orchestral works by Beethoven automatically became a significant occasion, and as no such concert had taken place in a decade local musicians and music lovers had been anticipating the event since it had been announced, several weeks earlier.

"The latest news in Vienna is that Beethoven is to give a concert at which he is to produce his new symphony, three movements from the new mass, and a new overture," twenty-seven-year-old Franz Schubert had written to an absent friend on March 31, 1824. The new symphony was known to be much longer than any previous work in the genre and to contain choral and solo vocal parts—unprecedented in the symphonic literature. These facts raised curiosity to an unusually high level.

Beethoven had finished the colossal work a month or so before Schubert's letter was written, and on March 10, 1824, he had written to B. Schott's music publishing house in Mainz offering both "a new grand solemn mass with solo- and choral-voices [and] large orchestra . . . which I hold to be my greatest work," and "a new grand symphony, which ends with a finale (in the style of my piano fantasy with chorus, but far greater in content) with solos, and chorus of singing voices, the words from Schiller's immortal well-known Lied: To Joy."

If you are in any way creative in your work, you know the feeling of having reached a certain point with a project, beyond which you can do no more without either going mad or running the risk of causing more harm than good by further tampering. "Here I stop," you say. With terribly mixed feelings—relief and regret, confidence and insecurity, self-satisfaction and self-disgust, among others—you turn in your work, and from that moment the work takes on a life of its own, separate from yours. During a relatively brief interim period you may be able to make alterations or tighten a few nuts and bolts, on the basis of suggestions from editors or others or as a result of second thoughts of your own, but even then the work is no longer entirely yours: It has been handled by outsiders who do not know exactly what you were thinking or feeling while you were shaping it. Nor, for that matter, do *you* remember exactly what you were thinking or feeling all those days, weeks, months, or years ago. Your work is no longer yours alone.

Beethoven probably had thoughts and realizations of this sort whenever he turned a new piece over to one of his publishers. We know that he worked long and hard at most of his compositions—that he was a write, rewrite, and re-rewrite man, not a wholly spontaneous creator. His goal was "not just to create music, but to create music of the highest artistic worth," according to Beethoven scholar Barry Cooper, thus there was a great deal of "sketching and related labor," an ever-repeated attempt to "reach something unattainable." Since Beethoven knew that perfection was impossible—that he could go on for the rest of his life making changes and adjustments—he probably needed to tell himself, as he completed each of his works, "This is the best I can do now," and then send it off for performance or publication, or both.

But one can hardly keep from wondering what his thoughts were when he completed certain pieces—pieces in which and through which he had explored new paths, done things that he knew would shake up and probably puzzle the musical establishment, and in effect rechanneled the riverbed of music history. This must have been so not only in such obvious cases as the "Eroica" Symphony, with its unprecedented length; bold harmonic, rhythmic, and textural innovations; shocking beginning (the traditionally slow first-movement introduction had been compressed into two quick, powerful chords played *forte* by the entire orchestra); and more or less equal distribution of weight among the first, second, and fourth movements, with only the third to give a bit of emotional respite. It must have been true also of works such as the often-passed-over Second Symphony, whose jagged first movement—about seven minutes of music, not counting the repeat of the exposition—contains the indications *forte, fortissimo, sforzando* (reinforced, strongly accented), *forte-piano,* or *sforzando-piano* at more than 260 points, and the instruction "crescendo" at 17 points. The Second sounds euphoniously high-spirited to our ears, but in 1803, at the time of its premiere, it gave listeners some serious jolts. The critic for Vienna's high society newspaper, *Zeitung für die elegante Welt,* went so far as to describe it as "a gross monster, a hideously writhing wounded dragon that refuses to expire, and, though bleeding in the finale, furiously thrashes about with its extended tail." And there was comparable head scratching over other Beethovenian innovations: the harmonically ambiguous, meandering opening of the First Symphony; the ominous-sounding timpani, tuned in diminished fifths, in Florestan's aria in the opera *Fidelio;* the use of four light, solo timpani strokes to begin the Violin Concerto; the violent starting and stopping in the first movement of the Fifth Symphony and the merging of the third and fourth movements into a single continuum; the imitations of nature in the "Pastoral" Symphony (although in this case the precedents were many); the tempestuousness and vehemence of many parts of the piano sonatas; and above all, the unprecedented technical demands that the vast majority of Beethoven's works made on instrumentalists and singers.

When he completed the Ninth Symphony, he must have known that it would provoke equally strong or even more puzzled and astonished reactions than his earlier works had done. What, we wonder, must have run through his mind as the ink dried on the last notes, words, bar lines, and dynamic indications on the last page of the score, and as he prepared to hand it over to copyists and began to think about where first to present it to the world?

Arrangements for that presentation were eventually made and, as Schubert's letter indicates, the symphony was not the only new work on the program. The day before the concert, a bill posted at various strategic points in the city proclaimed:

Grand Musical Academy [that is, concert] by Herr L. van Beethoven, will take place tomorrow 7 May 1824, in the I[mperial] R[oyal] Court

Theater next to the Carinthian Gate. The following pieces of music are the newest works by Herr Ludwig van Beethoven. First. Grand Overture. Second. Three grand Hymns, with Solo and Choral Voices. Third. Grand Symphony, with Solo and Choral Voices entering in the Finale, to Schiller's Ode, to Joy. The solo parts will be taken by D[emoise]lles. Sontag and Unger, and Herren Haizinger and Seipelt. Herr Schuppanzigh is leading the orchestra, Herr Kapellmeister Umlauf is directing the whole, and the Music Society is doing the favor of strengthening the chorus and orchestra. Herr Ludwig van Beethoven himself will take part in the direction of the whole. Entrance prices are as usual. Boxes and single seats may be obtained on the day of the per-

Playbill announcing the Ninth Symphony's premiere.

formance at the theater's ticket office, in Kärnthnerstrasse No. 1038, at the corner house by the Carinthian Gate, on the first floor, during the usual office hours.

The "grand overture"—*Die Weihe des Hauses* (*The Consecration of the House*)—that would open the program is not one of Beethoven's masterpieces, but it contains a theme that bears an unmistakable resemblance to an important subject in the first movement of the Ninth Symphony. The "three grand hymns" that would come next were the Kyrie, Credo, and Agnus Dei sections of the *Missa Solemnis*—the great Mass that was by far the most significant piece of religious music Beethoven ever created; it had been completed the previous year but had been performed only once, in Saint Petersburg, just one month prior to the Vienna concert, and not in its composer's presence. And the "grand symphony" that came third on the program was, of course, the Symphony No. 9 in D minor, op. 125, which was, in fact, being presented for the first time anywhere.

Listeners would already have been straggling into the Kärntnertor Theater—a standard, horseshoe-shaped, Italian-style house—by the time Beethoven arrived: Seats on the main floor and in the gallery were occupied on a first-come, first-served basis; only boxes were reserved. Accounts conflict as to who participated in the event, although all the performers named in the concert announcement translated above were certainly present. Within a few years, the young soprano Henriette Sontag would become the Maria Callas of her day, idolized wherever she went. Caroline Unger, her slightly older contralto colleague, did not lag far behind in celebrity: Even Gaetano Donizetti and Vincenzo Bellini eventually wrote opera roles specifically for her. Six months before the first performance of the Ninth, Anton Haizinger had sung the lead tenor role in the world premiere of Weber's opera *Euryanthe,* which also took place at the Kärntnertor Theater; in the German-speaking world, Haizinger was already one of the best-known singers of his generation, although he was only twenty-eight. Bass Joseph Seipelt, the oldest (thirty-seven) and least well-regarded member of the vocal quartet, was a last-minute replacement for Joseph Preisinger, who had not been able to deal with the higher notes that his part demanded.

The composer's friend Ignaz Schuppanzigh, a respected forty-seven-year-old violinist who had taken part in the first performances of many

The soprano Henriette Sontag. *(From an anonymous engraving.)*

of Beethoven's chamber and orchestral works, "led the orchestra." In other words, he was probably placed on a slightly raised platform in front of the musicians, sometimes playing the violin and sometimes using his bow to give cues and other indications to the musicians. Michael Umlauf—a forty-two-year-old violinist and composer who ranked only fourth among the six music directors in the Austrian emperor's employ but whom Beethoven considered dependable—"directed the whole," which means that he, too, gave cues but was also responsible for coordinating the orchestra, chorus, and soloists. Yet the announcement also states that Beethoven would "take part in the direction of the whole"—a frightening prospect for participants and listeners alike, given the composer's deafness and the complexity of the works being presented. According to most sources, however, Beethoven's role was limited to giving a basic tempo indication at the beginning of each movement, and it is not at all far-fetched to imagine that Umlauf and Schuppanzigh instructed orchestra musicians, chorus members, and soloists not to pay attention if the composer intervened elsewhere, because he could easily have thrown the proceedings into complete disarray. (Thomas Forrest

Kelly, in a thorough and fascinating chapter on this event in his book *First Nights: Five Musical Premieres,* points out that Umlauf had already saved Beethoven from disaster at performances of other works, combining musical competence with "what must have been a gift for diplomacy.")

Some expert observers described the Kärntnertor Theater's house orchestra of forty-five players as the best professional ensemble in the city, but even if this was true the group was not large enough to fulfill the Ninth Symphony's requirements. For this concert, Beethoven demanded a large string section and two players on many of the individual wind parts, plus one timpanist and three percussionists—which would have added between 85 and 100 players, although we don't know the exact number. Some of Vienna's leading professional musicians joined the ensemble, and the best available amateur instrumentalists in town were recruited to fill out the ranks. Nor do we know the exact size of the chorus, except that it numbered between 80 and 120 singers. On May 6, at the final rehearsal for the following day's concert, the composer had stood at the theater's stage door and had embraced, one by one, each of the amateur orchestra and chorus members who were participating, gratis, in the proceedings.

Much of the program presented technical difficulties that our professional orchestras and expert choruses have long been able to solve with relative ease but that the half-professional, half-amateur forces that participated in the concert of May 7, 1824, would have found virtually insurmountable. Professional symphony orchestras did not exist in Beethoven's day; major theaters in the larger cities had house orchestras whose members also played occasional symphony concerts, but in even the best of these ensembles changes in personnel were frequent and sometimes extensive. The basic required level of accuracy and internal discipline was incalculably lower than the standard that would be achieved within the following hundred years, thanks in large part to the rapid development of the conducting profession, which was still in its infancy in Beethoven's day. Schuppanzigh attempted to teach the string players their parts in the course of a few "separate rehearsals"—sectional rehearsals, we would call them today—but there were no rehearsals for the full orchestra without the chorus. And the half-amateur chorus, whose task was, if anything, even more terrifyingly difficult than that of the orchestra, seems to have had only five or six rehearsals before it practiced together with the orchestra.

Worse still, the concert was taking place before the works on the program had been published, thus all the performers were reading from handwritten copies, many of which were hard to decipher. Some of the manuscript choral parts were lithographically duplicated, but that certainly did not improve their legibility. Beethoven's worry over this problem is practically tangible in a brusque letter that he sent to an unidentified copyist not more than ten days before the premiere:

> Copy everything exactly as I have indicated; and use some intelligence here and there. For, of course, if bars are copied on pages differently from those of the manuscript, the necessary connections must be observed; and the smaller notes too; for almost half of your notes are never exactly on or between the lines. If all the movements of the symphony are going to be copied as you have copied the first Allegro, the whole score will be useless—I need the solo vocal parts which have already been copied, and also the violin parts and so forth which have not yet been checked, so that instead of one mistake there may not be 24.

Rehearsals for the vocal soloists may have begun as early as March. Beethoven had first encountered Sontag and Unger the previous year, when they were seventeen and twenty years old, respectively, and he seems to have attempted typically clumsy flirtations with both of them. "Two women singers called on us today," he wrote to his brother Johann, "and as they absolutely insisted on being allowed to kiss my hands and as they were decidedly pretty I preferred to offer them my mouth to kiss." But early in March 1824, Schindler wrote to Beethoven that Sontag had had to cancel some of her work because she had drunk some bad wine—a gift that Beethoven had received from an admirer and had passed on to her and to Unger with no ill intentions. "She vomited fifteen times the night before last. Last night she was better. With Unger the effect was in the opposite direction. What a pair of heroines! . . . Sontag was supposed to go to the rehearsal of the Court concert yesterday morning. When she heard that she stood to lose the 24 ducats, she sent word that she had recovered from her illness and would come. Both beauties send you their regards and ask for a better and more wholesome wine in future."

When the young ladies began to go over the parts they were to sing in Beethoven's new works, their horror at the cruel difficulties imposed by his unorthodox and often downright unidiomatic vocal writing swamped their admiration for his genius. And when Beethoven refused to make changes in these parts, Unger called him a "tyrant over all the vocal organs" and added, presumably with a sigh, "Well then we must go on torturing ourselves in the name of God." But she later recalled, about those rehearsals in general and that encounter in particular:

> I still see that simple room in the Landstrasse, where a rope served as bell-pull, and in the middle a large table on which the excellent roast and that capital sweet wine were served. I see the room next door, piled to the ceiling with orchestral parts. In the middle of it stood the piano. . . . Jette [Henriette] Sontag and I entered that room as though entering a church, and we attempted (alas in vain) to sing for our beloved master. I remember my insolent remark that he did not know how to write for the voice, because one note in my part in the symphony lay too high. He answered, "Just learn it! The note will come." His words spurred me on to work from that day on.

Beethoven did provide an alternative C-sharp to a high E-natural in the bass's recitative—the symphony's first sung line—but when that expedient proved insufficient, the bass Preisinger was replaced by Seipelt, as previously mentioned. (The final score retained both versions.) Any good solo bass or bass-baritone ought to be able to sing the original high E and the various Es and Fs and even the F-sharp that occur later in the part without undue difficulty; much more problematic is the series of high F-naturals that the entire bass section of the chorus is required to sing in the passages "Seid umschlungen, Millionen!" ("Be embraced, ye millions!") Beethoven must have wanted to create a feeling of striving, of reaching for heaven, at this intense moment, and he evidently accepted the risk that a less than first-rate bass section might produce a canine howl rather than the most human of exhortations.*

---

* Pierre Boulez, during a public interview (conducted by Ara Guzelimian at the Judy and Arthur Zankel Hall, Carnegie Hall, New York, on January 17, 2008), mentioned that in writing highly virtuosic passages in his composition *Sur Incises*, what had interested him was precisely the risk factor, not the virtuosity in itself. Generally speaking, the most inventive composers write for talented performers who are willing and able to work hard and take risks.

According to Helene Grebner, a young soprano from the chorus who described the event to the conductor Felix Weingartner more than seventy years later, "Beethoven sat among the performers from the first rehearsal onwards, to be able to hear as much as his condition would permit." Weingartner's report continued:

> Her description of him is the same as the one that has been handed down to us: a thickset, very robust, somewhat corpulent man, with a ruddy, pockmarked face and dark, piercing eyes. His gray hair often fell in thick strands over his forehead. His voice, she said, was a sonorous bass; he spoke little, however, for the most part reading pensively in his score. One had the tragic impression that he was incapable of following the [sound of the] music. Although he appeared to be reading along, he would continue to turn pages when the movement in question had already come to an end.

A brand-new score that required innovatory approaches to technique; a mixture of professional and amateur instrumentalists and singers who were not accustomed to working together; vocal soloists who considered some segments of their parts unsingable; hard-to-read, error-ridden manuscript parts for players and singers alike; and grossly insufficient time for study and preparation: Under these conditions, only two rehearsals of the complete ensemble were held! One wonders whether even 50 percent of this new music could have been presented intelligibly, let alone convincingly, at the concert of May 7. Leopold Sonnleithner, an amateur musician (and the nephew of Joseph Sonnleithner, the librettist for *Fidelio*), was present at most of the rehearsals, preliminary and final, and forty years later he recalled:

> The whole symphony, especially the last movement, caused great difficulty for the orchestra, which did not understand it at first, although leading musicians . . . were playing in it. The double-bass players had not the faintest idea what they were supposed to do with the recitatives [at the beginning of the finale]. One heard nothing but a gruff rumbling in the basses, almost as though the composer had intended to offer practical evidence that instrumental music is absolutely incapable of speech.

And yet, the concert took place. Beethoven had invited the Austrian emperor, Francis I, as well as the rest of the imperial family, but they were all out of town; even Francis's brother, the Archduke Rudolph, archbishop of Olmütz—an assiduous amateur musician who had studied composition with Beethoven and was his most powerful patron—could not be present, and the royal box remained empty during the performance. The rest of the theater, however, was packed with an audience that included many of Beethoven's other aristocratic patrons, a substantial number of cultivated admirers from the bourgeoisie, and many musicians, most of whom counted as members of the lower class and were anything but upwardly mobile. Beethoven, who, in the depressed Viennese economy of the 1820s, was constantly looking for ways to raise money, had backed the event himself in the hope of earning a fair sum from it, and he must have been pleased to see a full house, for financial reasons as well as for its significance as a tribute to his art.

In our day, even people who can recall the impression the Ninth made on them the first time they heard it cannot possibly imagine what sort of effect it had on members of the audience on May 7, 1824. The symphony can move us more today than it could have affected people in 1824, in the first place because even the most modest of our professional orchestras can play it much better—thus also make it more comprehensible—than the Kärntnertor Theater orchestra could have done at the time, but also because of the simple fact that a work created long ago and that has been revered for many decades is overlaid with extra strata of emotions. The Pantheon in Rome is in itself a brilliantly constructed building, but the fact that it has stood on the same spot on earth for nineteen centuries, and our awareness that its creators continue to speak to us through it across all those centuries, contribute overwhelmingly to its impact on observers who care about such things. For us, the Ninth is both an extraordinary, living musical organism and a milestone in the history of civilization; for listeners in 1824, it had not yet taken on milestone significance, and as living musical organisms went it was a difficult one to cope with.

Nevertheless, the audience at the first performance greeted the work enthusiastically. At the end (or after the second movement, according to some sources), the applause was tremendous, but the deaf Beethoven, still poring over his manuscript, was unaware of the ovation until

Fräulein Unger tugged at his sleeve and made him turn to see the crowd's clapping hands and waving hats and handkerchiefs. He bowed gratefully.

"The current musical winter season could not have been brought to an end more worthily and brilliantly than by a great musical academy [concert] in which the greatest genius of our time demonstrated that the true artist knows no stagnation," wrote the anonymous author of an article that appeared in the German music review *Cäcilia*. The article continues:

> Forward, upward, is his watchword, his cry of victory. *Beethoven* offered a grand overture, three hymns from his new mass, and his new symphony, whose last piece ends with a chorus on Schiller's lied, "An die Freude." One can say nothing more than what the connoisseurs recognized and unanimously declared: *Beethoven* has outdone everything we have previously had from him; *Beethoven* has advanced still further onward!!
>
> These new artworks appear as the colossal products of a son of the gods, who has just brought the holy, life-giving flame directly from heaven.

Yet the enthusiasm of the first audience and of many of the critics present was almost certainly stimulated more by the music's sheer physical power and by general respect for its aging composer (at fifty-three, Beethoven had already surpassed by a decade the average life span of an early-nineteenth-century Viennese male) than by any substantial comprehension of what the gigantic new work was intended to communicate. "He certainly gave the old wigs something to shake their heads about," wrote his former pupil, the piano pedagogue Carl Czerny, in commenting to a friend about how the "new symphony breathes such a fresh, lively, indeed youthful spirit; so much power, innovation and beauty as ever [came] from the head of this ingenious man." But Czerny presumably had the advantage of being able to familiarize himself with the work by playing the score at the keyboard. About the choral movement in particular, most listeners' sentiments were probably voiced by the anonymous reviewer in Germany's *Allgemeine musikalische Zeitung* (*Universal Musical Journal*), who wrote that "this truly unique Finale would be still more imposing if it were in a more concentrated form"—in other words, shorter and with an easier-to-follow structure—and who added, heartlessly: "The composer himself would share this view, had not cruel fate robbed him of the means of hearing his own creations." The contribution of the vocal soloists and chorus was summed up in a single sentence in the *Wiener allgemeine Theater-Zeitung* (*Viennese Universal Theater Journal*): "The singers did what they could."

But the puzzled reactions are understandable. After all, the Ninth Symphony was a proto-Romantic vision transformed into sound, irrationality rendered plausible, foolish idealism made realizable. In 1824, not even Beethoven, let alone that first group of casual and no doubt thoroughly flummoxed listeners, could have grasped the magnitude of what had been accomplished.

"Austrians-Asstrians"

PLACE: A FOURTH-FLOOR APARTMENT IN A BUILDING AT LANDSTRASSE
   323, VIENNA
TIME: ABOUT 5:30 P.M., MAY 7, 1824

Where is that ass Schindler? I can't find my black frock coat—maybe he knows where it is. It seems that I'm doomed to be surrounded by cretins and thieves unworthy of breathing the same air that I breathe. I'm hungry but I don't want to eat anything now: My nerves are in such a state, I wouldn't be able to control my bowels. This damned concert! If only it brings in enough money to keep my head above water for the next few months. I can't bear this constant, eternal scrounging—I, who have given so much! I shouldn't have let myself be persuaded to give the new symphony's first performance here. These horrible Austrians-Asstrians! "We, your reverent admirers and disciples"— or whatever it was that those shit-heads wrote. Someone probably remembered that all my other symphonies were performed here first and wanted the tradition to continue. But how I survive is of no interest to the local gentry, as long as they can bask in the reflected glory. Hypocrites, villains all! What could I have been thinking? I must have had a moment of weakness—vanity must have made me believe their sugary words of praise. My God, I've lived among the Viennese for—how long now?—over thirty years. Karl? Karl! *Terrible: I no longer hear my own voice even when I shout. I'm not even sure that I shouted.* Karl? Ah, there you are. Has Schindler sent a message? No? What time is it? Dear God! I told him to be here by five. What? Write in the notebook, damn it! I told him half past five? You think your uncle is such an old pisser that he can't remember what he's told others? *He's pointing at my head and smiling. . . .* Ah, so you like my haircut! It was about time, no? Ha! The barber washed and trimmed my hair—he said that it's still very thick, considering my age. *But how gray it's become—I hadn't looked in a mirror in a long time.* Yes, this time I made sure it was dry before I went outside; I don't want to get sick again. Where are you going? . . . The door? . . . Oh, there you are, Schindler. Where have you been? I told you to be here at five. What? Half past five? Never mind; you're here. Where's my black frock coat? The tailor . . . What will I do? What? Write, damn it, don't shout! The green one? Yes, you're right, in the half-light of the theater few people will notice what color it is. *My God, what a bootlicker! Look at that face—the face of a foxy servant. And he thinks he belongs in the realm of art! I'll never forget the time he asked me why I didn't write a finale for my C minor piano sonata—as if I could have brought the piece crashing down to earth after having made it soar higher than the stars in the long second movement! "Over the canopy of stars," as the chorus sings in the new symphony. I told him that I hadn't had time to write a finale—I thought he would catch my irony, but he took me seriously! Now what's he writing? I should . . .* All right, I'll put the coat on and we can go to the theater—but don't you "Oh-great-master" me! Just look after the thieves who run the box office! *Even if my green frock coat were covered in shit it would be too good for the sniveling Viennese. Think of what I'm giving them today: my soul, my life, everything I have to give, everything I am! They will like it or not, they will accept it or not, but they* can't *understand it, they can't know where it comes from, what it has cost. "All men will be brothers," said Brother Schiller, but it won't happen in my lifetime, it won't happen in Karl's lifetime, and it probably won't happen for hundreds of years. The men of today aren't brothers to me. They are beggars, slaves, clods. I soar above them as my music soars above the music of my contemporaries. We exist on different planes. For them, that other line of Schiller's would be more to the point: "Against stupidity, even the gods fight in vain."* All right, let's go, then.

No one knows what Beethoven was thinking in the late afternoon of May 7, 1824, in the hours immediately prior to the first performance of his Ninth Symphony, but some of the composer's thoughts probably went in directions suggested by this imagined monologue, or one-sided dialogue. Love for humanity and contempt for human beings; a sense of his own musical superiority and physical frailty, and special concern with his bowels; affection inextricably bound up with affliction: All of these and many other emotions, notions, and conditions, along with the nervousness inherent in backing, organizing, and participating in a major concert dedicated entirely to his own latest works, must have made Beethoven even more difficult than usual that day—and he could be difficult under the best of circumstances. Many of his rogue-and-peasant-slave descriptions of his contemporaries are well known, as are his clumsy puns about Austrians-Asstrians (even more far-fetched in the original German—*Österreicher-Eselreicher*—than in English), his fraught relationship with his nephew, Karl, and his mistrust of Anton Schindler. At the time of the Ninth's premiere, Karl was seventeen years old; about his place in his uncle's biography, more anon, but in any case he was a boy with "normal" interests and little understanding of or patience with his uncle's incomprehensible artistic aspirations and highfalutin principles. Schindler, a Moravian-born violinist—twenty-nine years old in 1824—is remembered today only because he functioned as a sort of secretary to Beethoven in an on-again, off-again relationship that lasted from 1816 until the composer's death.*

And then there are the *Konversationshefte*, or conversation books, in which Beethoven's friends and other interlocutors jotted down whatever

---

* Schindler's stupid, insensitive remark about the Piano Sonata in C minor, op. 111, which was to remain Beethoven's final—and, many would say, his most extraordinary—statement in a genre that he had immeasurably enriched and indeed transformed in the course of three decades, was reported by Schindler himself in his untrustworthy biography of the composer: "I ventured in my innocence to ask Beethoven why he had not written a third movement appropriate to the character of the first." If Schindler's tale is to be believed, the composer responded with evident sarcasm, which Schindler did not pick up: "He replied casually that he had not had time to write a third movement, and had therefore simply expanded the second." The concrete fact is that Beethoven still had four active years ahead of him after he had completed op. 111 and could easily have added another movement had he so desired; the less concrete fact is that the second movement of op. 111 takes the listener so profoundly into Beethoven's heart and—allow me the hyperbole—into the heart of the universe that anything that followed it would have been impossibly anticlimactic.

they had to tell the deaf musician. After the composer's death, Schindler appropriated the conversation books, <u>burned</u> many of those that contained uncomplimentary references to himself, and <u>forged and excised</u> entries in others; but the following quotations are authenticated excerpts from some of the 137 notebooks that still exist. On May 6, 1824, the day before the Ninth's premiere, Schindler wrote: "We'll take everything with us immediately now—we'll also take your green coat, which you can put on in the theater for conducting. The theater is dark anyway, no one will see that it is green." At this point, Beethoven said something, to which Schindler replied in writing—apparently with comic intent, because he switched from the formal *Sie*, which he normally used with Beethoven, to the familiar *du*, as if he were addressing God: "O great master, you do not own a black frock coat! So the green one will have to do, in a few days the black one will be ready." In my invented monologue, I have transposed the conversation to the following day, but Beethoven's impatience with Schindler's teasing and his all-too-prescient worry over how much money the concert would net him are well documented, as is his growing inability to control the volume of his voice when he spoke. "You talk too loud," Karl had written in one of the notebooks during a conversation in April 1824, not long before the premiere. "People don't need to know our business." Karl was embarrassed by the situation; we can only be touched by it.

Music lovers who visit <u>Vienna</u> today get such a strong dose of secondhand nostalgia about Beethoven, Schubert, and company that they are easily misled into believing that the Vienna of the 1820s was a place in which high culture was universally respected, genius dwelt at every street corner, and outstanding music making was always to be heard. The hard truth is that terms such as "crossover," "kitsch," and "dumbing down" could as easily have been applied to the cultural life of Vienna in Beethoven and Schubert's day as to that of major cities throughout the Western world in our own.

Most Viennese music lovers in the post-Napoleonic period clamored to hear the forebears of today's firebrand virtuosi, schlock-mongers, and half-pop, half-serious opera singers. In 1822, for instance, large crowds turned out to hear not only the eleven-year-old pianist <u>Franz Liszt,</u> who would prove to have staying power, but a whole slew of juvenile ivory ticklers engaged in a free-for-all to see who could play more notes per second than any of the others. Not to mention the excitement created, during Beethoven's Viennese years, by Carl Czerny's monster arrangement for sixteen (count 'em!) pianists of Rossini's *Semiramide* Overture, and the eight children of Basilius Bohdanowicz who sang a single aria over and over, each time in a different language, and then squeezed together before a piano keyboard to play a piece in synch.

The distinction between art and spectacle seems to have been even blurrier in those days than it is now; certainly, listening to a Beethoven symphony was much more an elitist activity in the first quarter of the nineteenth century than it is in the first quarter of the twenty-first. As to genius dwelling down the street: Of the approximately two hundred musicians in Vienna who earned at least part of their living from composition during those years, most of today's music lovers would recognize the names of Haydn, Beethoven, Schubert, and no one else.

Beethoven's disgust with what he perceived as a general decline in taste and a particular neglect of himself in the Vienna of the 1820s could hardly have been greater, which is why, while he was completing the Ninth Symphony during the first two months of 1824, he seriously considered holding its premiere in Berlin. But news of his proposed defection soon leaked out and provoked a strong reaction. Toward the end of February, probably only a few days after he had put the finishing touches to the symphony's score, thirty prominent Viennese citizens sent him a petition, begging him to allow the Ninth's premiere to take place in their city. "Out of the wide circle of reverent admirers that surrounds your genius in this your second native city, a small number of disciples and lovers of art approach you today to express long-felt wishes, and timidly to proffer a long-suppressed request," the plea began. It continued with flattering comments about "your worth and what you have become for the present as well as the future," with assurances that the supplicants' wish was "also the wish of an unnumbered multitude" and that their request was "echoed loudly or in silence by everyone whose bosom is animated by a sense of the divine in music." They then laid it on even thicker, by telling Beethoven that he was the only survivor of the "sacred triad," the other members of which were Haydn and Mozart, and that his two predecessors had created "great and immortal works . . . within the lap of their home"—a statement that refrains from mentioning that Haydn and Mozart also created many "great and immortal works" while they were abroad. Of course, "Beethoven's name and his creations belong to all contemporaneous humanity and every country that opens a sensitive heart to art," they said, yet "it is Austria that is best entitled to claim him as her own." (As it happens, Beethoven, the only non-Austrian member of the "sacred triad," was also the only one of the three who composed nearly all of his significant music in Austria.)

After having referred disparagingly to the popularity of Rossini's music ("a foreign power has invaded this royal citadel"), the letter continued:

> Do not withhold any longer from the popular enjoyment, do not keep any longer from the oppressed sense of that which is great and perfect, the performance of the latest masterworks of your hand. We know that a grand sacred composition [the *Missa Solemnis*] has joined the first one [the Mass in C, op. 86] in which you immortalized the emotions of a soul, penetrated and transfigured by the power of faith and super-terrestrial light. We know that a new flower grows in the garland of your glorious, still unequaled symphonies. . . . Do not disappoint the general expectations any longer!

The letter—signed by seven aristocrats and various well-known local bureaucrats, musicians, music publishers, and the piano maker Andreas Streicher—is valuable not only as proof of the esteem in which Beethoven was held in his adoptive city but also because it demonstrates how deeply the notion that great music could be both "immortal" and widely disseminated had taken hold in Europe within Beethoven's lifetime. Pre-nineteenth-century audiences had tended to lose interest in music that failed to follow the dictates of fashion. Bach, who was born in 1685 and whose works were already stylistically passé at the time of his death sixty-five years later, would have been delighted but astonished to learn that his music would be venerated and widely performed nearly three centuries after it was written. He may have believed in the hereafter, but he wrote for the here and now—for the church ceremonies and court occasions that took place as his life unfolded and for the instruction of the musicians of his day. Haydn (1732–1809) and even Mozart (1756–1791) still worked within the specific-piece-for-specific-occasion system, although the fact that Mozart began at the age of twenty-eight to keep a catalogue of his works, and the even more significant fact that he and Haydn published as many of their compositions as possible, demonstrate composers' dawning ambition to have their works survive them, perhaps even for a considerable time.

Not until Beethoven's day, however, did winning a place in posterity become a major goal—the greatest goal, for many composers. With the rise, in his lifetime, of the bourgeoisie, middle-class families were able to give their children music lessons, and *Hausmusik*—music in the home—became the home entertainment system of the 1800s. The equipment required for making it comprised a piano, one or more other instruments and/or voices, and printed music, the demand for which increased almost exponentially. This phenomenon occurred just as the figure of the Romantic genius—the artist as a being unhampered by normal constraints—was taking hold. The music of the brilliant, eccentric Beethoven circulated widely, and the conviction that this music would become "deathless" was a logical consequence of both his persona and the diffusion of his works. In the letter from his Viennese admirers, the reference to "the many who joyfully acknowledge your worth and what you have become for the present as well as the future" is an exceptionally significant sign of the times: The arts were no longer to be considered mere "means and objects of pastime." Composers were becoming the high priests, perhaps even the gods, of a secular religion; the best among them were expected to create works that would endure, and they were seen, in addition, as representatives of ethnic and nationalistic characteristics, however loosely defined. In this instance, the person or persons who framed the letter implied that Germanic music was profound whereas music from certain other ethnic areas (Italy, although unmentioned, was the most obvious object of derision) was frivolous. The letter chides Beethoven for having "looked on in silence as foreign art took possession of German soil and the honored home of the German muse, while German works gave pleasure only by echoing the favorite tunes of foreigners." But it also pumps him up by telling him that he is "*the one man whom all of us are compelled to acknowledge as foremost among living men in his domain.*"

In a conversation book entry, the writer Carl Joseph Bernard, a friend of Beethoven's, informed the composer that the letter-cum-petition had been conceived at a Viennese beer parlor by some cultural patriots who were dismayed by the popularity of Italian opera. Beethoven was not at all displeased by the document, but its subsequent appearance in two theater journals angered him: People would believe, he felt, that he had instigated the publication and perhaps even the writing of the letter. But his anger eventually subsided.

No doubt there were important practical considerations as well as concessions to his Viennese supporters behind Beethoven's decision to let the concert take place in the Austrian capital. His health had often been shaky in the previous months and years, and he must have been daunted by the prospect of more than two hundred hours of bone-jostling travel by horse-drawn coach from Vienna to Berlin and back—a journey that would have been punctuated by nights and meals in inns of dubious quality. Once a serious option to stay home had turned up, Beethoven took advantage of it.

That decision made, proposals and counterproposals about the choice of a venue, a date, and the musicians who would be invited to participate in the concert quickly began to occupy much of Beethoven's time. According to music historian Mary Sue Morrow, Beethoven's frustrations over organizing concerts throughout his Viennese years were "felt by all musicians trying to work within the city's inadequate concert structure," but the difficulty of his music made it unfit for "the existing concert format." Each Viennese theater of any significance had not only its own orchestra and chorus but also its own *Kapellmeister* (music director, with duties as conductor) and *Konzertmeister* (concertmaster, or principal first violin, who also had to lead the orchestra—which is why, in Britain, the principal first violin is still today called the leader). Count Palffy, who ran the Theater an der Wien, where the first public performances of many of Beethoven's masterpieces, including the Third, Fifth, and Sixth symphonies, had taken place, was willing to host the event there, and several dates in late March were proposed. But Franz Clement, the house's concertmaster and the man who, eighteen years earlier, had given the first performance of Beethoven's only violin concerto, was now on the composer's long blacklist. Beethoven wanted his friends Schuppanzigh and Umlauf as concertmaster and music director, respectively, probably because he knew that he could persuade or bully them into doing things his way. Holding the performance during Lent would probably have reduced ticket sales, too, and in 1824 Easter oc-

The Kärntnertor Theater, Vienna, circa 1840. *(After an anonymous engraving.)*

curred late, on April 18. It was only on or around April 23 that Beethoven reached an agreement with Louis Antoine Duport, manager of the Kärntnertor Theater, to hold the event there, with Schuppanzigh and Umlauf in command, and the precise date was not set until six or seven days later—a mere week before the concert took place.

There were other problems. Beethoven was no economic wizard—he had never even learned to multiply—but he deeply feared that if the prices of admission to this special event were not raised above the theater's normal prices, his hope of realizing a substantial profit from the concert after having covered the fees for the use of the theater and its orchestra and for the copyists' work would evaporate. "After talks and discussions lasting for six weeks I now feel cooked, stewed, and roasted," he wrote to Schindler sometime in April. "What on earth is to be the outcome of this much discussed concert, if the prices are not going to be raised? What will be left over for me after such heavy expenses, seeing that the copying alone is already costing so much?"

The police authorities refused to allow the prices to be raised—we do not know why—and Beethoven had to contend again with the authorities for permission to include the *Missa Solemnis* excerpts in the program, because laws in the rigidly Catholic Austria of the Restoration period forbade the performance of liturgical works in secular venues. Sometime in April, before he had decided to hold the concert at the Kärntnertor Theater rather than the Theater an der Wien, Beethoven wrote to Dr. Franz Sartori, head of the Central Book Censorship Office:

> Sir!
>
> As I am told that the Imperial and Royal Censorship will raise objections to the performance of some church works at an evening concert in the Theater an der Wien, all I can do is to inform you that I have been invited to arrange this performance, that all the compositions required have already been copied, which has necessitated considerable expenditure, and that the time is too short to arrange forthwith for the production of other new works—
>
> In any case only three church works, which, moreover, are called hymns, are to be performed.—I urgently request you, Sir, to interest yourself in this matter in view of the fact that, as it is, there are so many difficulties to cope with in any undertaking of this kind. Should permission for this performance not be granted, I assure you that it will not be possible to give a concert and that the entire cost of having the works copied will have been met to no purpose—
>
> I trust that you still remember me—
>
> I am, Sir, with kindest regards, your most devoted
>
> > Beethoven

This appeal did not work: Austrian bureaucrats could not have imagined, in 1824, that millions of people in the twenty-first century who have never heard of their emperor, Francis I, would hold Beethoven's name and works in high esteem. Permission was granted only after Count Lichnowsky, one of Beethoven's patrons, helped the composer's friends to approach Count Sedlnitzky, the notorious chief of the imperial police force, who gave the required nod.

Plans for the concert caused Beethoven so many headaches that he decided more than once to cancel it, only to repersuade himself to proceed. In the end, despite its reasonable success as an artistic event and the signs of esteem and affection that the composer culled from it, the concert was <u>all but a disaster from a financial</u> point of view. By the time Beethoven had covered all of his expenses, he netted only about four hundred florins—barely enough to cover a few months' rent. At a dinner that he gave a few days later at a restaurant in the Prater, Vienna's main park, to thank Umlauf, Schuppanzigh, and Schindler for their help with the concert, his anger over the economic outcome boiled over, and he became so abusive that his guests walked out. He eventually patched up relations with all of them, but a letter to Schindler demonstrates that he was as undiplomatic as ever in expressing his opinions of others. "I do not accuse you of having done anything wicked in connection with the concert," he wrote. "But stupidity and arbitrary behavior have ruined many an undertaking." And as if that weren't clear, or insulting, enough, Beethoven compared <u>Schindler</u> to a sewer: "Stopped-up sluices often overflow quite suddenly." He went on to say that he would rather compensate Schindler for his assistance by giving him small gifts "than *have you at my table*. For I confess that your presence irritates me in so many ways. . . . For owing to your vulgar outlook how could you appreciate anything that is not vulgar?! In short, I love my freedom far too dearly." Not the gentlest of apologies, perhaps, but by no means one of Beethoven's rudest letters, either.

A <u>repetition of the concert</u> with some program alterations took place at twelve thirty on Sunday, <u>May 23, 1824</u>—three weeks after the premiere—not at the Kärntnertor Theater but at the <u>Grosser Redouten-saal</u> in the Hofburg (royal palace), in a different part of town. The hall was not even half full, perhaps in part because the weather was good that day and many people wanted to take advantage of it.* As a result, earnings were eight hundred florins below expenditures, and Beethoven would have been out of pocket had not Duport, the impresario for this event as he had been for the premiere, generously insisted on paying him the five hundred florins that had been guaranteed. The disappointed and

---

* The <u>Grosser Redoutensaal</u>, used in Beethoven's day mainly as a ballroom but occasionally as a concert venue, still exists, although it has undergone several major renovations in the last two centuries; the most recent and extensive reconstruction was necessitated by major fire damage in 1992. But the complaints voiced by more than one early-nineteenth-century observer about the hall's overly reverberant acoustics can easily be understood today: however lovely it is to look at, the Redoutensaal is essentially a vast shoebox made up of hard, reflecting surfaces. The echo effect must have turned loud passages played by numerous musicians into gibberish.

disgruntled composer left Vienna to spend the summer in the country, as was his custom. He put his latest symphony behind him and set to work on the first of what was to become a series of five of the most extraordinary string quartets (many musicians would say *the* most extraordinary, without qualification) ever written—his valedictory works.

But the Ninth Symphony would not gather dust on a shelf. Slowly at first, but then with rapidly increasing velocity and vigor, it began a life of its own, separate from the life of its creator.

"An endlessly painful state"

Beethoven's life story has been approached through documents, first-person testimony, historical context, anecdote, educated and uneducated guesswork—including posthumous psychoanalysis—and, most interestingly but most dangerously of all, through his works. The interpretation of his life (as, for that matter, of any life) is exceedingly difficult and open to endless controversy, and one cannot seriously consider parsing a life without having some idea of how it unfolded.

The story begins on the banks of the Rhine, in the town of Bonn. From 1949 to 1991, when Bonn was the capital of the German Federal Republic, a standing joke among resident politicians and civil servants described the city as only half the size of Chicago's cemetery but twice as dead. In a word: provincial, especially in comparison with West Berlin, Munich, Hamburg, Frankfurt, Cologne, and several other West German cities. But oddly enough, in 1770, when Beethoven was born there and when the city's population was barely ten thousand—one-fiftieth the size of the metropolitan area's population two centuries later—Bonn was not considered quite so insignificant a backwater.

In the eighteenth century, "Germany" meant several dozen independent or interdependent states, large, medium-sized, and small. Bonn was the capital of the electorate-archbishopric of Cologne, although the city of Cologne, fifteen miles to the north, was and still is larger than Bonn. In an era in which the notion of separating church and state was still in its infancy, the archbishop of Cologne, who resided with his court in Bonn, was one of the seven or eight rulers who, upon the death of a holy Roman emperor, were called upon to elect a successor; thus

Market square, Bonn, eighteenth century.

the term "elector." Not surprisingly, an appointment to the position of elector-archbishop had far less to do with the tenets of the Roman Catholic faith than with the realities of political life. Maximilian Friedrich, who held the post during Beethoven's childhood, was a jovial fellow whose religious principles were flexible enough to allow him to have a mistress and whose clear-sighted approach to politics allowed him to share her with his prime minister, who, it seems, fathered all the children. The shared mistress and child bearer, Countess Caroline von Satzenhofen, was abbess at an important local convent, as a reward, no doubt, for the profundity of her religious convictions. But if devout citizens were bothered by this ever-so-slight infringement of the most talked-about of the Ten Commandments, they kept their opinions to themselves. Bonn thrived, after all, thanks to the presence of the archiepiscopal court, and much of the town's population consisted of petty officials—whose families constituted a sort of protobourgeoisie—and of the lower-class clerks, artisans, laborers, and servants who provided the palace with goods and services.

In Bonn, as in much of the rest of Europe, court musicians were artisan-servants, and the Beethoven family produced several representatives of the category. The composer's grandfather, also named Ludwig van Beethoven, hailed from Mechelen, a few miles north of Brussels, in Flanders, but moved to Bonn in 1733, at the age of twenty-one, to take a job as a singer in the electoral chapel. Since his personal honesty was as highly regarded as his musicianship, he was eventually named court music director. His son, Johann, born circa 1740, also became a court singer as well as a teacher of the rudiments of piano and violin technique. In 1767, Johann married twenty-one-year-old Maria Magdalena Keverich, daughter of the chief cook at the elector's summer palace; she had married for the first time at sixteen and had been widowed less than three years later. Johann and Maria Magdalena's first child, Ludwig Maria, was born in April 1769 but lived only six days; their second child, born in December 1770, was also named Ludwig (without the "Maria"), after his grandfather. The composer's exact date of birth is unknown; he was baptized, however, on December 17, and inasmuch as baptisms in those days usually took place within a day or so of birth, Beethoven's birthday is generally celebrated on December 16.

What is certain is that this Ludwig grew up under difficult economic conditions and that he was much loved by his mother but received little affection from his father—and felt little for him. Johann's character was weaker than that of his own father, and he was an alcoholic, although scholars differ as to whether this condition had already manifested itself during his son's childhood. The composer later claimed that he somewhat resembled his grandfather, but whether he meant physically or in other respects is not clear; Kapellmeister Beethoven died a few days after his grandson's third birthday, thus the younger Ludwig had few if any firsthand recollections of his grandfather. But the grandson would have heard many tales from local musicians and courtiers of the elder Ludwig's honesty and reliability.

Not long after Grandfather Beethoven's death, Johann began to give piano and violin lessons to little Ludwig. Several people who knew the boy well and lived long enough to see him achieve fame bore witness to the cruelty of Johann's teaching methods: He forced his son to practice the piano for long hours, used corporal punishment when the boy did not do what was expected of him, dragged Ludwig out of bed at all hours to perform for his own drinking companions, and humiliated him for perceived deficiencies. Even allowing for post-facto exaggeration on the part of those who claimed to have observed these doings and for the fact that stern discipline and corporal punishment were then considered necessary for proper child rearing, one may confidently assume that Beethoven's earliest musical studies were not a source of pure pleasure for him. This leads to a strong and probably not wholly misguided temptation to imagine that music making must always have retained at least a slight negative component, even in his maturity.

By the age of seven the boy was performing relatively complicated works in public. Shortly thereafter, his father put his musical education in the hands of other local teachers. When Ludwig was nearly nine, he became the pupil of Christian Gottlob Neefe, an accomplished composer and keyboard player, who had arrived in Bonn to become music director of the court theater and was later appointed court organist as well. Under Neefe's tutelage, Beethoven blossomed, and by the winter of 1782–83 the teacher was able to make special reference—in an article he published in Carl Friedrich Cramer's *Magazin der Musik*—to

> Louis van Betthoven [*sic*], son of the aforementioned tenor, a boy of eleven [*sic;* he was twelve] and of the most promising talent. He plays the piano very skillfully and with power, reads at sight very well, and I need only say that he plays mainly Sebastian Bach's *The Well-Tempered Clavier,* which Herr Neefe put into his hands. Whoever knows this collection of preludes and fugues in all the keys—which might almost be called the *non plus ultra* of our art—will know what this means. So far as his other duties permitted, Herr Neefe has also given him instruction in thoroughbass [the seventeenth- and eighteenth-century art of accompanying from a sort of musical shorthand—a bass line with numbers over it to indicate the notes to be played above it]. He is now training him in composition and in order to encourage him has had nine variations for the pianoforte, written by him on a march, engraved at Mannheim. This young genius deserves help to enable him to travel. He would certainly become a second Wolfgang Amadeus Mozart, were he to continue as he has begun.

The march variations mentioned by Neefe were on a theme by Ernst Christoph Dressler and became Beethoven's first published work. (His last substantial work for the piano—completed about ten months before the Ninth Symphony—was also a set of variations, but this time on a waltz theme rather than a march. The composition, known as the "Dia-belli" Variations, stands alongside Bach's "Goldberg" Variations as one of the towering masterpieces in the genre.)

By the age of thirteen, Ludwig had become assistant court organist to Neefe, but outside the musical sphere his formal schooling had come to a close when he was ten, as was the case with most other boys in his day. Beethoven's writing style remained unrefined, and his mathematical skills began and ended with addition and subtraction; he did, however, learn to speak, read, and write French, badly but fluently (he seems to have been called Louis, the French form of his name, throughout his childhood and adolescence), and he was a voracious reader, endlessly curious about the world around him—increasingly so as the years went by. Yet throughout his boyhood, what counted most was his explosive musical talent. Neefe nourished it well; everything else was secondary.

The young Beethoven began to attract the attention of several local aristocratic families that provided encouragement and in some cases friendship outside his own dismal domestic surroundings. When he was sixteen, he traveled to Vienna (it is not known whether the trip was paid for by Elector Max Franz—successor to Maximilian Friedrich—or by a group of local people who believed in the young man's future) to study with Mozart, Beethoven's senior by nearly fifteen years; the well-known tale of the audition, during which the initially inattentive older composer was suddenly impressed by his young visitor's remarkable capacity to improvise at the keyboard, has never been confirmed by reliable testimony, but Beethoven almost certainly heard Mozart play and may have had a few lessons with him. A letter from home, however, alarmed Beethoven with the news that his beloved mother, who had long been suffering from consumption, was gravely ill: He would have to go back to Bonn as quickly as possible if he wished to see her again before she died.

Maria Magdalena Beethoven passed away a few weeks after Ludwig's return home, and her already shiftless husband began to sink deeper and deeper into alcoholic unreliability. Ludwig was thrust into the position of chief breadwinner for himself, his father, and his two younger brothers, Caspar Carl and Nikolaus Johann, then ages thirteen and eleven. To a man who had given him shelter in Augsburg and lent him some money for the remainder of his hasty return trip to Bonn, Ludwig reported that his mother had died after a great deal of pain and suffering. She was such a kind, loving mother to me, and my best friend. Oh, who was happier than I when I could still utter the sweet name, mother, and it was heard—and to whom can I say it now? To the silent images of her in my imagination? As long as I have been here I have had very few happy hours. For the whole time I have been plagued by asthma, and I am afraid that it may develop into consumption. To this is added melancholy, which for me is almost as great an evil as my illness itself. . . . Fate is not favorable to me here in Bonn.

In short, a conflicting mix of characteristics and states of mind—pride, a sense of inadequacy, depression, and mild hypochondria complicated by legitimate worry about contracting the disease that had killed his mother—had already settled deep inside him, and the new conditions he faced, added to his grief over his mother's death and his disappointment at having had to return from brilliant Vienna to provincial Bonn, seemed to increase his unhappiness exponentially.

Yet his remaining years in Bonn were productive ones. Beethoven was by then one of the elector's official court organists, and beginning at the age of eighteen he also played viola in the court orchestra—an experience that provided him with invaluable practical knowledge and allowed him to participate in performances of some of the most recent and significant products of European musical culture, including Mozart's operas *The Abduction from the Seraglio, The Marriage of Figaro,* and *Don Giovanni.* He also gave piano lessons, took part in some of Bonn's other musical activities, and composed prolifically, although the surviving works from that period are significant only because of who and what Beethoven became in later years. Finally, in his twenty-second year, he made up his mind to return to Vienna. Mozart had died the previous year, at thirty-five, but Count Waldstein, who had become Beethoven's most important patron in Bonn, wanted the young man to study with the sixty-year-old Haydn. "With the help of assiduous labor you will receive Mozart's spirit through Haydn's hands," Waldstein wrote to his protégé. Early in November 1792, Beethoven set out from Bonn, surely not foreseeing that he would never see his native town again.

Vienna, like Bonn, was a Catholic city, and it was the capital of the empire dominated by the Hapsburg dynasty, which had strong connections with Catholic Bonn. But Rhineland Germans like Beethoven thought of Vienna as southern, lighthearted, and somewhat unserious, thanks to the strong influence of both Italy and the Balkan regions and the large numbers of transient or permanent residents from southern and eastern Europe. Beethoven must have been impressed not only by Vienna's beautiful palaces and cosmopolitan atmosphere, but also by its sheer size: The city's population in 1790 was about 250,000—twenty-five times that of Bonn.

Haydn proved to be anything but an ideal teacher for the willful young musician, and Mozart's spirit—like the spirit of any other extraordinary individual—was untransmittable. Yet within a decade Waldstein's wildly high hopes had been realized and surpassed in ways that the generous count could never have imagined. Beethoven studied composition not only with Haydn but also, and more substantially and fruitfully, with Johann Georg Albrechtsberger and Antonio Salieri, Mozart's old rival, and he quickly attracted widespread attention as a pianist, thanks in particular to his skills at improvising elaborate, imaginative variations and fantasies on any theme or motif presented to him. He may not have been capable of turning out masterpieces when he was still in his teens, as Mozart had been before him and as Mendelssohn was to be after him, but in his mid-twenties his original genius began to burst forth, torrentially. Beginning in 1795, when Beethoven's three groundbreaking trios for piano, violin, and cello were published as opus 1, his reputation as a serious composer grew and spread. Between that year and 1802, the tenth anniversary of Waldstein's prophecy, Beethoven produced his first twenty piano sonatas, first two sonatas for cello and piano, first eight sonatas for violin and piano, first three concertos for piano and orchestra, first six string quartets, and first two symphonies; and many musicians and music lovers in Vienna and beyond began to grasp the fact that, with the possible exception of the aging Haydn, Beethoven was the most brilliant living composer—certainly the most promising representative of the younger generation. His compositions revealed not only exceptional technical gifts but also exceptional boldness of invention, emotional power, and spiritual depth.

Early in the same period, however, Beethoven began to experience auditory disturbances, and by the end of it the disturbances had become acute. In October 1802, in a rented room in the peaceful village of

Louis van Beethoven

Beethoven in 1801.
*(Engraving by C. T. Riedel
from a drawing by
G. Stainhauser von Treuberg.)*

Heiligenstadt—now part of the city of Vienna—Beethoven wrote a lengthy, emotionally charged will in which he described his condition. The document was nominally addressed to his brothers but was, in fact, addressed to everyone he knew and probably to posterity. He never gave it to anyone, but he held on to it for the rest of his life, through dozens upon dozens of moves from one apartment to another in Vienna and surrounding areas; it was discovered among his papers after his death, a quarter century later.

O ye men who consider or declare me hostile, obstinate or misanthropic, how greatly you wrong me, you do not know the secret cause of what seems thus to you. My heart and my soul, from childhood on, were filled with tender feelings of good will, I always felt like performing great deeds, too. But just consider that for six years I have been afflicted with an incurable condition, made worse by incompetent physicians, deceived year after year by the hope of an improvement and now obliged to face the prospect of a *lasting disability* (the healing of which may take years or even be quite impossible)[;] born with an ardent, lively temperament, also susceptible to the diversions of society, I was, at an early age, obliged to cut myself off, to live my life in solitude; if, once in a while, I attempted to set all this aside, oh, how harshly would I be driven back by the doubly sad experience of my bad hearing, and yet it was not possible for me to say to people: speak louder, shout, for I am deaf; ah, how would it be possible for me to reveal a weakness in the *one sense* that should be perfect to a higher degree in me than in others, the one sense that I once possessed to the highest degree of perfection, a perfection that few others in my profession have ever possessed.—Oh, I cannot do it, so forgive me if you see me draw back from you, when I would gladly join together with you[;] my misfortune hurts me doubly inasmuch as I will surely be misunderstood because of it; for me there can be no recreation in people's company, no conversation, no mutual exchange of ideas[;] I can venture into society only as much as is required by the most urgent needs, I must live like an outcast; if I approach people, I am overcome by a burning anxiety, inasmuch as I fear to find myself in danger of allowing my condition to be noticed.—So it has been for this last half year, which I have spent in the country; advised by my sensible physician to spare my hearing as much as possible, he almost concurred with my present natural disposition: although sometimes, carried away by the longing for companionship, I let myself be tempted by it. But what a humiliation when someone stood next to me and heard a flute from afar and *I heard nothing* or someone *heard the shepherd* sing, and I again heard nothing; such experiences brought me almost to despair, little was lacking to make me put an end to my life.—Only *art* held me back, ah it seemed to me impossible to leave the world before I had brought forth all that I felt destined to bring forth, and so I muddled on with this wretched life— truly wretched, for a body so touchy that even a slight variation can transport me from the best state to the worst one.—*Patience*—it is said—I must now choose as my guide; this I have done.—My resolve should endure, I hope, until the relentless Parcae see fit to break the thread; perhaps things will go better, perhaps not; I am steadfast.—To have been forced to become a philosopher as early as my 28th year, this is not easy. Almighty God! you look down into my innermost being, you know it, you know that the love of mankind and an inclination to do good dwell therein. Oh men, if you read this sometime, think then, that you have wronged me, and let the unfortunate one be consoled at finding someone like himself, who despite all nature's obstacles has yet done all that lay in his power to be numbered among the ranks of worthy artists and men. . . . So it has come to pass—I hurry joyfully toward death;—if it comes before I have had the opportunity to fulfill all my artistic capabilities, then it will still have come too soon, despite my hard fate, and I shall wish that it had come later.—Yet even then I shall be content, for will it not free me from an endlessly painful state?

Beethoven was a writer—a writer of music, usually, rather than words, but in any case a person accustomed to using self-expression for catharsis. Maybe the very act of admitting, on paper, that he was becoming deaf, and of consolidating and giving voice to his thoughts about his terrible condition and about its impact on his life, had a liberating effect on him. This we cannot know. But what we do know is that the works he completed in the months and years after he had written this extraordinary will—which also contained specific instructions as to how his property was to be distributed after his death, and which has become known as the "Heiligenstadt Testament"—bear witness to a major change in his development. To say that he broke new ground is to understate the matter grossly: Beethoven altered the course of Western music. In the astonishingly individualistic compositions that he produced between the ages of thirty-two and forty-two, he extended the boundaries of tonality, lengthened and transmuted the old forms, and allowed intensely personal expression much freer rein than it had previously known in music.

None of this happened overnight. In Beethoven's earlier works, as in many of the compositions, early or otherwise, of his predecessors—Mozart, Haydn, and others—there are plenty of suggestions and anticipations of things to come, of the specific types of expression that Beethoven would expand almost beyond recognition. Yet by doing what he did, by not only appropriating previous methods but also bending them radically, Beethoven asserted the right of the artist to break old rules and make new ones. His willfulness, his refusal to equate artisanship with what he saw as High Art, helped—if only by example and as a side effect—to create the cult of genius that would become virtually a sine qua non of nineteenth-century culture. "The rules don't permit it? Very well: *I* permit it!" Beethoven had reportedly said in response to conservative musicians' criticisms of an unorthodox passage that he had written. Proclamations of this sort—not necessarily by Beethoven himself—became banners and battle cries for the Romantics. Listen, for instance, to the Beethovenian ring of the nineteen-year-old Ralph Waldo Emerson's words in this journal entry from December 1823:

> Who is he that shall controul me? Why may not I act & speak & write & think with entire freedom? . . . Who hath forged the chains of Wrong & Right, of Opinion & Custom? And must I wear them? Is Society my anointed King? . . . I am solitary in the vast society of beings; I consort with no species; I indulge no sympathies. I see the world, human, brute & inanimate nature; I am in the midst of them, but not of them; I hear the song of the storm,—the Winds & warring Elements sweep by me—but they mix not with my being.

Even a drastically abbreviated list of the works that Beethoven brought into being during the decade that music historians have long referred to as his "Middle Period" leaves one with a sense of wonder bordering on disbelief: the Third ("Eroica"), Fourth, Fifth, Sixth ("Pastoral"), Seventh, and Eighth symphonies; *Leonore* (the name he gave to the first and second versions of his only opera); the Fourth and Fifth ("Emperor") piano concertos; the Violin and Triple concertos; the "Waldstein," "Appassionata," and "Les Adieux" piano sonatas; the Ninth ("Kreutzer") and Tenth (G Major) violin sonatas; the Third Cello Sonata, op. 69; the String Quartets op. 59, nos. 1 to 3 ("Razumovsky"), and op. 74 ("Harp"); the "Ghost" and "Archduke" trios for piano, violin, and cello; the *Coriolan, Egmont,* and three *Leonore* overtures; the Choral Fantasy for piano, orchestra, and chorus; and the Mass in C Major. Probably only Mozart and Schubert, in the last ten years of their brief lives, produced in a single decade as much music that is still performed frequently all over the world as Beethoven produced between 1803 and 1813. During the same period, Hegel wrote his University of Jena lectures, later published as *Phänomenologie des Geistes* (*Phenomenology of Spirit* or *of the Mind*), which were crucial to establishing his reputation as a philosopher; Goethe gave the world *Faust,* Part One; Schiller produced *Wilhelm Tell;* and Blake's *Milton* and the first two cantos of Byron's *Childe Harold's Pilgrimage* appeared. But none of these works—not even *Faust*—has occupied as much space in its specific area as Beethoven's works of that decade have occupied in theirs.

These were the works that gave birth to the familiar image of Beethoven as a tempestuous genius who shook his fist at fate and, Jove-like, loosed musical lightning bolts that welded the rationalistic Enlightenment ideals of the just-ended eighteenth century, in which he had spent roughly the first half of his life, to the stormy Romantic individualism of the newborn nineteenth. By the time he reached middle age, his startling originality had made him a European musical icon, and his much-discussed intransigence and eccentricity had become a symbol of untrammeled artistic freedom.

It is impossible to explain in nontechnical terms what Beethoven actually did that was so revolutionary. Charles Rosen, in his study *The Classical Style: Haydn, Mozart, Beethoven*—which has become a classic in its own right since its first appearance in 1971—takes some 450 pages to describe to the musically initiate, using technical terminology and musical examples, what happened to Western music during the three-quarters of a century between the death of Bach and the death of Beethoven. The subject is enormous, and any attempt to communicate its outlines in only a few paragraphs must begin with a backward glance at European music history.

Early Christian music—Ambrosian and Gregorian chant—consisted essentially of single, unaccompanied melodic lines. Late in the twelfth century, composers at Notre Dame in Paris began to employ two vocal lines simultaneously, and over the following four centuries listeners' ears gradually became accustomed to ever more complicated harmonic textures. Toward the end of the sixteenth century, groups of Florentine intellectuals, poets, and musicians—generically referred to as the Camerata Fiorentina—became interested in ancient Greek writings on musical theory and tried to re-create the ways in which classical Greek dramas might have been sung or intoned over relatively light instrumental accompaniment. The result was the birth of opera, and this new musical genre was seen—perhaps more in retrospect than by its creators and early practitioners—as, in part, a reaction against the densely harmonic writing that then dominated European art music, both sacred and secular. A plaque on the Bardi Palace in Florence, where members of the Camerata, including Galileo's father, helped to establish the new form, refers explicitly and chauvinistically to opera as a reaction against "Flemish barbarism"; the term "Flemish," in this case, was a catchall for composers born north of the Alps, although many of them had received some of their training in Italy and had worked there, and most of the important Italian composers of the day, including Giovanni Pierluigi da Palestrina and Carlo Gesualdo, wrote music that was just as complex, harmonically, as that of their northern counterparts.

During the seventeenth century, opera gradually came to dominate Italian secular music; flowing and often florid vocal lines were accompanied by relatively simple harmonic formulas in the instrumental parts. But in Germany, and especially in predominantly Protestant northern and central Germany, harmonic and contrapuntal complexity continued to hold sway. This German High Baroque style culminated in the works of Johann Sebastian Bach, which, however, had already become unfashionable more than a decade before his death, in 1750. A new approach to musical expression began to develop—an approach that at first combined the most hackneyed and predictable Baroque harmonic progressions with melodic lines and rhythmic patterns that were simple to the point of dullness. In other words, the early works in this gradually evolving new style combined the basic elements of old German and relatively new Italian musical trends but—not surprisingly—fell far short of the best achievements of either.

This is not the place for investigating terms such as "style galant" and "Sturm und Drang," with which music historians who deal with this period contend, or for discussing the works of Bach's most musically prominent sons or of the Stamitz family or of other figures active in the evolution of European music in the mid-eighteenth century. What one does need to know, however, is that by the beginning of the last quarter of that century the new trends had solidified and crystallized into what we call, for the sake of convenience, the Classical style. Rosen chooses 1775 as the approximate date after which "the new sense of rhythm which displaces that of the High Baroque becomes completely consistent." In retrospect, we can see that the style's most brilliant exponents at that time were Haydn, who was forty-three years old in 1775, and Mozart, who was only nineteen but was already producing works of astonishing maturity. Beethoven, who would eventually carry the style to its outer limits, was not yet five years old.

Neither Haydn nor Mozart rejected Bach's work—nor did Beethoven. On the contrary, their admiration for the relatively small quantity of their great predecessor's music that was then in circulation grew as they themselves matured, and so did its influence on their music. And, in a different but comparable way, so did the influence of Bach's contemporary George Frideric Handel, whom Beethoven, even at the end of his life, was reported to have considered the greatest of all composers. But the features that most clearly distinguish the masterpieces of Haydn and Mozart and virtually all the works of Beethoven from those of the great Baroque masters are formal concision and lightning-quick expressive changes. In other words, whereas Baroque composers generally (not always!) wrote music that functioned in blocks—an aria whose character was fundamentally tragic throughout, for instance, or a jubilant instrumental movement, or a cantata chorus entirely dedicated to expressing the concept of hope for the Resurrection—the great masters of the Classical style set contrasting themes in close juxtaposition, often passing smoothly but rapidly from the triumphant to the tranquil, from passion to playfulness, from tragedy to consolation, from light to darkness and back again.

Mozart was probably the greatest master ever of musical chiaroscuro, of instantaneous light-dark character shifts in both instrumental music—music that speaks in an exclusively nonverbal way—and vocal music, whose character is to some extent determined by the text it sets. Beethoven, however, was no dilettante in this respect, and he was one up even on Mozart where intentionality was concerned. There is a dimension of willfulness, of self-assertiveness, in his works that does not exist in his predecessors' music. In Beethoven, the ego not only drives the proceedings; it is often also their subject and always a strongly felt presence. The first movement of Mozart's last symphony, nicknamed the "Jupiter," is as powerfully assertive—and as joyous, as lyrical, as playful—as the first movement of Beethoven's Third ("Eroica") Symphony, but Beethoven's movement has a self-referential quality that is not present in Mozart's. (This is not a value judgment: If I were told that one or the other of them had to be canceled from my aural memory, I would be incapable of making a choice.) And the same quality is present, in one way or another and to greater or lesser degrees, in virtually all of Beethoven's music. Even in his religious music, we no longer hear either the pure, profoundly devotional emotion of Bach's sacred music or the "sweetness of sin" that Stravinsky claimed to hear in Mozart's sacred music; instead, we hear Beethoven asking God what in the world is going on, what He is doing to humanity in general and to Ludwig van Beethoven in particular—and why. This insertion and assertion of the first person is one of the principal elements that set Beethoven apart from his predecessors and contemporaries and that contributed to the international fame that he achieved during his fourth decade.

He enjoyed the recognition, but, inevitably, it was also a burden to him. In 1812, toward the end of his incredibly prolific "Middle Period," he sent a grateful but self-admonishing letter to a young girl who was studying music and who had written him a praiseful note.

> Do not rob Händel, Haydn, and Mozart of their laurel wreaths. They are entitled to theirs, but I am not yet entitled to one. . . . Persevere, do not only practice your art, but endeavor also to fathom its inner meaning; it deserves this effort. For only art and science can raise men to the level of gods. . . . The true artist has no pride. He sees unfortunately that art has no limits. He has a vague awareness of how far he is from reaching his goal; and while others may perhaps admire him, he laments that he has not yet reached the point to which his better genius only lights the way for him like a distant sun.

It may be that Beethoven simply could not keep up the sustained outburst of creative energy that he had maintained from 1803 to 1813, and that this fact explains why that period was followed by some relatively fallow years. Between late 1813 and 1820 the only major new works that he completed were the String Quartet op. 95 ("Serioso"); the three piano sonatas op. 90, op. 101, and op. 106 ("Hammerklavier"); the two cello sonatas, op. 102; and the song cycle *An die ferne Geliebte* (*To the Distant Beloved*). Even if in his entire life Beethoven had produced nothing but the seven compositions just mentioned, he would still have to be counted among the titans of Western music, yet in terms of sheer productivity this seven-year period cannot be compared either to the previous one or to the one that was to follow.

But there were also substantial personal reasons for the hiatus. Genius, pride, and morbid sensitivity—especially about his deafness—cohabitated uncomfortably in Beethoven and made his life miserable. His solitariness, rudeness, and lack of the most basic practical abilities made him the best-known Viennese eccentric of his day, and even simple, everyday human contacts were difficult for him. On the one hand, it would be wrong to believe that Vienna's musicians and music lovers felt only respect or awe for Beethoven, or that, at a personal level, they thought of him as merely a half-deranged, pitiable fellow. The sense of awe existed, certainly, and Beethoven's eccentricities did cause comment and amusement, just as the considerable degree of withdrawal from society created by his deafness stirred feelings of pity in many observers; but many people felt genuine warmth toward him—and he did have a strongly expansive, friendly side to his nature, and a wild sense of humor. On the other hand, Beethoven had trouble dealing even with well-intentioned friends, let alone the landlords and servants whom he regarded as his natural enemies, and the love relationships that he longed to have with women were rendered impossible by a combination of unattainable idealism and intolerant moralistic notions: He was looking for someone like Leonore, the heroine of his opera—someone submissive but brave, feminine but masculine, virginal but sensual, intelligent but without doubts about what is good and what is evil—which meant that his hopes for marriage were nothing but mad daydreams. (Whether Beethoven suffered from venereal disease is a long-debated issue, thus whether the strongly moralistic streak in his declared beliefs about good and bad behavior was a consequence of the disease is a matter of speculation once or even twice removed from the range of biographical usefulness.) In addition, beginning in 1815, when his brother Caspar Carl died, leaving a nine-year-old son, Beethoven—thanks to an out-of-kilter sense of duty and the completely misguided notion that he would make a wonderful father—became embroiled in a ruinous series of legal battles with his sister-in-law over custody of the child, named Karl. This was the most obvious cause of the slowdown in Beethoven's artistic activity during that period.

But there must also have been deeper reasons for it. He must have sensed that the musical and spiritual veins he had been mining through the first dozen years of the nineteenth century had been exhausted and that he had to seek new sources within himself. Much later in the century, Friedrich Nietzsche wrote about the importance, for a creative person, of knowing how to wait, of allowing ideas to gestate naturally, and Beethoven certainly possessed that knowledge instinctively and to an exceptional degree. Together, the years 1813 to 1820 may well have formed the most important period of all in the history of his musical development—the period during which he was marshaling his internal forces and unconsciously, but probably also consciously, preparing for something completely different.

Yet "the imagination must not pine away," says Charlie Citrine, the protagonist of Saul Bellow's *Humboldt's Gift*—and Beethoven could easily have subscribed to the rest of Citrine's statement: The creative mind "must assert again that art manifests the inner powers of nature." The subconscious may be refreshed by sleep, but then the time had to come when "waking was true waking." Beethoven seems to have started out along the path toward full waking in 1819, when he learned that his pupil and patron, the Archduke Rudolph, was to be installed as archbishop of Olmütz (present-day Olomouc in the Czech Republic). The composer wrote to tell Rudolph that he intended to write a Mass for the occasion—the *Missa Solemnis* would be the result—but his congratulatory letter is, as Lewis Lockwood points out in his landmark study, *Beethoven: The Music and the Life,* a typical mix of "expressions of homage, some avuncular advice, stoic wisdom, firm reminders of Beethoven's artistic superiority, and resistance to any hint of subordinate status." From a purely psychological point of view, the mix is an update—thirty-two years on—of the previously quoted letter that the sixteen-year-old Beethoven had sent to his benefactor in Augsburg on returning to Bonn from his abortive first trip to Vienna, but the apologetic tone of the adolescent boy has been replaced by the alternately assertive, condescending, and at times downright offensive tone of a mature artist who firmly believes that he will be remembered long after his illustrious addressee has been forgotten.

> However numerous may be the congratulations which have been pouring in to you, my most gracious lord, yet I know only too well that this new honor will not be accepted without *some sacrifices on the part of Y.I.H.* [Your Imperial Highness] . . . There is hardly anything good—without sacrifice[,] and it is precisely the nobler and better man who

seems meant for this more than others, so that his virtue may be put to the test. . . . As for Your Imperial Highness's masterly variations [on Beethoven's theme "O Hoffnung," from *Fidelio*] . . . I noticed numerous little slips, I must however remind my illustrious pupil "La Musica merita d'esser studiata" [music deserves to be studied]—in view of Your Imperial Highness's very fine talents and really excellent gifts of imagination it would be a pity not to press forward. . . . Y.I.H. can thus create in two ways, both for the happiness and welfare of very many people and also for yourself. Musical creators and benefactors of humanity have not been found so far in the present world of monarchs. . . . I did not know how to interpret Your Imperial Highness's command that I should come, and again your intimation that Y.I.H. *would let me know when,* for I never was a courtier, am still not, and shall never be able to be one. . . . God knows my innermost being, and even if appearances may perhaps be against me, everything will be cleared up one day *for me.*

Could anyone less famous, and less eccentric, than Beethoven have remained unpunished in Restoration-era Vienna for a written statement like this one about the absence of benefactors of humanity among monarchs—addressed, furthermore, to the brother of one of the most powerful monarchs of the day? But Rudolph was accustomed to receiving all sorts of communications from his music teacher, including one in which the composer told him of the sorry effects of a laxative that his doctor was having him take at the time. In the case of the letter quoted at length above, one can easily imagine the thirty-one-year-old archduke and archbishop-elect shaking his head, sighing, "Ja, der Beethoven . . . ," and telling a secretary to file the letter away—which is why we have it today.

About the composer's politics, by the way, the historian David B. Dennis has noted that "Beethoven has been designated a precursor of every major political orientation in modern German history," from enlightened despotism to revolutionary idealism. He was an admirer and a detractor of Napoleon, a composer of revolutionary music and of patriotic music, a man who flattered rulers and who treated rulers with contempt. "Beethoven," Dennis wisely concludes, "was all of these things, but not any one of them." He would almost certainly have counted himself among those who—as his contemporary William Blake put it—

"imputed Sin & Righteousness / To Individuals & not to States." But during his last decade, Beethoven seems to have favored, as an ideal, rule by a wise individual similar to the late-eighteenth-century Austrian emperor Joseph II, or by an elite of wise individuals, or by an English-style constitutional monarch—in short, by a person or group of persons who would give free rein to all noncriminal forms of expression. In writing to thank King Frederick William III of Prussia for allowing him to dedicate the Ninth Symphony to him, Beethoven underlined the fact that "Your Majesty is not only the father of Your Majesty's subjects, but also the protector of the arts and sciences." (The king wrote back: "In view of the acknowledged excellence of your compositions, I have had great pleasure in receiving the new work you have presented to me. I thank you for sending it, and send you the enclosed diamond ring as a token of my sincere esteem.")

Beethoven's contempt for most human beings conflicted with his all-embracing love for humanity. He hoped, and may even have believed, that art would somehow transcend the constrictions imposed on us by our "mortal coil" and would gradually teach us to achieve a godlike status. He himself, Ludwig van Beethoven, in his exceptionally overburdened mortal coil, would never manage to attain that new condition, but the thing that he felt had been planted in him, the force or capacity that he did not understand but had learned to live with, allowed him to create moments of transcendence in and for himself and others. There were many periods in his life when economic worries might have made him nod in agreement with Samuel Johnson's statement "No man but a blockhead ever wrote, except for money," but had he lived long enough to read the second part of *Faust*, which was not published until five years after his death, he would much more readily have agreed with Goethe's statement that beautiful words (or—why not?—notes) "must come from the heart. / And when the breast overflows with longing, / One looks around and asks who will partake."*

---

* The quotation is from Act III:

Helena: So sage denn, wie sprech' ich auch so schön?
Faust: Es ist gar leicht, es muss von Herzen gehn. Und wenn die Brust von Sehnsucht überfliesst, Man sieht sich um und fragt—
Helena:—wer mitgeniesst.

Helen: So tell me, then, how may I, too, speak so beautifully?
Faust: It's quite easy, it must come from the heart. And when the breast overflows with longing, One looks around and asks—
Helen:—who will partake.

In the works of his last years Beethoven delved ever more deeply into his subconscious while affirming ever more strenuously the artist's obligation to use self-revelation as a means toward the achievement of worldwide human harmony. I call this process the universalizing of the intimate. His *Missa Solemnis* (which, in the end, he did not complete until three years after Archduke Rudolph's installation as archbishop), Ninth Symphony, last three piano sonatas, "Diabelli" Variations for piano, and last five string quartets are above all a search for transcendence. In them, he carried the process of universalizing the intimate as far as and probably further than any other musician had or has ever done; at the very least— as Maynard Solomon, a lifelong student of the composer's life and works, has written—in these works Beethoven "forever enlarged the sphere of human experience available to the creative imagination."

The question of whether we ought to read artists' lives into their works ceases to matter in Beethoven's last years. His late works *were* his life. Deafness was to Beethoven what exile has been to others, and "the condition we call exile," according to the exiled Russian poet Joseph Brodsky, "accelerates tremendously one's otherwise professional flight— or drift—into isolation, into an absolute perspective: into the condition in which all one is left with is oneself and one's own language, with nobody or nothing in between." By the mid-1820s, the external events in Beethoven's life—quotidian and banal events, such as his constant changes of dwelling, or dramatic and upsetting ones, such as his nephew Karl's attempted suicide—were nothing but an exoskeleton; the vital substances had been distilled into music—his "own language," as Brodsky put it, "with nobody or nothing in between" it and himself. Weary and careworn though he was, Beethoven did not want to die, but he did want to exist in an ideal Elsewhere—an Elsewhere that he then created for himself and for anyone who was or is or will be willing and able to enter. By March 26, 1827, when his devastated body and exhausted spirit ceased to be, Beethoven had given everything that he had in him to give. Maybe he would eventually have achieved even higher transcendence than he reached in the finale of the Sonata op. 111 or the twenty-fourth and thirty-first variations of the "Diabelli" set or the "Benedictus" of the *Missa Solemnis* or the third movement of the Ninth Symphony or the *Grosse Fuge* or the entire String Quartet op. 131; but we—the rest of us— cannot imagine him, let alone anyone else, going any further in that direction. Wonderful musical creations by other geniuses followed and continue to follow, but no one since Beethoven has gone further than he went along the path to transcendence. When, a quarter century after Beethoven's death, Schumann described the twenty-year-old Brahms as the musician of the future and a sort of successor to Beethoven, he entitled his article "New Paths"—unconsciously summoning up the perceptive phrase in the poet Franz Grillparzer's funeral oration for the composer from Bonn: Beethoven's successors, Grillparzer had written, would have to "begin anew, for he who went before left off only where art leaves off."

In many ways, Beethoven was—is—much more modern than we are. "We live 'as if,' " says the protagonist of Claire Messud's novel *The Last Life*, "as if we knew why, as if it made sense, as if in living this way we could banish the question and the 'as if'ness itself, the way we speak and act as if our words could be comprehended." Beethoven, in his terrifying isolation and his terrible pride and his unsurpassed capacity to transform experience into organized sound complexities, went beyond that stage. In the last quartets, and certainly in the Ninth Symphony, he obliterated the "as if"ness of comprehension, and then went on to obliterate obliteration—to dance on obliteration's ashes.

Struggle, stress, and strain: words often used in discussions of Ludwig van Beethoven's life and art. His predecessors, including Bach and Mozart, experienced plenty of struggle, stress, and strain in their daily lives but probably not in their creative lives, or at least not to so great a degree. The lines between art and artisanship were blurred in their time. With consummate skill, they rapidly conceived and composed the works commissioned of them, because for them the distance between aspiration and achievement in art was almost nonexistent, once they had mastered the tools of their trade. Besides, Bach and Mozart lived with a worldview according to which everything happened as God willed. They understood pain as well as Beethoven—the Agnus Dei of Bach's Mass in B minor and all four movements of Mozart's String Quintet in G minor come immediately to mind as exemplars of that pain—but, unlike Beethoven, they weren't constantly demanding to know *why* pain was endemic to and ever present within the human condition. This is not meant to belittle Bach or Mozart: Their music is as great as Beethoven's!

But Beethoven was a modern man. He did believe in some form of divinity as a Source or Prime Mover, but he took nothing at face value; everything had to be probed and questioned. Despite his colossal gifts and skills, he was unable to proceed directly from aspiration to achievement; even determining the substance of his aspirations was no easy task for him. The first part of his creative process was the struggle, not to decide where he wanted to go but to understand where he *needed* to go, and then to clear what seemed to him the best possible trail for reaching his destination.

As he aged and as his deafness worsened, eventually cutting him off almost completely from normal social intercourse, Beethoven became increasingly preoccupied by abstract problems, and the more such problems preoccupied him the harder it was for him to reconcile his mental, spiritual, and creative life—*real* life, for him—with what other people called real life. He paid an inestimably high price for the privilege, if privilege it was, of making such unprecedented explorations. (Was it a privilege for *him* to enrich *our* lives? The notion is appallingly selfish on our part.) He had helped to initiate and had then developed and completed an entire cycle in the history of musical expression, yet it is significant that Grillparzer, in the funeral address, felt compelled to refer to what many had considered misanthropy on Beethoven's part. "He fled the world because, in the whole range of his loving nature, he found no weapon to oppose it," said the poet, who had observed Beethoven firsthand. "He withdrew from mankind after he had given it his all and received nothing in return." But, as Elsa Morante wrote, "Those who flee from love cannot find peace in solitude."

I found myself thinking about that love, that withdrawal, and that turmoil as I left the courtyard and entranceway of the house at Ungargasse 5 in Vienna, crossed the street, looked back at the building, and imagined Beethoven walking through its doorway on May 7, 1824, en route to the Kärntnertor Theater for the first performance of what would remain his last symphonic gift to humanity.

PART TWO

1824, or How Artists Internalize Revolution

The Establishment reestablished

Even if the Austrian emperor and his family had been in Vienna and had attended the premiere of the Ninth Symphony at the Kärntnertor Theater, they would not have been inclined to pay much attention to the finale's message of brotherhood, joy, and, implicitly, freedom. They were absolutists who, like monarchs in much of the rest of Europe, had recently lived through a quarter century of violent challenges to the established order; now that that order had been reestablished, they were prepared to use any means at their disposal to prevent further upheavals.

As a political concept, the term "restoration" means that a system or regime once ousted from power has been restored to its former position. Each restoration has its own complex network of underlying conditions, but one condition—resentment—is probably common to all: resentment on the part of the winners for having been ousted in the first place, and resentment on the part of the losers for finding themselves in a new-old situation—one they thought had been eliminated once and for all, but that has come back to dominate their lives. Restoration is a recipe for long-term, all-around bitterness. But in Europe during the years in which Beethoven was writing the Ninth, the bitterness was tempered by exhaustion.

Between 1789 and 1815, the French revolutionary and Napoleonic wars had torn Europe apart. From the Atlantic's eastern shores all the way to Moscow, clashing ideologies had been transformed into clashing armies; the liberty-equality-fraternity banner was quickly bloodied by the revolutionaries' excesses, and its motto was then subverted by Napoleon, who used the ideal of exporting the Revolution as a tool for achieving domination of the whole Continent. However shocking the effects of the infant French Republic's guillotine may have been, the eighteen to forty thousand chopped-off heads that it produced during the Terror of 1792–96 were a statistical trifle in comparison with the results of the foreign wars that followed. Between 1796 and 1815, an estimated two and a half million soldiers and one million civilians met their deaths in the Napoleonic Wars. During virtually any one of Napoleon's major battles, two or three times as many people were killed as had been executed by order of the Committee of Public Safety or other French Revolutionary groups throughout their existence. In the battle of Borodino alone, on September 7, 1812, the opposing armies of Russia and France jointly lost far more soldiers than the United States would lose during a dozen years of fighting in Vietnam, and the revolutionary and Napoleonic wars lasted twice as long as the Vietnam War, four times as long as the Second World War, and six times as long as the First World War.

Little wonder, then, that in April 1814, when the defeated Napoleon (who, by the way, was Beethoven's senior by only sixteen months) was sent into exile on the Tuscan island of Elba, an enormous sense of relief pervaded millions upon millions of Europeans, including many of those who had approved of the emperor's goals or had in any case opposed the restoration of power to their countries' most reactionary forces. Entire peoples were worn out, entire nations drained, by warfare that had begun to seem eternal, and the Old World's old leaders did not fail to grasp the fact that their power, so long threatened or usurped, would soon be secure again. They arranged to meet in Vienna the following September to decide how the "liberated" Continent was to be carved up among them.

The Congress of Vienna ran on for the better part of a year. Toward the end it was thrown into confusion by news of Napoleon's clandestine return to the Continent and attempt to regain power, but his defeat at Waterloo in June 1815 and his subsequent exile to the remote African island of Saint Helena truly ended an era of upheaval. Dominating the Congress from start to finish were the four chief architects of Napoleon's downfall: the British foreign minister, Viscount Castlereagh (Robert Stewart, 2nd Marquess of Londonderry), in representation of the prince regent, the future King George IV; Tsar Alexander I of Russia, representing himself—although several of his advisers, including the influential Count Karl Robert von Nesselrode (of German origin), were on hand; the French foreign minister, Talleyrand (Charles-Maurice de Talleyrand-

The Congress of Vienna. *(Drawing by J.-B. Isabey, 1815.)*

Périgord), negotiating on behalf of King Louis XVIII—younger brother of the beheaded Louis XVI (the latter's son, Louis XVII, had died in a revolutionary prison at the age of ten); and, most important, the Austrian foreign minister, Prince Klemens von Metternich, representing the Hapsburg king, Francis I. Another significant participant, King Frederick William III of Prussia, came accompanied by his relatively liberal-minded chief advisers, Prince Karl August von Hardenberg and Baron Wilhelm von Humboldt, and was much wooed by other delegates, most of whom agreed that Prussia had to be prevented from forming too close an alliance with Russia. All of these men were intent on gaining the best possible advantages for their respective countries, and, reasonably enough, none of them completely trusted any of the others: According to a well-known adage of diplomacy, nations have interests, not friends, and the same may be said of their chief representatives.

No good reason surfaced for trying to reestablish the Holy Roman Empire, the thousand-year-old supranational political structure that had already been tottering toward extinction before Napoleon officially abolished it in 1806. In its place, and from the ruins of Napoleon's crumbled Confederation of the Rhine, Metternich created a German

Confederation—thirty-nine states of various sizes, of which Austria and Prussia were the most powerful and over which Austria presided. In terms of territorial extension, however, the greater part of the vast, reconstituted Austrian Empire—Beethoven's home for most of his life—lay outside the German Confederation's boundaries and included not only present-day Austria but also most or all of present-day Hungary, the Czech Republic, Slovakia, Slovenia, Croatia, and Serbia, as well as large chunks of present-day Germany, Romania, Italy, and Poland. Prussia and Russia divvied up the rest of Poland; Sweden annexed Norway; and Russia kept Finland—which it had taken in 1809—along with the various territories and political entities that later formed much of the European part of the Soviet Union. Talleyrand, one of the greatest figures in the history of diplomacy—thus also one of the most ambiguous ones—managed to ensure that France would maintain most of its prewar borders, on the understanding that it would support Austria and Great Britain in preventing Russia from expanding westward and would look unfavorably upon any Russo-Prussian entente.

Regency Britain and Louis XVIII's France were constitutional monarchies—liberal not by the standards of our day but by those of theirs—whereas Russia, Prussia, and Austria were absolutist monarchies. This significant difference and, to a lesser extent, religious divergences among the nations (European state religions included Roman Catholicism, Russian Orthodoxy, Anglicanism, several Protestant faiths, and, in parts of the Balkans, Islam) inevitably created mistrust and misunderstandings, but so high had been the cost of the Napoleonic Wars that there would be no further Continent-wide conflicts for a whole century. The seeds of this long period of relative peace, and of the repression that was part of the bargain, were sown at the Congress of Vienna.

Partly because he shone at gala social events and was an inveterate rake, partly because he wished to make the Congress drag on for an outrageously long time so that he would increase his chances of wresting concessions from visiting colleagues eager to return home, Metternich made sure that Vienna would provide the most splendid entertainments for its illustrious visitors. Among the cultural activities organized for the Congress's guests was a concert at the Grosser Redoutensaal on November 29, 1814—a concert that consisted entirely of music by Beethoven. According to Lewis Lockwood, Beethoven's international standing was so high that he easily became the Congress's "musical hero," despite the fact that "most of the gathered nobility preferred ballroom music to Beethoven." (Metternich himself loved Italian opera and detested Beethoven's music.) Beethoven "shamelessly cultivated this role" at the Congress, says Lockwood, "by hurriedly composing the bombastic cantata *Der glorreiche Augenblick* ('The Glorious Moment') for the assembled heads of state, along with a flashy polonaise for piano" dedicated to the tsarina.

Beethoven's recent *Wellingtons Sieg* (*Wellington's Victory*—another, more spectacular potboiler, for full orchestra with percussive sound effects), and the Seventh Symphony, which had been given its first public performance a year earlier, were heard together with *Der glorreiche Augenblick* on the concert of November 29. With the exception of the symphony, these works were blatant attempts to curry favor with the aristocrats present in the city and to ride the tide of patriotic euphoria that followed hard upon Napoleon's defeat. But as a freelance musician the composer could ill afford to pass up an opportunity to earn much-needed cash—especially under disastrous postwar economic conditions—through the publication and dissemination of potentially popular works. The concert was so successful that it was repeated, for the composer's financial benefit, on December 2 and again on Christmas Day. Beethoven then "let himself be persuaded," according to Lockwood, to participate in a concert at the Rittersaal (Knights' Hall) on January 25, 1815. He also let his pupil Archduke Rudolph, the Austrian emperor's brother, and Count Razumovsky, the Russian ambassador to Austria, present him to the assembled crowned heads and other dignitaries.

Although the entertainments that Metternich provided for his foreign guests included not only music but also complicated erotic entanglements, many of the delegates complained about the Congress's length. According to the tsar, Metternich was "the best master of ceremonies in the world," but he added that "it would be hard to find a worse minister." Talleyrand—evidently frustrated by the slow pace of the proceedings—claimed that his Austrian colleague "held aloof inertia to be a kind of superior genius," and he described most of his fellow delegates as "too frightened to fight [that is, argue with] each other, too stupid to agree." Nevertheless, the Congress did eventually come to an end, and its final declarations were presented for signature on June 9, 1815, a few days before the battle of Waterloo.

Relief + regret + repression = Romanticism?

One of the most remarkable and panoramic descriptions of the battle of Waterloo unfolds in *The Charterhouse of Parma,* a novel written in 1839 by Marie-Henri Beyle—better known by his nom de plume, Stendhal—who had been attached to the French army off and on throughout Bonaparte's rule as first consul and reign as Emperor Napoleon I. Over a hundred years later, the English novelist and man of letters Ford Madox Ford declared that "the most depressed pages of Tolstoy's *War and Peace* read like inadequate witticisms" in comparison with Stendhal's description of the Waterloo battlefield. Early in *Charterhouse,* Fabrice del Dongo, the novel's impetuous young protagonist, runs away from his aristocratic, ultraconservative father's home to serve Napoleon; he observes the battle that puts a decisive end to his hero's career, then wonders how he can possibly make something of himself now that the revolutionary-imperial adventure has been snuffed out. And the same predicament dominates the lives of the wholly different young male protagonists of Stendhal's two other, earlier, fictional masterpieces, *The Red and the Black* and the unfinished *Lucien Leuwen.* All three characters seem to be consciously or subconsciously obsessed with one question: What do we do, now that Napoleon is gone and all the enthusiasm-engendering excitement is over?

Stendhal, who was born in 1783, was curious about how the Napoleonic era, viewed as a bygone epic, would affect post-Waterloo youths, because he knew so very well what the emperor's reign—which he called "the despotism of glory"—had meant to young people of his own generation. He had witnessed and subscribed to the initial idealism, to the notion that France's mission was not only to repulse the armies of the foreign monarchies allied against the forces of the Revolution but also to liberate all of Europe from the tyranny of absolutism. As the wars dragged on, however, he had seen those ideals subverted, reduced to hollow, meaningless slogans and used as an excuse for conquest, with all of its accompanying devastation. Later, in the aftermath of Napoleon's de-

Stendhal. *(Portrait by S. Valeri.)*

feat, Stendhal became one of the first literary figures to perceive the relationship between the death of the Revolution and the flowering of Romanticism—Romanticism understood as a sublimation of the liberating principles of a revolution that had first exploded across Europe and then imploded on itself. (For the sake of clarity: The term "Romanticism" generally refers to late-eighteenth-century and early- to mid-nineteenth-century artistic and intellectual tendencies that combined anti-dogmatic Enlightenment ideals with a strong emphasis on emotion and instinct. The German writer and musician Ernst Theodor Amadeus Hoffman [1776–1822], a protagonist of the movement, considered Haydn and Mozart, as well as Beethoven, to have been Romantic composers; the fact that today Haydn and Mozart are generally considered exemplars of the Classical style and Beethoven is seen as a transitional figure from Classicism to Romanticism demonstrates the terminology's fluidity. Writing in 1810, Hoffmann described Beethoven in particular as "a pure Romantic," whose music "sets in motion the lever of fear, of awe, of horror, of suffering, and awakens that infinite longing which is the essence of Romanticism.")

A good case can be made for the notion of Romanticism as a child of the

French Revolution and a grandchild of the Enlightenment. Although the Revolution had failed in the short run, it partially succeeded in the long run: The various forms of parliamentary democracy—liberal-conservative, social democratic, federalist, and so on—that seem to be solidly in place today in most of Europe and North America and in many parts of the rest of the world, are to a great extent descended from the Enlightenment and the Revolution. But during the period from 1815 to 1848, Europeans did not know that within a few generations freedom of speech, of the press, and of religion would be available to a significant portion of humanity. Members of Beethoven's generation witnessed the last years of the Enlightenment and then the birth, transformation, subversion, and demise of the Revolution, and members of the following generation had the still more depressing experience of witnessing only the phases of subversion and demise. The inward-searching nature of artistic developments after the Congress of Vienna was in part a subconscious, self-defensive tactic for avoiding despair over the condition of Restoration Europe.

Anyone who has lived under repressive regimes in more recent times will understand the phenomenon: In order to survive, you are forced to pretend to believe in something in which you do not believe and that you may, in fact, detest; at the same time, you cannot help but wonder of what conceivable use or consequence your survival could be under such circumstances. But the Romantics, who lived not only before Hitler and Stalin but also before Darwin, Marx, Freud, and Einstein, did not possess as vast a gamut of uncertainties—not to mention nihilistic beliefs and attitudes—as later generations would have at their disposal. Although the despair factor was as present in the human psyche in the early nineteenth century as it is today and as it has been throughout human history, the search for absolute meaning was still a reasonable option two hundred years ago. Many commentators have described Romanticism as the inspiration behind Europe's striving toward freedom, but that notion seems to me less sustainable than the converse: The European aspiration for freedom was the inspiration behind Romanticism. And what Stendhal seems to have grasped earlier than anyone else is the fact that the Romantics were not the children of the Revolution, but rather its orphans.

The British historian Eric Hobsbawm treaded on thin ice when he declared, in his 1962 study, *The Age of Revolution: 1789–1848,* that "artists were in this period directly inspired by and involved in public affairs." Never before had they been more politically committed, he said, and he added that "even the apparently least political of arts, music, had the strongest political associations." He called Mozart's *Magic Flute* (1791) a propagandistic opera on behalf of the highly politicized Masonic Order; pointed out that Beethoven had dedicated the "Eroica" (1803–4) to Bonaparte "as the heir of the French Revolution"; reminded readers that Goethe was "a working statesman and civil servant" and Pushkin a political exile; and described Balzac's *Comédie Humaine* novels as "a monument of social awareness."

It is true that artists, like everyone else, exist within given periods and environments; whatever their character, whatever the range of their intelligence and emotions, and however long- or shortsighted their ideas and beliefs may be, they are children of their time and place. Every artist works within and reacts to a given social reality or series of realities, and in this sense the artists who were active between 1789 and 1848 were no different from those who were active at any other time in the past or who are active today. The French Revolution did indeed have a liberating effect on artists and intellectuals, some of whom began to take sides on humanistic and occasionally even on political issues, and the repression that followed the Congress of Vienna managed to put only a partial, temporary halt to dissenting expression. Up to this point, Hobsbawm's ideas are reasonable. But he seems unwilling to confront the fact that the calm brought about by repression was greeted with a great sigh of relief by many artists and thinkers.

Take, for instance, Georg Wilhelm Friedrich Hegel, who was born in 1770—the year of Beethoven's birth—and who lived through the entire French revolutionary and Napoleonic period. A little over a year after Waterloo, Hegel, who greatly influenced later generations of ethical and political philosophers, gave his inaugural lecture as professor of philosophy at the University of Heidelberg. In it, he declared that the time had at last arrived when "philosophy may expect attention and love again; when this science, well-nigh stricken dumb, can lift up its voice again and may hope that a world which had become deaf to it may lend an ear to it once more." (Replace the words "philosophy" and "science" with "music" and "art," and Beethoven could have pronounced the sentence verbatim.) Referring to the just-ended war decades, Hegel said that the

G.W.F. Hegel.
*(Lithograph by
J. L. Sebbers, 1828.)*

"distress of our time" had emphasized "the petty interests associated with the meaner side of our daily life," and that the pressures and struggles of the "real world" had been not only a constant, concrete occupation but also a constant mental preoccupation: They had absorbed "all the power and force of mind." During the years of strife, people's lives had been so completely dominated by "the objective world" that a "higher inner life, a purer spirituality, could not maintain itself in freedom, and better natures were captivated by those interests and to some extent sacrificed to them." To achieve inner life, the spirit had to be able to "turn inward and concentrate itself within itself." According to Hegel, the new, peacetime conditions presented an opportunity for the development of religious devotion and pan-German patriotism, but he also hoped that "alongside the political and other interests bound up with our everyday life," the arts and sciences—the life of the mind—would "flourish once more."

In this same lecture, Hegel, again harking back to the just-ended revolutionary and Napoleonic period, described the "German nation" as having "hewn its way out of the crudest conditions"—imposed by those nasty French, of course—and of having "saved its nationality, the basis of all vital life." He was convinced that philosophy, for instance, had "disappeared without a trace" from other European countries (once again, he was referring mainly to France), whereas "the German nation has pursued it as a possession peculiarly its own" and has "acquired the higher calling of being custodians of this holy fire."

This is but one among many examples of how the defeat of Napoleonic France led to ethnic and nationalistic reactions against French culture's century-long reign in western Europe—and nationalism became one of the main strains of Romanticism. The Italian poet and essayist Giacomo Leopardi referred to this developing situation at the beginning of his "Discussion of the Present State of Customs in Italy"—an essay drafted in March 1824, just a few weeks after Beethoven had completed the Ninth Symphony. Leopardi, who was by no means anti-French, noted that "a sort of equality of literary, civil, and military reputations" among the major European nations had emerged during the nine years since Waterloo and the conclusion of the Congress of Vienna, and he allowed that this newfound equilibrium was in part "a result of

Giacomo Leopardi.
(Wood engraving after a contemporary painting.)

the growth of commercial exchange and the habit of traveling," accompanied by the desire of "every nation" (by which he meant those nations' educated classes) "to get to know as deeply as possible the languages, literatures, and customs of other peoples." The wars that Napoleon had undertaken to extend French influence had, in fact, produced the opposite effect: Since the time of Louis XIV, said Leopardi, all other European nations had conceded cultural primacy to France, but because France was now "abased by her losses" the other nations were able to flourish.

Not that France had lost its intellectual way: In the year 1824 alone, the French mathematician and physicist Nicolas Léonard Sadi Carnot published his book *Réflexions sur la puissance motrice du feu* (*Reflections on the Motive Power of Fire*), which comprised what later became known as the second law of thermodynamics; the French engineer Claude Burdin invented and built the first real hydraulic turbine; the gifted painter Théodore Géricault—creator of the astonishing *Raft of the Medusa*—died at the age of thirty-two while trying to complete a remarkable series of paintings of deranged and insane people; Charles Augustin Sainte-Beuve and other leading literary figures founded the pro-Romantic newspaper *Le Globe;* and twenty-two-year-old Victor Hugo published his first book, *Nouvelles odes et poésies diverses,* to immediate acclaim. France was still in excellent mental shape. But Leopardi's point was simply that other European nations were beginning to achieve intellectual and cultural parity with France.

Leopardi lived most of his brief life (1798–1837) in an isolated corner of one of central Italy's culturally repressed Papal States. The belief, which he stated in the 1824 essay quoted above, that "Europe's civilized nations, that is, principally, Germany, England, and France herself, have set aside their age-old national prejudices," proved to have been wishful thinking, to everyone's misfortune, yet his comments on the newly resumed flow of ideas demonstrate his keen awareness of the opening up of international travel, commerce, and communication in post-Napoleonic Europe. Virtually no one travels for pleasure or on nonessential business in a war zone, and much of Europe had been a war zone for two decades. Since Waterloo, however, people who had long kept as close to home as possible were now able to go virtually wherever they wished, if they had the means to do so—to such an extent that by 1824 even Samuel Taylor

Coleridge, who was not normally given to cranking out doggerel, gave in to the temptation to satirize British tourists.

> Some are home-sick—some two or three,
> Their third year on the Arctic Sea—
> . . . .
> But O, what scores are sick of Home,
> Agog for Paris or for Rome!
> Nay! tho' contented to abide,
> You should prefer your own fireside;
> Yet since grim War has ceas'd its madding,
> And Peace has set John Bull* agadding,
> 'Twould such a vulgar taste betray,
> For very shame you must away!
> . . . .
> Keep moving! Steam, or Gas, or Stage,
> Hold, cabin, steerage, hencoop's cage—
> Tour, Journey, Voyage, Lounge, Ride, Walk,
> Skim, Sketch, Excursion, Travel-talk—
> For move you must! 'Tis now the rage,
> The law and fashion of the Age.
> . . . .
> Of all the children of John Bull
> With empty heads and bellies full,
> Who ramble East, West, North and South,
> With leaky purse and open mouth,
> In search of varieties exotic
> The usefullest and most patriotic,
> And merriest, too, believe me, Sirs!
> Are your Delinquent Travellers!

But tourism hardly constituted the principal stuff of which post-1815 Europe was made, nor was it even a significant factor in the new scheme of things. The physical difficulty and high cost of travel in those last years

---

* British equivalent of Uncle Sam.

before railroad tracks began to spread across the Continent meant that pleasure trips were reasonable undertakings only for those with strong constitutions and fat wallets. The word that most fittingly characterizes Europe during the decade that elapsed between the opening of the Congress of Vienna and the completion of the Ninth Symphony is "repression," not "travel" or even "communication." The regimes represented at the Congress spent the following years enforcing the basic tenets of ultraconservatism that had been established there. Dissensions inevitably broke out and amendments and regroupings proved necessary, but the overall situation was clear. By 1818, Restoration France had demonstrated that it was not about to rock the boat again; consequently, it was admitted not only to the reorganized, Continent-wide family of nations, known at the time as the Concert of Europe, but to equal partnership with the leading members. At the Congress of Aix-la-Chapelle in October of that year, the Quadruple Alliance (Austria, Britain, Prussia, and Russia) became a Quintuple Alliance that included France. In 1822, when a rebellion broke out in Spain, the alliance gave France the responsibility of dispatching troops to maintain the status quo—just as, two years earlier, Metternich's Austria had intervened to quash revolts in the Italian kingdoms of Piedmont-Sardinia and the Two Sicilies. Among the major powers, only Britain opposed such interventions, on the grounds that most of the rebels were seeking constitutional reform under their respective monarchs rather than opting for out-and-out revolution. But trans-Channel objections were overruled on the Continent, and Britain virtually withdrew from the Concert of Europe.

The brutal measures imposed by the interventionists were in keeping with Metternich's policy of total repression of any word or deed that smacked even slightly of liberalism. A generation earlier, during the reigns of Joseph II (1780–90) and Leopold II (1790–92), Austria had been one of the most enlightened nations in Europe. According to the historian Adam Bunnell—a Roman Catholic priest—Emperor Joseph "wanted to eliminate the wide gap that separated the rich from the poor in his lands. He wanted all to have a chance to be educated, to be enlightened Christians as he thought he and his circle were. Above all, he wanted to eliminate what many considered . . . the preying of the church on the superstition of those who knew no better. He introduced tolerance for non-Catholics and believed in bettering *this* world through education and reform." Leopold, who succeeded Joseph in 1790, made sure that his sons, and especially Crown Prince Francis, were brought up with modern ideals. "The princes must, above all, be convinced of the equality of man," he had written. "They should be made to realize . . . that their entire existence must be subordinate to their duties. They must regard it as their highest duty to listen and to comfort. . . . They must understand that one may never receive individuals in a bored, disdainful, distracted, ill-humored, or choleric manner; that one must give one's full attention to such persons, whatever their station."

To the end of his reign, Francis stood by his father's precepts—he was famously kind and attentive to individual subjects—but the French Revolution had made him alter his way of applying them. As early as 1793, only a year after Francis had ascended to the throne, and the year in which his aunt Marie Antoinette, queen consort of Louis XVI of France, was guillotined, his chief of police, Count Johann Anton Pergen, had written to the governors of Austria's provinces: "In the present conditions when the cult of liberty has gained so much ground and all monarchical governments face great unrest, the ordinary arrangements for peace and security are inadequate. Every government must secretly set all forces in motion for the good of the state, in order to convert those in error and to wipe out through effective countermeasures all dangerous impressions that might have been instilled in any class of subjects by sneaking agitators."

The young Beethoven, who had arrived in Vienna from his native Bonn in 1792, laughed at the idea of a French-style revolution in his adoptive city. Although he wrote to a friend in Bonn, on August 2, 1794, that "several *important people* have been locked up" and that "it is said that a revolution is to break out," he immediately added: "I believe that so long as an Austrian has his *brown beer* and *sausages,* he won't revolt." In the same letter, however, he mentioned that the gates to the suburbs were to be shut each night at ten o'clock, that the soldiers had loaded their muskets with live ammunition, and that people dared not speak up for fear that the police would take them into custody.

Two upheaval-strewn decades later, the authorities' attitudes had congealed to such an extent that even hard-won previous concessions— such as the abolition, back in Joseph II's day, of the papacy's secular authority—were renounced in order to bolster the monarchy's power.

"Many eras witnessed tyrannical governments," commented the historian E. H. Gombrich, "but what gave a special characteristic to life under Metternich was the sense of deep and widening disappointment." Count Joseph Sedlnitzky, Pergen's successor as police chief, proved to be the most dedicated of watchdogs, and he was dog-like also in his devotion to his masters, Metternich and the emperor. At first, the student associations, known as *Burschenschaften,* and other nationalist organizations throughout the German Confederation demonstrated angrily against the repressive measures, but in 1819, when a member of one such group assassinated the reactionary playwright and diplomat August von Kotzebue, Metternich demanded that the *Burschenschaften* be outlawed, that publications that expressed political dissent be banned, and that university students and professors who deviated or seemed to deviate from official policy be expelled. These repressive new laws, known as the Carlsbad Decrees, were made permanent in 1824, and they effectively turned the confederation's member nations—especially Austria—into prototypes of the modern police state. Professional spies and amateur informants flourished throughout the Hapsburgs' domains, and nowhere more so than in Vienna, where every market and tavern was plagued by at least one pair of ears eager to intercept any untoward opinion in order to show off their possessor's fidelity to the emperor. Even Beethoven's conversation books demonstrate the uneasiness of average citizens: Not many months after the Carlsbad Decrees had been issued, someone abruptly ended a café chat with the composer by writing in one of the books: "another time—just now the spy Haensl is here."

Beethoven, whose relatively liberal sympathies, love of freedom, and contempt for authority were well known, was considered too eccentric and out of touch to be potentially dangerous; others were less fortunate. Even the nationalistic but otherwise largely apolitical poet and playwright Franz Grillparzer was constantly forced by state censors to rewrite parts of his works, some of which were banned altogether simply because the censors were afraid of having overlooked hidden subversive meanings that were not, in fact, to be found in the texts. And in 1820, twenty-three-year-old Franz Schubert was arrested, allegedly for having insulted the police but really because he was on friendly terms with the poet Johann Senn, who was arrested at the same time, imprisoned, and sent into exile. So far as is known, Schubert was not punished by the police, but he must have been deeply frightened by his too-close encounter with imperial repression. What is certain is that he and Senn never met again.

The seething magma of protest in the German-speaking world would eventually erupt into the revolution of 1848, but throughout the 1820s and '30s it remained mostly subterranean. In three short lines, the poet Hoffmann von Fallersleben (the pseudonym of August Heinrich Hoffmann) broadly satirized the timid, café-frequenting rebels of the day: "And they chatter, leaf [through the gazettes], search, / And finally come to the conclusion: / 'Another little piece of apple pie!' " No matter how intensely artists and intellectuals detested the political situation in which they found themselves, they could express their aversion in only the most oblique ways. Aversion led to introversion, to the concentration on intensely personal thoughts, feelings, and states of being and the transformation of them into artistic expression—to Romanticism, in a word.

Britain's government may have looked liberal in comparison with the politically antediluvian regimes excogitated and run by Metternich and his likeminded brethren in Germanic Europe, but the tactics it adopted to quell domestic unrest were no gentler than those deployed in more reactionary nations. In particular, workers' protests over their miserable living conditions were immediately and sometimes violently repressed. Eleven protesters were killed and four hundred injured in Manchester's Peterloo massacre of August 1819, and three months later Parliament passed the infamous Six Acts, which severely limited freedom of speech and assembly. Yet in 1824, the year of the Ninth Symphony, Parliament first passed a law that allowed workers to unionize and then—in an early, tentative move toward democratic progress—established the National Gallery, "for the benefit of all."

At the same time, however, Britain continued to expand its empire by conquering more and more of Africa and southern Asia after having lost much of its North American stronghold to the young United States. In 1824, the British occupied Mombasa, in Kenya; Rangoon, in Burma; and Melville Island, off the northern coast of Australia, and signed treaties with Holland for the acquisition of the latter's possessions in India and the Malay Peninsula, including the island of Singapore. The British favored the struggles for independence of Spain's South American colonies, not out of benevolence toward the colonists, much less toward the indigenous populations, but in order to ensure that Spain would never be in a position to reacquire its lost wealth, power, and influence. In December 1823, with the encouragement of King George IV's government, U.S. president James Monroe issued a declaration—now known as the Monroe Doctrine—that warned European countries to cease all interference, especially attempts at colonial expansion, in the Western Hemisphere; support from Britain, the world's greatest naval power, was imperative, because the United States was not yet strong enough to enforce such a policy on its own. This entente helped the South American liberators Simón Bolívar and Antonio José de Sucre to abolish the last remnants of Spanish rule on their continent—a mission that they accomplished in the year of the Ninth Symphony.

The same message to Congress in which President Monroe asserted his now famous doctrine—which was tucked in among reports on the postal service, road repairs, the surveying of harbors, and the like (in 1824, the Erie Canal neared completion, and Upper Canada's Welland Canal, which would also benefit the United States, was begun)—contained an anomalous but remarkable paragraph, much neglected in history books, about, of all places, Greece.

> A strong hope has been long entertained, founded on the heroic struggle of the Greeks, that they would succeed in their contest, and resume their equal station among the nations of the earth. It is believed that the whole civilized world takes a deep interest in their welfare. Although no power has declared in their favor, yet none, according to our information, has taken part against them. Their cause and their name have protected them from dangers which might ere this have overwhelmed any other people. The ordinary calculations of interest and of acquisition, with a view to aggrandisement, which mingle so much in the transactions of nations, seem to have had no effect in regard to them. From the facts which have come to our knowledge, there is good cause to believe that their enemy has lost forever all dominion over them; that Greece will become again an independent nation. That she may obtain that rank is the object of our most ardent wishes.

In the eyes of educated western Europeans as in those of the American president, Greece was significant not only as the cradle of Occidental civilization but also as the birthplace of democracy; for many of them, the Greek wars of independence from Ottoman Turkey symbolized or at least hinted at the democratic ideals that were being repressed all across Europe. Had people spoken out in favor of freedom at home, they would likely have faced unpleasant consequences, but their Christian governments could not easily have prevented individuals and private organizations from supporting the oppressed—and conveniently distant—Christian Greeks in their opposition to the dominant Muslim Turks. (Note, by the way, the odd fact that Monroe did not name the power from which the Greeks were seeking independence.) But unlike the young American republic, which was ill positioned, politically, economically, and geographically, to intervene in European affairs, governments east of the Atlantic could have aided the Greeks but didn't. For instance: George Canning, Britain's foreign minister at the time, favored the Greek cause but opposed direct intervention in it. Yet in England as elsewhere in Europe, the Greek insurrection became a romanticized, sublimated form of rebellion, and the man who most potently symbolized Romantic rebellion became fatally involved in the Greek struggle.

Lord Byron fights "freedom's battle"

It is the evening of May 7, 1824. In Vienna, the Ninth Symphony's plea for universal brotherhood is being heard in public for the first time. But seven hundred miles to the southeast, in the mud-choked Greek town of Missolonghi, a sealed coffin containing the crudely embalmed corpse of George Gordon Byron, 6th Baron Byron, floats in the darkness of a caulked cask filled with 180 gallons of spirits. The most idolized poet of the age has been dead for two and a half weeks, but his remains have yet to begin the five-week-long sea voyage that will take them back to his native England.

Like Beethoven, who was seventeen years his senior, Lord Byron appeared to his contemporaries as an embodiment of Romanticism—a wild genius, unaccountable to common standards of behavior, dominated only by his ego. But, again like Beethoven, Byron is known today as a far more complicated personality. Aristocratic pride and radical political beliefs, an overheated libido and a great capacity for tenderness, a tremendous appetite for women counterbalanced by strong homoerotic tendencies, a beautiful countenance offset by a clubfoot (about which he was even more sensitive than Beethoven was about his deafness), extremes of morbidity and mordancy, of blackguardly egotism and boundless generosity: These and many other contradictory characteristics combined to make the poet one of the most engagingly enigmatic figures in our culture's history.

Byron was born in London in 1788 to a good-hearted but irascible mother—a descendant of King James I of Scotland—and to a profligate father who died when his son was three. Young Byron's early childhood was as impoverished as Beethoven's had been, but the future bard's penury came to an abrupt end when a childless great-uncle left the Byron family's title and estates to his ten-year-old nephew. Byron attended Harrow and Cambridge, began to publish remarkably accomplished poetry when he was eighteen, and at twenty-one set out on a two-year trip, through parts of Portugal and Spain but mainly around the eastern Mediterranean.

In Greece he conceived and set to work on the autobiographically tempestuous narrative poem *Childe Harold's Pilgrimage,* which, if we indulge our imaginations, can be seen as a counterpart to segments of Beethoven's early storm-and-stress works in minor keys, including the Piano Trio op. 1, no. 3; the piano sonatas op. 2, no. 1, op. 10, no. 1, and op. 13 ("Pathétique"); the Cello Sonata op. 5, no. 2; and the String Quartet op. 18, no. 4. There is much more posturing in *Childe Harold* than in Beethoven's early published works (although, on second thought, maybe we simply have a harder time identifying musical posturing than verbal posturing), but dark, roiling elements are common to both. Byron's poem also contains clearly reasoned musings on various subjects, especially the disastrous modern condition of the once-glorious Hellenic world. In the second of *Childe Harold*'s four cantos, Byron upbraided contemporary Greeks as "the hopeless warriors of a willing doom" and invoked a "gallant spirit"—someone who would call the nation back "from the tomb." Was he baiting himself? The seeds of the half-idealistic, half-suicidal adventure that would lead him to an early death fifteen years later seem to have been sown in 1809.

After his return to England, Byron's first speech in the House of Lords was an ultraradical declaration on behalf of the frame workers, or weavers, of Nottinghamshire. Many of these factory employees were being driven out of work by the introduction of a new, more efficient type of mechanical frame, or loom, into the textile industry; there had been rioting, and many of the new frames had been broken—as a result of which a bill had been introduced in Parliament to make frame breaking a capital offense. In a letter written two days before he made his speech, Byron explained his position on a problem that affects our postindustrial society two centuries later as profoundly as it affected laborers at the time of the Industrial Revolution. He described the workers as "a much injured body of men sacrificed to [the] views of certain individuals who have enriched themselves by those practices which have deprived the frame workers of employment. . . . My own motive for opposing [the] bill is founded on it's [*sic*] palpable injustice, & it's [*sic*] certain inefficacy.—I have seen the state of these miserable men, & it is a disgrace to a civilized country.—Their excesses may be condemned, but cannot be subject of wonder."

The speech established Byron's liberal credentials and brought him notoriety in political circles, but the publication a few days later of the first two cantos of *Childe Harold's Pilgrimage* brought him immediate fame in all educated circles within Britain and, soon thereafter, throughout the Western world. Other works followed quickly, and all were virtually automatic bestsellers. Byron's celebrity and good looks led him into a series of affairs with well-connected married women, including, most scandalously, his half sister, Augusta Leigh. Early in 1815 he married Annabella Milbanke, also of aristocratic descent, but by the time their daughter was born at the end of the year the marriage had broken down, in part thanks to widespread rumors about Byron's liaison with Augusta.

The scandal had one even more dramatic consequence than Annabella's decision to leave her husband: Byron's permanent departure from England in the spring of 1816. He spent several months in Switzerland—much of the time in the company of Percy Bysshe Shelley and his circle (including the social philosopher William Godwin's stepdaughter, Claire Clairmont, who bore Byron a second daughter early in 1817)—then moved on to Italy, where he lived for nearly six years. There he began to purge his poetry of the Romantic melancholy and high-flown self-dramatization that had already given the adjective "Byronic" to the En-

Lord Byron, by H. Meyer. *(After G. H. Harlow, stipple engraving, 1816.)*

glish language and to write in the sharper, wittier style that had always characterized his robust, pungent, and exhilaratingly entertaining personal correspondence. The tempestuous, self-absorbed *Childe Harold* of Byron's twenties gave way to the alternately waspish and meditative *Don Juan* of his thirties.

At Venice, his base for two years, he turned out a remarkable quantity of literature while indulging his sexual appetites with a succession of short-term mistresses and numerous local prostitutes. Then, in 1819, a more serious attachment to the nineteen-year-old Countess Teresa Guiccioli led him to abandon Venice, first for Ravenna, where Teresa and her elderly husband lived, then for Pisa, to which the countess's father and brother had to flee because of their connection with the subversive Carbonari movement for Italian reunification—a movement with which Byron also became involved—and finally to Genoa.

By early 1823, domestic life with Teresa had begun to bore Byron, and he readily accepted an invitation from the London Greek Committee to represent them on-site in aiding the Greeks' struggle against the Turks. A considerable portion of his fortune was channeled into the project: Byron not only leased and equipped a ship to transport him to Greece but also helped finance Greek military efforts—no easy task, since the Greeks were split into conflicting factions, each of them eager to enlist the support of the famous and, above all, wealthy Englishman. For months after his arrival in August 1823 on the island of Cephalonia, a British protectorate, Byron dedicated himself to creating a semblance of unity among the various factions, and only in December (the same month in which President Monroe declared his support for Greek independence) did he feel ready to travel to the mainland. After a close brush at sea with the Turks, he arrived at the town of Missolonghi on January 5, 1824, and there, together with the Greek nationalist leader Prince Alexander Mavrocordatos, he began to plan the capture of the remaining Turkish strongholds on the Gulf of Corinth.

It is easy to wax ironical about Byron's motives in the entire Greek affair—easy to point to his interest in smart uniforms and his fixation with heroic deeds. But Byron had almost always sided with radical-libertarian causes at home and abroad and had loved Greece since his first visit there in 1809–10. His support for Greek independence was sincere, and once he arrived in Missolonghi he threw himself wholeheartedly into the fray. "His house was filled with soldiers," reported Julius Millingen, a young, pro-Greek English physician who had attached himself to Byron's entourage. "His receiving room resembled an arsenal of war, rather than the habitation of a poet. Its walls were decorated with swords, pistols, Turkish sabres, dirks, rifles, guns, blunderbusses, bayonets, helmets, and trumpets . . . ; and attacks, surprises, charges, ambuscades, battles, sieges, were almost the only topics of his conversation with the different capitani."

Perhaps Millingen had expected Byron to discuss pentameters and hexameters with "the different capitani," and to decorate his makeshift

Missolonghi dwelling with objets d'art. But the poet's internal life was an unknown to the young doctor as to the military people. Byron had fallen in love with his page, Loukas Chalandritsanos, a handsome fifteen-year-old boy; his love was unreciprocated. Two and a half weeks after his arrival at Missolonghi, Byron wrote what later generations have seen as his valedictory poem.

> "On this day I complete my Thirty-sixth Year"
> Missolonghi, Jan. 22, 1824.

> 'T is time this heart should be unmoved,
>   Since others it hath ceased to move:
> Yet, though I cannot be beloved,
>   Still let me love!

> My days are in the yellow leaf;
>   The flowers and fruits of love are gone;
> The worm, the canker, and the grief
>   Are mine alone!

> The fire that on my bosom preys
>   Is lone as some volcanic isle;
> No torch is kindled at its blaze—
>   A funeral pile.

> The hope, the fear, the jealous care,
>   The exalted portion of the pain
> And power of love, I cannot share,
>   But wear the chain.

> But 't is not *thus*—and 't is not *here*—
>   Such thoughts should shake my soul, nor *now*,
> Where glory decks the hero's bier,
>   Or binds his brow.

> The sword, the banner, and the field,
>   Glory and Greece, around me see!
> The Spartan, borne upon his shield,
>   Was not more free.

Awake! (not Greece—she *is* awake!)
    Awake, my spirit! Think through *whom*
Thy life-blood tracks its parent lake,
    And then strike home!

Tread those reviving passions down,
    Unworthy manhood!—unto thee
Indifferent should the smile or frown
    Of beauty be.

If thou regret'st thy youth, *why live?*
    The land of honourable death
Is here:—up to the field, and give
    Away thy breath!

Seek out—less often sought than found—
    A soldier's grave, for thee the best;
Then look around, and choose thy ground,
    And take thy rest.

This is not one of Byron's finest poems, but it strikes the reader by its zigzagging from the private to the public and back again. Byron contrasts the fact that he is in the autumn of his life—"the yellow leaf" (he is not posturing here: The average life expectancy of a European male in those days was about forty years) with the youthful "fire that on my bosom preys" and with the "hope," "fear," "care," and "pain" of love that he still experiences. But he then contrasts these private woes with public concerns for Greece—although these, too, are made personal by his thirst for carrying out what he perceives as heroic deeds. Yet while he is indulging in a final self-exhortation, in the name of heroism, to extinguish his "reviving passions," show indifference to "the smile or frown of beauty," and seek an "honourable death," he is also saying that for purely private reasons he prefers death to the loss of his youth; that a soldier's grave is worthier of him than any other sort of grave; and that he is ready to look around, choose his ground, and take his rest.

The emotional structure of this poem differs radically from the one that Beethoven hit upon for the Ninth Symphony. Byron's poem crescendos from private anguish to public heroism but then diminuendos back to private anguish and preoccupation with death—soul death and physical death; content-wise, it is in A-B-A form. Beethoven's symphony, as I understand it, swirls continuously upward from despair to struggle to acceptance to joy; content-wise, it is in a dynamic A-B-C-D form within which its creator's private miseries are transformed into something all-embracing, something that exists here and now but also everywhere and at all times in human experience. Byron remains touchingly intimate. Beethoven forces us to climb to a higher vantage point: He universalizes the intimate.

In February 1824, just as Beethoven was completing the Ninth and a few weeks after Byron had written "On this day I complete my Thirty-sixth Year," the poet took ill. He had not yet fully recovered when, early in April, he developed a persistent fever, and this led his physicians to recommend bleeding. That Byron was fully aware of the perils of entrusting himself to the medical men of his day is clear from a letter that he had written to his friend Francis Hodgson in 1810, during his first visit to Greece. In it, he characterizes the doctors who had looked after him during an illness as "assassins" and says that he was so sure that one of them, Romanelli, would cause him to die that he actually wrote his own facetious epitaph: "Youth, Nature, and relenting Jove / To keep my *lamp in* strongly strove, / But *Romanelli* was so stout / He beat all three—and *blew* it *out.*"

"Youth, Nature, and relenting Jove" had bested Byron's doctors in 1810, but in 1824 medical incompetence joined forces with persistent illness, disappointment in love, and disillusionment with the greedy and untrustworthy soldiers available to him for his grand undertaking, and killed him. Byron died at Missolonghi on April 19, eighteen days before the premiere of the Ninth Symphony.

Four decades later, the English poet and critic Matthew Arnold compared Byron and Shelley unfavorably, as writers, with their fellow High Romantics Wordsworth, Coleridge, Keats, and Sir Walter Scott, but prophesied that posterity would remember Byron and Shelley much longer than the others. Wordsworth and company did not "apply modern ideas to life," according to Arnold, whereas Byron and Shelley had attempted to bring a liberating spirit to English letters. Arnold's predictions count for little today—all six of the writers he was assessing, with the possible exception of Scott, are considered major figures in English literature—but the fact that Byron, four decades after his death, was still seen as a battler for the modern spirit says a great deal about his significance for nineteenth-century liberal thinkers.

Byron and Beethoven were vastly divergent in background and personality. Byron's self-absorption, which subsided considerably from his twenties to his thirties, from the "pure" Romanticism of *Childe Harold* to the irony-tempered Romanticism of *Don Juan,* might have diminished even further had he, like Beethoven, lived into his fifties. They were similar insofar as they felt contempt for most human beings, but Beethoven seems to have been more concerned than Byron with reaching out toward humanity in the abstract. What is compelling, however, in the convergence of Byron's death and the unveiling of Beethoven's final symphony is the fact that the handsome, wealthy, amoral, urbane poet and the unkempt, economically unstable, moralistic, rough-hewn composer had simultaneously come to similar conclusions about contemporary European civilization. Although revolutionary and Napoleonic Europe had turned into a vast graveyard, both men believed that postrevolutionary and post-Napoleonic Europe had become an equally vast prison for the human spirit. Byron, whose ego displayed itself through histrionics rendered tolerable by self-mockery, would probably have greeted the ideals and sentiments expressed in the Ninth Symphony's finale with a mixture of hope, skepticism, and barbed irony. Beethoven, on the other hand, wanted to help light the way for humanity; he wanted human beings to realize their high ethical potential, and he probably felt, deep down, that such a feat would coincidentally have made them worthy of himself. Yet however great was the distance that separated the two Bs' world outlooks, Byron's martyrdom—which is how the poet's death was perceived in liberal circles—and the premiere of Beethoven's Ninth Symphony remain the most emblematic events of 1824 in the history of Romanticism's evolution.

Absolute rulers and an anarchic writer

"You are sad about Byron, but I am very glad of his death, as a sublime theme for poetry." Alexander Sergeyevich Pushkin was only twenty-five years old in June 1824, when he made this bitterly ironic statement in a letter to Prince Pyotr Andreyevich Vyazemsky, a friend from school days, but the poet had already crammed experience after experience into his life. He was familiar with glory and misery, freedom and despotism, exaltation and depression, sexual excess and rejection in love.

News of Byron's death two months earlier was spreading across Europe; the English poet's remains were on the high seas as Pushkin wrote his letter to Vyazemsky, and the letter also contains Pushkin's opinion of the cause for which Byron had given his life: "About the fate of the Greeks one is permitted to reason, just as of the fate of my brothers the Negroes—one may wish both groups freedom from unendurable slavery. But it is unforgivable puerility that all enlightened European peoples should be raving about Greece." He had seen plenty of Greek "bandits and shopkeepers" in Odessa in the previous weeks and months, and they didn't seem to have much to do with "Themistocles and Pericles"—in other words, with fifth-century B.C. Athens, where democracy was born and the arts flourished.

Pushkin's phrase about "my brothers the Negroes" refers to his descent, on his mother's side, from Abram Hannibal, an Abyssinian who had been sold into slavery and later adopted and ennobled by Peter the Great; Hannibal's great-grandson was proud of his African ancestry. On his father's side, Pushkin was descended from the old Russian boyar nobility. These double aristocratic ties had made his parents into snobs, although there was precious little cash to support their arrogance. They didn't care much for their son, but good connections and a partially successful exam helped him to land, in 1811, in the first class of students at the new Imperial Lyceum, the prestigious secondary school that Tsar Alexander I had founded at Tsarskoye Selo, near Saint Petersburg. Pushkin's versifying talent, like Byron's, was precocious and prodigious—by the age of fifteen he was publishing high-quality poetry—and there was considerable resemblance between their talents for dissipation as well. Nor did belonging to the aristocracy prevent Pushkin from developing radical political ideals any more than it had impeded similar tendencies in Byron. Some of the poems that Pushkin wrote in his late teens expressed liberal notions and could be circulated only in manuscript, in a sort of tsarist-era samizdat. But the imperial censors did their job well: In May 1820, at the time of his twenty-first birthday, Pushkin was banished to Russia's southern provinces, by direct order of the tsar.

Exile humiliated the proud young poet and frustrated the enthusiastically debauched Saint Petersburg social butterfly; when—even whether—that exile might end depended entirely on the unpredictable states of mind of the tsar and his advisers. But exile was a boon to Pushkin's long-term personal and artistic development, thus also to world literature. By the end of 1820, Pushkin had been allowed to travel in Caucasia and the Crimea, had begun to study English—mainly in order to read Byron in the original—and had set to work on his narrative poem "The Prisoner of the Caucasus," which, after its publication two years later, so touched the tsar that he considered pardoning Pushkin—although in the end he allowed reasons of state to prevail over his feelings. Through the first half of 1824, Pushkin was in Odessa, the Black Sea port where, he said, "everything breathes, diffuses Europe." It was from there, at about the time of the Ninth Symphony's premiere in Vienna, that he sent a letter that got him into worse trouble than ever with Russia's absolute ruler. He told a friend that when he read the Bible,

> the Holy Spirit is sometimes to my liking, but I prefer Goethe [who was still alive] and Shakespeare. You want to know what I am doing. I

Alexander Sergeyevich
Pushkin. *(Portrait
by A. P. Yelagina, after
original [1827] by
V. A. Tropinin.)*

am writing the motley stanzas of a romantic poem—and I am taking lessons in pure atheism. An Englishman is here, a deaf philosopher, the only intelligent atheist I have yet met. He has covered some thousand pages with writing to prove *qu'il ne peut exister d'être intelligent Créateur et régulateur* [that an intelligent being, a Creator and regulator, cannot exist], destroying in passing the flimsy evidence of the immortality of the soul. His philosophic system is not so consoling as it is usually thought to be, but unfortunately it is the most plausible.

The "romantic poem" was Pushkin's novel in verse, *Eugene Onegin*—generally considered his masterpiece, and certainly the work by which he is best known—which he had begun the previous year and would finish in 1831. The deaf English philosopher was a medical doctor named Hutchinson who later became an Anglican minister—which suggests that Pushkin took the doctor's speculations more seriously than their propounder did. The imperial censors intercepted and read the letter, and the drift of its contents was reported to the tsar, whose religious beliefs were becoming ever more orthodox, not to say bigoted. Fortunately, the ruler of all the Russias did not see the tribute to his old archenemy Napoleon that Pushkin wrote into his poem "To the Sea" ("K moriu"), which also dates from 1824:

> He vanished, mourned by freedom,
> Leaving the world his crown.
> Sound forth, rise up in storm:
> He was, O sea, your singer.
> . . . .
> Like you, he was powerful, deep, and gloomy.
> Like you, he was indomitable.
> . . . .
> The fate of the earth is everywhere the same:
> Where there is a drop of virtue, already on watch
> Is either enlightenment or tyranny.

This poem, written three years after Napoleon's death, supports Stendhal's hypotheses about the profound, ineradicable impression that the emperor had made on early-nineteenth-century youths all over Europe, regardless of whether their countries had been France's allies or enemies, and the despair that young people felt after Napoleon's defeat by the forces of reaction. Rightly or wrongly (or both), to Pushkin and his contemporaries Napoleon had represented the principles of the French Revolution, and he was even seen by young Romantics like Pushkin as a fellow spirit, "powerful," "deep," "gloomy," "indomitable," and a "singer" of the sea, or, in other words, of the world's mysterious abysses.

But even without the ode to Napoleon, Pushkin's letter on atheism was sufficient to make the tsar decide to increase the young man's punishment by having him transferred from pleasant Odessa, with its temperate climate, Italian opera house, and flirtatious aristocratic ladies, to a remote estate that belonged to the poet's mother's family at Mikhailovskoye in the province of Pskov, eight hundred miles to the north. There Pushkin spent the last two years of his six-year exile, increasingly frustrated over his confinement but finding consolation, or at least occupation, in his work. During that period he made considerable progress on *Onegin* and completed his play *Boris Godunov* and his poem "The Gypsies," all of which had been started in 1823 or '24 and touch upon the subject of individual suffering. In *Boris Godunov*, however, as in the Ninth Symphony, intense individual suffering is expressed within the context of humanity's suffering and striving for freedom—hopeless striving in Pushkin's work, idealized striving in Beethoven's; and, as in Byron's "On this day I complete my Thirty-sixth Year," so in *Boris* questions of personal ambition are set off against questions that concern large segments of our species. Pushkin considered *Boris* one of his most important works, but the tsar's censors could not tolerate it.

The real Tsar Boris (ca. 1551–1605) was responsible for many constructive policies as well as an unusual degree of openness toward western Europe, but his highly suspicious nature led him to commit unjust and often brutal acts against his enemies, actual or only potential. Pushkin's main concern, however, was not biographical accuracy. From the play's first scene, he created parallels between sixteenth-century Russian history and recent European history—parallels that no reasonably perceptive reader of the day would have failed to notice. One of the characters, Prince Vortynsky, in his dialogue with another prince, mentions the old Varangian guards—the Varangians having been a noble class from which they both were descended—but goes on to say:

> . . . 'Tis no easy thing for us to vie
> With Godunov; the people are not wont
> To recognise in us an ancient branch
> Of their old warlike masters; long already
> Have we our appanages forfeited,
> Long served but as lieutenants of the tsars,
> And he hath known, by fear, and love, and glory,
> How to bewitch the people.

Here, the Varangians look suspiciously like Europe's prerevolutionary aristocracy—both represent a decadent, ineffectual Establishment—and Boris is made out to be the same sort of daring usurper as Napoleon.

Pushkin's contemporaries would also have made an automatic connection between what one of the play's characters refers to as the dynastic political "sins" and "dark and evil deeds" of sixteenth-century tsars and the complicity of the current tsar, Alexander I, in the murder of his father, Paul I. Nor can passages like the following lament have gone over well with the authorities:

> . . . Is there any safety
> In our poor life? Each day disgrace awaits us;
> The dungeon or Siberia, cowl or fetters,
> And then in some deaf nook a starving death,
> Or else the halter. Where are the most renowned
> Of all our houses, where the Sitsky princes,
> Where are the Shestunovs, where the Romanovs,
> Hope of our fatherland? Imprisoned, tortured,
> In exile. Do but wait, and a like fate
> Will soon be thine.

Despite the lip service paid to the Romanovs—Alexander I's family, which reigned over Russia from 1613 until the Bolshevik Revolution of 1917—the list of cruel and arbitrary punishments meted out by an unpredictable, despotic tsar cannot have been appreciated on high, especially since Pushkin went so far as to put this rebellious speech in the mouth of a nobleman named Pushkin, and to have Tsar Boris say, a little further on: "I like not the seditious race of Pushkins."

Toward the end of the play, the dying Boris tells his young son how to govern with the cruel cynicism proper to an absolute ruler:

> For many a year experienced
> In rule, I could restrain revolt and treason;
> They quaked with fear before me; treachery
> Dared not to raise its voice. . . .
> Of late I have been forced to reinstate
> Bans, executions—these thou canst rescind;
> And they will bless thee. . . .
> At the same time, little by little, tighten
> Anew the reins of government; now slacken;
> But let them not slip from thy hands.

And in the final scene, when the false pretender Dmitri is proclaimed tsar and the people are incited to "Shout: Long live the Tsar Dmitri Ivanovich!" the play ends with the extraordinary stage direction: "The PEOPLE remain silent."

Pushkin wrote *Boris Godunov* during the worst period of his internal exile; his isolation was in many respects comparable to that of the deaf Beethoven of the 1820s, and what literary historian and Pushkin scholar Stephanie Sandler has written about how to absorb *Boris Godunov* could also provide a clue for how to listen to the Ninth Symphony, or, for that matter, for how to approach any work of art. "Whether we can take pleasure in reading or watching *Boris Godunov* depends on how much we are able to be like Pushkin," she says, adding that "we must be something other than a passive audience," and that "we as listeners must work to imagine what it was like for Pushkin to write the play as he did. . . . We must be willing to see ourselves in this play, willing to play the parts assigned to us."

In other words, if we try to imagine the work as its creator conceived it, we will have a more vivid, multidimensional view of it. But Pushkin, who was nearly three decades younger than Beethoven, differed from the composer inasmuch as he still hungered for acceptance, recognition, and more: "I want glory so that your ears will be stricken / With the sound of my name every hour, so that you / Will be surrounded by me, so that everything, everything / Around you will reverberate loudly with talk of me," he wrote in 1825. Beethoven, by 1825, had known the hollowness of recognition and glory and was beyond longing for acceptance.

By the time *Boris Godunov* was ready for publication, Alexander I had died, a revolt by antiauthoritarian liberals had been staged and easily put down, and the rebels—later called Decembrists, because their uprising took place in December 1825—had been imprisoned, exiled to Siberia, or executed. Pushkin had been on friendly terms with several leading Decembrists, some of whose deeds had been inspired, at least in part, by his poetry. But the new tsar, Nicholas I—Alexander's younger brother—recognizing Pushkin's popularity as an author, decided to put an end to the poet's exile and, in the fall of 1826, granted him a lengthy private audience in Moscow. Nicholas seems to have appreciated Pushkin's frankness—the young author told him that had he been present at the time of the Decembrist revolt he would have been among the rebels—and when Pushkin complained of the absurd rigors of official censorship, the tsar declared that from then on he himself would read Pushkin's works in manuscript and act as his personal censor.

For a short time, Pushkin was euphoric over Nicholas's promise, but he soon realized that the tsar, who was no literary expert, merely handed the troublesome poet's manuscripts to the chief censors, who acted in what they believed to be their master's interests. In the case of *Boris Godunov,* this meant that publication was permitted only after a six-year delay and the imposition of many textual changes. The play was not performed until long after Pushkin's death, and only recently has an uncut edition of the uncensored version, completed in 1825, been issued.

The fact that Pushkin began to work on *Boris Godunov* in the year of Beethoven's Ninth Symphony is, on the face of things, purely coincidental; the Russian poet may never even have heard of the German composer, and it was above all his intensive reading of Shakespeare in 1824 that made him want to write for the theater. There may well be a connection, however, to Byron, since the English poet's verse dramas exercised a strong influence on his Russian counterpart—as did Byron's death. But the fact that Pushkin chose to write about despair and oppression just when Beethoven and Byron were dealing with the same matters, and when the likes of Alexander I, Metternich, and Charles X were doing their best to make despair and oppression as endemic as possible throughout Europe, is, I believe, not mere coincidence: The theme was airborne across the Continent, and it was a cause as well as a manifestation of Romanticism, which was both inspired by and an inspirer of Europe's aspiration toward freedom.

Interlude

If there is a hidden thread that connects Beethoven's Ninth Symphony to the works created in and around 1824 by other significant artists, it is precisely this quest for freedom: political freedom, from the repressive conditions that then dominated Europe, and freedom of expression, certainly, but above all freedom of the mind and spirit. To a hypothetical observer who, in 1824, had heard of Beethoven, Byron, Pushkin, and the other major figures who have appeared or will appear here, the points of contact among them would have seemed tenuous, perhaps even nonexistent. But from a twenty-first-century perspective, the connection seems almost too obvious.

Napoleon had nearly managed to unify Europe, despite the Continent's geographic, climatic, ethnic, linguistic, gastronomic, and religious diversity. Notwithstanding his ultimate defeat, he had brought mutually distrustful national cultures closer together, sometimes on purpose, more often by accident. Cultural cross-pollination undoubtedly moved more slowly and affected fewer classes of people in 1824 than it does today, but among the European aristocracy and bourgeoisie it was already strongly present.

We have so far observed a composer from the Rhineland living in Vienna, an English poet dying in Greece, and a Russian poet moving through various parts of his vast homeland; we will now have a look at a couple of key artistic figures in Paris, which in many ways remained Europe's cultural capital even after Waterloo—the place where artists had to prove themselves in order to be taken seriously elsewhere—and from there we will return to the Rhineland, to observe one of the most remarkably transnational, liberty-advocating, and modern-spirited artists of the day.

France after Napoleon:
Paintbrush and pen replace cavalry and cannon

While Beethoven's last symphony was being heard for the first time, while Byron's corpse was awaiting transport from Greece to England, and while Pushkin was expressing skepticism about the Greek cause, twenty-six-year-old Eugène Delacroix—scion of a once well-to-do, now shabby-genteel family that had served the French military or diplomatic corps under all of the recent regimes—was working on a painting intended to draw attention to the Greek rebellion and, by extension, to the issue of freedom versus oppression. Yet when I look at *Scenes from the Massacres at Chios* (a Greek island), Delacroix's canvas then in progress, I sense that he was one of the many artists of the post-Napoleonic period who felt so relieved to be able to lead a normal life—whatever they thought of the reactionary regimes that had resumed their stranglehold on the Continent—that the presence of political-historical or even humanistic issues in their work was less important than the presence of the personal. Preoccupation with events had given way to a more intense focus on exploration of the self.

On January 25, 1824, for instance, Delacroix had used only a few words ("j'ai commencé la femme trainée par le cheval") to note in his diary that he had begun to paint the figure of a Greek woman being dragged off by a Turkish horseman—an important feature of the *Massacres at Chios*. But the focus of his entry that day was entirely personal, not political. Reflecting on the characters of likable people, he wrote that they "make you think for a moment that they are yourself, a bit; but you quickly fall back into your sad individuality." His concern is with psychology and personal situations, not with the world of events—which helps to explain why, for all its freedom-loving spirit, *The Massacres at Chios* is a study in pose and color rather than a paean to the Greek rebellion or a means for arousing revulsion over the horrors of war. Delacroix's friend Stendhal, who had observed such horrors firsthand, went so far as to claim that the figures depicted looked more like plague victims than war victims.

And yet the painting also illustrates suffering unmitigated by glory, which probably explains why it offended many of its early viewers. From a later perspective—our own—it is a "vast and terrible and overwhelm-

Scenes from the Massacres at Chios, by Eugène Delacroix.

ing canvas": This is how the narrative voice in Margaret Drabble's novel
The Sea Lady describes it. The work is seen as a "masterpiece of Eros and
of Death" and "as an emblem, as a paradigm, of two of the great intellectual and aesthetic causes of the last four decades of the twentieth century," which Drabble's narrator identifies as feminism and Orientalism.
The novel's two protagonists—a young English couple—

> gazed at the eerily silent and stoic scene of butchery. It was the beauty
> that appalled. To the right of the painting, the curving torso of a young
> Greek woman was voluptuously displayed as she was twisted back-
> wards against the prancing horse of her Turkish conqueror. Her figure
> was conventionally beautiful, beautiful in the manner of conventional
> sado-masochistic fantasies: her upstretched arms and manacles of

bondage, her swooning head, her bared breasts, her rapture, her immi-
nent rape and her enslavement to her turbaned ravisher were designed
to arouse the viewer, and not with pity. But the naked Parisian model
was but one motif, rearing herself up to one side of the large and
crowded canvas. Who had posed for the dark-haired, heavy-lidded
dead woman in the foreground with the fair-haired child clinging to
her lower body? Who had posed for the strangely indolent reclining
dying man with the staring knowing eyes? Who had posed for the
handsome chiselled old woman to the right of the centre of the pyra-
mid of death, with her bared and wrinkled chest and her transfixing
prophetic Sibylline gaze? It was wrong to admire, and yet the work was
wonderful. Its wonder was shaming.

Delacroix could not have anticipated either the feminist movement
or the gravity of the clash between the Islamic world and the Western
world in our day, but surely many of the people who saw *Scenes from the
Massacres at Chios* when it was new felt the same sort of disconcerted admiration that it arouses in many of today's observers. The painter himself
may well have understood and even worked to elicit these mixed emotions, although his primary concern was almost certainly that of making
the maximum communicative impact, regardless of the subject matter.
On the very day—Friday, May 7, 1824—on which Beethoven was participating in the first performance of the Ninth Symphony, Delacroix, in
Paris, made a diary entry about his painting in progress. "The human
spirit is strangely made," he said.

> I think I would have agreed to work on [this painting] while perched
> atop a bell-tower; today, the idea of completing it is only a nuisance;
> this is all because I was away from it for a long time; the same is true of
> my painting and of all possible tasks for me. A thick crust must be
> pierced in order to give oneself to something with all one's heart; it is
> an intractable terrain that repels plowshare and hoe. But with a bit of
> stubbornness, its hardness suddenly vanishes. It abounds in flowers and
> fruit. . . . But when something bores you, don't do it. Don't run after
> vain perfection. Some things that the mob considers failings are what
> often give life. . . . I don't like reasonable painting at all. I can see that
> my disorderly spirit needs to give itself a shake, undo things, take a

hundred different tacks before reaching the goal, the need for which preys on me in everything. . . . If I haven't writhed like a snake in the hands of an oracle, I am cold. I must recognize and submit to this, and I am very happy to do so. Everything that I've done well has been done thus.

These statements ("Don't run after vain perfection," "If I haven't writhed like a snake in the hands of an oracle, I am cold") could almost be described as a mini-manifesto of Romanticism, or at least of anti-Neoclassicism. Although Delacroix described himself as a "pure classicist," he was widely seen, in his day—and is still seen today—as the High Romantic painter par excellence. "Painting is nothing but a bridge set up between the mind of the artist and that of the beholder," he wrote, thereby setting up a bridge of his own from Romanticism to Impressionism and beyond, to abstract art. But the line between conservatism and radicalism is often a blurry one. The Paris Salon of 1824, at which *The Massacres at Chios* was exhibited, included not only another important Romantic canvas, *The Hay Wain,* by the Englishman John Constable—whose use of color influenced Delacroix—but also Jean-Auguste-Dominique Ingres's *The Vow of Louis XIII,* which was seen at the time as an anti-Romantic work.* Yet the "Romantic" radical Delacroix found Beethoven's radically individual music hard to love, whereas the "Neoclassical" Ingres—Delacroix's senior by eighteen years—adored it and considered the composer a true Olympian. "The symphonies of Beethoven are grand, terrible, and also of an exquisite grace and sensibility," he said, and his sympathetic understanding was aided by his abilities as a fine amateur violinist—competent enough to play chamber music with the likes of Paganini and Liszt.

Delacroix was born before Bonaparte became first consul, and he lived through the First French Empire, the Restoration, the revolution of 1830, the reign of the "bourgeois king" Louis-Philippe, the revolution of 1848, and most of Napoleon III's Second Empire. It is no wonder, then,

---

* Constable's compatriot William Blake, who was sixty-seven and ailing, began his pen and ink and watercolor painting of *Beatrice Addressing Dante from the Car* in 1824 and worked on his illustrations to *The Book of Job.* Blake considered himself, and indeed was, independent of every artistic trend or movement, yet his very independence jibed in many ways with Romantic individualism. "I must Create a System, or be enslav'd by another Man's," he had written in his poem *Jerusalem.* "I will not Reason & Compare: my business is to Create."

that, having physically survived so many regime changes, he clung to his work in order to survive mentally and spiritually. However closely his humanitarian principles may have resembled those of Beethoven, Byron, and Pushkin—all of whom he outlived by many years—his day-to-day concerns did not. In 1863, shortly after Delacroix's death, Charles Baudelaire, who had known him for two decades, wrote a substantial tribute to him in *L'Opinion nationale;* his words seem to reflect the painter's ideas accurately, and they certainly sum up a way of thinking about art that was common in post-Napoleonic Europe, as well as prototypically Romantic. According to Baudelaire, Delacroix frequently repeated the formula "Nature is nothing but a dictionary." In other words, nature was something to be consulted but not copied; reality and art are two different things. But Baudelaire also emphasized the concept of the artist—in any of the arts—as a "translator," someone who converts internal impulses into expression. What, he asked, is the

mysterious something that Delacroix, to our century's glory, has translated better than anyone else? It is the invisible, the impalpable, it is dreams, it is nerves, it is the *soul;* and he did this using no other means than contour and color; he did it better than anyone else; he did it with the perfection of a consummate painter, with the rigor of a subtle man of letters, with the eloquence of a passionate musician. . . .

Delacroix was passionately in love with passion and coldly determined to seek the means by which to express passion in the most visible way. In this dual personality we find, as it happens, the two signs that mark the most solid geniuses—extreme geniuses who surely are not made to please those timorous or easily satisfied souls who find sufficient nourishment in lax, limp, imperfect works. An immense passion redoubled by a formidable will—such was the man.

Baudelaire's insights on Delacroix say something basic about the creative personality, especially as it manifested itself in the Romantic era. You have to be either mad or bursting with the need for self-expression— or both—to dedicate yourself to art in a world in which art is little valued and less understood: thus the passion of which Baudelaire speaks. But only those artists who are capable of contemplating the results of that passion with the subzero coldness of self-criticism are likely to

achieve anything unusual. As far as the work of art—the final product—
is concerned, the Romantic Age was no different from any other period
in cultural history, and its artists are either remembered for the excellence
of what they produced or not remembered because that excellence was
lacking.

In 1823, '24, and '25, Delacroix's friend Stendhal was producing essays
that served as a manifesto of Romantic expression in literature and that
have come down to posterity under the collective title *Racine and Shakespeare.*

Stendhal was an unlikely Romantic. As a young man he had studied
mathematics, and throughout his life he shunned all forms of mysticism
and religion. "God's only excuse is that he does not exist," he said, in
what Nietzsche enviously described, decades later, as the best atheistic
joke ever made. In music, Stendhal adored the classically linear
chiaroscuro of Mozart and Rossini as opposed to the more unsettling
self-expression of Beethoven, whom he described as a composer of
"music with learned dissonances" and "the Kant of music"—no compli-
ment intended. He did, however, understand something of what
Beethoven was about: Referring probably to works such as the Fifth
Symphony and the "Appassionata" Sonata, he wrote of the German composer's "Michelangelo-like impetuosity." And in attacking musical conservatives for their protests over some difficult leaps in Rossini's vocal
writing, he said, "If you want discoveries to be made, let your ships sail a
bit haphazardly on the high seas. If people had never allowed their ears
to be astonished, would the fiery, singular Beethoven ever have followed
the wise, noble Haydn?"

In *Racine and Shakespeare,* Stendhal used seventeenth-century
France's most celebrated playwright as an example of a type of expression
that had had its day, whereas the even older English Bard was held up as
a proto-Romantic—the greatest proponent of ever-fresh emotional communication. "I am of the opinion that tragedies must now be fashioned
to suit us rational, serious, and somewhat envious young people in the
year of grace 1823," he wrote, pretending to be much younger than his
forty years. "In our day, the alexandrine verse [used by Racine and his
contemporaries] is more often than not a disguise for foolishness."
Stendhal's main point was that the Classicists' unbending adherence to

the alexandrine verse form and to the ancient Greeks' practice of maintaining unity of time and place had straitjacketed French dramatic writing since the time of Louis XIV, well over a century earlier. He viewed the prolongation of these confining rules and procedures as sheer reactionary stubbornness, not as an aid to intelligibility.*

The essays that comprised *Racine and Shakespeare* were severely criticized, not so much for their author's promotion of Romanticism as for his praise of poor old Shakespeare, who had been dead for more than two centuries. These rebukes had little to do with the Bard himself and a great deal to do with England's unpopularity among the French—an age-old dislike that had grown exponentially thanks to Britain's role in the defeat of Napoleon. Stendhal replied to his critics by sarcastically accusing them of believing that Shakespeare had been an aide-de-camp of the Duke of Wellington. And in a letter to an anti-Romantic that he included in *Racine and Shakespeare* (a letter dated May 5, 1824, two days before the premiere of the Ninth Symphony), the author prophesied that in forty years French playwrights would be creating mighty dramas in prose with titles like *The Return from the Isle of Elba,* based on recent history—dramas with plots that might take place "over seven months' time and distances of five thousand leagues," without a care for unity of time and place. To Stendhal, Romanticism in literature was nothing more or less than "the art of presenting literary works that are capable of giving as much pleasure as possible to peoples [that is, nations], in keeping with the current state of their habits and beliefs." So in a very important sense, he equated Romanticism with contemporaneity and the avant-garde, and he set it in opposition to hidebound conservatism.

In the repressive atmosphere of the time, Romanticism in the arts was often a proxy for, or at least a symbol of, forbidden political liberalism. In 1824, while Stendhal was writing his essays, ultraroyalists were creating greater divisiveness within France than the country had known since Napoleon's fall a decade earlier. Louis XVIII possessed sufficient political acumen to realize that a return to pure, prerevolutionary absolutism was impossible in his country, but the assassination by a Bonapartist of

---

* Two whole generations after Stendhal, the novelist Anatole France was still able to joke that he would be willing to convert his deepest, darkest secrets into alexandrine verses and have them declaimed every evening at the Comédie-Française, secure in the knowledge that no audience member would be paying attention to what was being recited.

Charles-Ferdinand Bourbon, Duc de Berry, Louis's nephew, in 1820, had given the upper hand to the political faction that was more royalist than the king. When Louis died, in September 1824, his ultraconservative younger brother, who ascended the throne as Charles X, immediately pressed for such unpopular, illiberal measures as compensation for aristocrats who had lost property during the Revolution (this move alone cost the country a billion francs), reinstatement of some of the Roman Catholic Church's secular authority, and silencing of the press. Shortly before Charles took the throne, Stendhal had written that for ten years, "France, which had seen its press enslaved" under Napoleon, "has enjoyed semi-freedom; but so far no man of genius, or even of talent, has shown up to take advantage of censorship's impotence." Under Charles, however, that half freedom was eliminated; the press simply had to comply with government decrees.

Stendhal believed in democracy, yet he was an intellectual elitist who knew that freedom of the press would not turn bad poets and writers into good ones. On the contrary, as he wrote shortly before Charles's accession,

> to avoid the ridicule that would undoubtedly affect them, these noble versifiers have prudently joined the political party in power. This party has currently managed to buy, openly or secretly, all but one or two of Paris's newspapers, so that the eccentric absurdities that these pseudo-bards want to pass off as Romantic poetry either sneak by unnoticed or are exaggeratedly extolled by the newspapers of the party under whose protection their authors are tidily lined up.

He was too much a child of the Enlightenment to be taken in by the self-indulgence and pompous self-esteem of fraudulent Romantics. "There are about a dozen poets in Paris who try, in their writings, to be as somber and eccentric as Lord Byron in his blackest fits," he wrote in an article published in the *New Monthly Magazine* in London in May 1824, shortly after Byron's death. "But their works resemble his more or less as tinplate thunder at the Opéra resembles a storm in the Alps."

For Stendhal, as for Delacroix, Pushkin, Byron, and Beethoven, artistic and intellectual achievement depended almost entirely on personal depth and professional excellence, rather than on their respective countries' political vicissitudes. But these artists were not apolitical; they internalized and sublimated revolution in an age of political repression and transformed it into what we call Romanticism. Some artists, however, more openly expressed their contempt for the regimes in power.

The French-German Christian-Jewish Romantic ironist

On May 24, 1824—the day after the Ninth Symphony's second performance, in Vienna's Grosser Redoutensaal—the poet and essayist Heinrich Heine was writing a letter to a friend when someone brought him a piece of news. He immediately set down his reaction. "As I write this I hear that my cousin, Lord Byron, died at Missolonghi. So that great heart, too, has ceased to throb!" he said. "Yes, that man was great; he discovered new worlds in anguish; Prometheus-like, he defied miserable men and their more miserable gods, and the fame of his name penetrated the icebergs of Thule and the burning deserts of the east."

Heine was referring not only to Byron's accomplishments as a poet, but also and above all to his stature as an opponent of received ideas, bourgeois morality, and the most obtusely reactionary, repressive regimes of the day. The twenty-seven-year-old German poet's observations about his spiritual "cousin" were particularly heartfelt because at the time he was, in a sense, a captive—an unwilling and anything but intrepid law student at the University of Göttingen, which he was attending only because the wealthy uncle who supported him was threatening to cut off funds if his nephew dropped out. Heine had already published some of the most beautiful lyric poetry in the German language and had been lionized in Berlin's highest cultural circles; how he felt about his exile in provincial Göttingen is clear from a devastatingly satirical segment of *Die Harzreise* (*The Harz Journey*), an account of a walking tour that he made in central Germany's Harz Mountains only a few weeks after Byron's death. He mockingly describes Göttingen as "famous for its sausages and university" and says that its inhabitants are "generally divided into students, professors, philistines and cattle," of which "the cattle class is the most important." Along the road that leads out of town, he meets two university officials who, he claims, were "charged with watching carefully that . . . no new ideas are smuggled in by a speculating assistant professor, instead of undergoing their regular decades of quarantine before coming to Göttingen."

Heine was a native of Düsseldorf, which is only about forty miles north-northwest of Beethoven's native Bonn. The two men's geographic and linguistic origins were similar, and their strong, irrepressible love of freedom was comparable, yet they could hardly have been more unalike in nature and in their approach to life. Beethoven was born into a dysfunctional, lower-class Catholic family; Heine was born (in 1797, within a year and a half of Delacroix and Pushkin) into a close-knit, middle-class Jewish family. As a boy, he idolized the French soldiers who occupied the Rhineland and abolished the ghettos in which the Jews had been forced to live. The Heines lost their comfortable bourgeois status when the father's business failed, and several family members, including the poet, eventually converted to Christianity in order to be able to accede to positions that were off limits to Jews; conversion was "an admission ticket to European culture," he said. Yet the Heines, unlike the Beethovens, remained united and loving.

Heine's perspective on history, politics, the creative mentality, Romanticism, and life in general not only characterized his poetry and prose but to a great extent also generated it. "Heine's eyes must have been as many-faceted as those of a fly," observed Ford Madox Ford. "He is at

Heinrich Heine. *(Woodcut facsimile after an engraving by L. E. Grimm, 1827.)*

once romanticist, realist, impressionist, folksong folk-lore German lyricist, French lost soul, Jewish Christian, and the one man who cannot have been descended from the brute beasts." He may have been "the most exquisite of all the world's lyrists since the great Greeks, perhaps the greatest of all the world's realistic-bitter romantics"; he was "of no place and of no race," and "there is no poet—there is, indeed, no other man— who resembles him." Writing less exaltedly only a few years after Heine's death, Matthew Arnold succinctly evaluated the "seven closely-printed octavo volumes" that comprised the American edition of the German poet's writings: "In the collected edition of few people's works is there so little to skip," he said.

At one time or another Heine was personally acquainted with many of the leading lights in German thought and literature of his day— Goethe, Hegel, the poet and translator August Wilhelm von Schlegel, not to mention Karl Marx and Friedrich Engels, among others—but he was the most modern of them all, including even Marx, his junior by twenty-one years. In their individual ways, the others were all idealists, whereas Heine, although he considered himself one as well and certainly kept in mind several important ideals for humanity, was too sharply observant and too much the ironist to have allowed ideals to blot out reality. His poem "Fragen" ("Questions"), for instance, from the *Nordseebilder* (*North Sea Pictures*)—written not many months after Beethoven completed the Ninth Symphony—employs High Romantic diction to express a proto-existential concept:

> By the sea, by the desolate night-time sea,
> Stands a youth-man,
> His breast full of woe, his head full of doubt,
> And with mournful lips he asks the waves:
>
> "O solve life's riddle for me,
> The agonizing, age-old riddle,
> Over which many heads have already brooded,
> Heads in hieroglyph-bedecked caps,
> Heads in turbans and black skullcaps,
> Bewigged heads and a thousand other
> Poor, sweating human heads—

> Tell me, what is the meaning of man?
> Where does he come from? Where is he going?
> Who lives up there, on golden stars?"
>
> The waves murmur their eternal murmur,
> The wind blows, the clouds fly by,
> The stars twinkle, indifferent and cold,
> And a fool awaits an answer.*

It is no surprise that Nietzsche, the great anti-idealist and idol smasher of the late nineteenth century, admired Heine's writings—although Heine, toward the end of his life, seemed to come down on God's side and on the side of his own Jewish heritage. In any case, the German-speaking public of Heine's day, which loved his lyric poetry, could not tolerate his barbed, unsparing wit or, probably, the fact that the poetry they so enjoyed was written by a Jew, albeit a converted one. Metternich liked Heine's lyrical works but felt compelled to proscribe his writings in Austria and its dominions. At about the time of France's "July Revolution" of 1830, which terrified absolutists across Europe, Heine's mordant attacks on every sort of established order and right-thinking belief led to the banning of his books in other German states, too, and the issuing of a warrant for his arrest. A Prussian foreign minister even requested that Heine be sentenced to death, perhaps as a result of the poet's verbal assault on Prussia's "philosophical-Christian soldiery, this conglomerate of pale beer, lies and sand. . . . The King of Prussia is a very devout man; he is a good Christian . . . and he believes in holy symbols," Heine wrote. "But, ah, I wish he believed in Jupiter, the father of the gods, who punishes perjury—perhaps then he would give us the promised constitution."

When the German federal diet included Heine in a decree promulgated "against the wicked, anti-Christian, blasphemous literature that wantonly treads all morality, modesty and decency underfoot," Heine replied that he had

---

* Parts of this poem could be read as a realistic counterfoil to some of the ecstatic lines from Schiller's "Ode to Joy" that Beethoven set in the Ninth Symphony: "Brothers, a loving Father must live / Above the canopy of stars. / Dost thou fear the Creator, world? / Seek him above the canopy of stars! / He must dwell above stars."

a better opinion of the Deity than those pious souls who imagine that He created man only for suffering. Yes, here on earth I would establish, by means of the blessings of free political and industrial institutions, that beatific state which, according to the opinions of the pious, will be realized only on the Day of Judgment and in heaven. . . . We have measured the earth, weighed the forces of Nature, reckoned the resources of industry, and behold!—we have found that the earth is spacious and wide enough for everyone to build his hut of happiness on it—that the earth can feed us all decently, if only every one of us works, and no one lives at another's expense—that it is no longer necessary to preach the blessedness of heaven to the large masses of the poor.

In 1831 Heine fled to Paris, where he immediately felt very much at home. "If anyone asks you how I am," he wrote to a friend, "tell him 'like a fish in water,' or rather, tell people that when one fish in the sea asks another how he is, he receives the reply: 'I am like Heine in Paris.' " This was because he saw the French as the "chosen people" of "the new religion, the religion of our day": liberty. Its "first gospels and first dogma" were written in French, he said; "Paris is the new Jerusalem, and the Rhine is the Jordan which separates the holy land of liberty from the country of the Philistines." All the greater, then, was his disillusion once he realized what France's revolutions had actually produced: "Not for themselves did the people bleed and suffer, but . . . for that bourgeoisie which is worth just as little as the noblesse whose place it took, with the same egoism. . . . The people have won nothing with their victory except regret and greater depravity." Nor did he hold higher hopes for American democracy, where, he said,

all men are equal—equal dolts, with the exception, naturally, of a few millions, who have a black or a brown skin, and who are treated like dogs. Actual slavery, which has been abolished in most of the northern American states, does not revolt me as much as the brutality with which the free blacks and the mulattoes are treated. . . . Americans make much of a to-do about their Christianity, and are zealous churchgoers. This hypocrisy they have learned from the English, who have bequeathed to them their worst characteristics. Material pursuits are their true religion; money is their God.

Heine spent the last twenty-five of his fifty-nine years in exile in Paris—the last eight of them confined to his room, as a result of a debilitating disease that eventually killed him. Long before Heine had immigrated to France, however, his writings, with their extraordinary mixture of High Romantic lyricism and disenchanted irony, were in many ways more Gallic than Teutonic. Although he was a poet, not a novelist, he often comes across as a sort of German Stendhal: Both writers observed life clearly, enjoyed to the full whatever delights it brought them without ever losing sight of the ridiculousness of all human enterprise, and chronicled the present while keeping an eye—a remarkably accurate, prophetic eye—on the future, to which both made themselves available in a "Beethovenian" way, through a striking combination of here-and-now self-assurance and awareness of their total insignificance in the cosmos.

Heine, by the way, showed little understanding of Beethoven's music—especially the late works, of which he said, "To me, it is a very meaningful fact that Beethoven was deaf at the end of his days, and even the invisible world of notes no longer had any reality in sound for him. His notes were only memories of notes, ghosts of lost sounds, and his last creations bear frightening marks of death on their foreheads." But Heine shared with Beethoven the belief that art had to be independent while remaining strongly connected to real life. "I am for the autonomy of art," he wrote in 1836. "It is not to be regarded as the handmaiden of religion or politics; it is its own definite justification, just like the world itself"— whereas barely a generation earlier very little art that lacked church, state, or aristocratic patronage had reached the public. But, Heine warned, "just as the giant Antaeus remained invincible so long as his feet touched the earth, so the poet remains strong and mighty so long as he stands on real ground, but loses his strength at once when he rises ecstatically into the blue."

Maybe the most similar element in the creative makeup of those two most dissimilar Rhinelanders, Beethoven and Heine, and the only element that allows us to bring them near each other in the pantheon of our collective Western cultural imagination, is the urgency with which they both needed to show humanity what it is—and what it could become. Just as Beethoven hoped, against all odds, for the day when "all men become brothers," so the clear-eyed Heine nevertheless managed to prophesy a "great confederation of peoples—the Holy Alliance of Nations" under which "we shall no longer need to sustain standing armies of many hundreds of thousands of murderers because of mutual distrust. We shall use our swords and horses to plow with and we shall win peace, prosperity, and freedom."

In a statement that could easily have been made by Beethoven, Heine wrote: "I know not if I deserve that a laurel wreath should one day be laid on my coffin. But lay on my coffin a *sword,* for I was a brave soldier in the Liberation War of humanity." Eighty-five years after Heine's coffin was lowered into the ground in Paris, his grave was demolished by order of Adolf Hitler. His ever-popular poem "Die Lorelei" continued to be printed in Nazi Germany, but it was identified as "a folk lyric of unknown authorship." What more fitting tributes could have been paid to the enduring power of Heine's pen/sword?

In a sense, every human being who has ever used his or her brain for nondestructive purposes counts as a brave soldier in humanity's War of Liberation, but the conjunction of Beethoven's last symphonic masterpiece with crucial works or events in the lives of so many other outstanding artists made 1824 a particularly fertile year in the history of that struggle. The fact that the Ninth Symphony, Byron's death, Pushkin's *Boris Godunov* and "To the Sea," Delacroix's *Massacres at Chios,* Stendhal's *Racine and Shakespeare,* and Heine's *Harz Journey* and *North Sea Pictures* all furthered, in one way or another, Romanticism's rear-guard action against repression underlines the significance of that speck of time. And perhaps these brief glances at those artists and their states of being at that moment will have helped to remind readers—as they reminded this author—that spiritual and intellectual liberation requires endless internal warfare against everything in ourselves that narrows us down instead of opening us up and that replaces questing with certitude.

Nearly two centuries later, the world still overflows with people who believe that truth not only exists but that it is simple and straightforward, and that *their* truths—be they political, religious, philosophical, moral, or social—constitute The Truth. Federico Fellini's characterization, a generation ago, of the fascist mentality as "a refusal to deepen one's individual relationship to life, out of laziness, prejudice, unwillingness to inconvenience oneself, and presumptuousness" describes the obedient adherents of most prefabricated beliefs, everywhere and at all times. The others—the disobedient, the nonadherents, those who think that the world is not easily explained and that human experience does not fit into tidy little compartments—are still fighting the eternally unwinnable War of Liberation. Until our sorry species bombs or gluts itself into oblivion, the skirmishing will continue, and what Beethoven and company keep telling us, from the ever-receding yet ever-present past, is that the struggle *must* continue.

The uniquely vital expressive power of the Ninth Symphony, which is one of the most striking products of human beings' attempts to continue the struggle, as well as to deepen their individual relationships to life, is the subject of the next part of this book.

PART THREE

Imagining the Ninth

The musical image

When I was in my mid-twenties and beginning what was to be a short-lived career as a conductor, I took a summer course in France with Louis Fourestier, the nearly eighty-year-old former music director of the Paris Opéra and Opéra-Comique who had been a co-founder, with Ernest Ansermet and Alfred Cortot, of the Orchestre Symphonique de Paris, and chief conductor of French repertoire at the Metropolitan Opera. On one occasion, Fourestier, whose musical personality had been shaped by such teachers as Vincent d'Indy and Paul Dukas, representatives of late French Romanticism, told me that in his opinion the best way to remember how one wanted a particular piece to "go" was to create a mental picture to fit it. The example he used was the third movement of the Ninth Symphony: When he was standing on the podium, ready to begin it, he would think of a young couple sitting on a park bench under a starry sky, holding hands and looking up at the empyrean in a mixture of awe and love; this image would put him in the right frame of mind, he said.

Fourestier was a highly trained, thoroughly professional musician and a lovable character, but his description and the philosophy behind it seemed to me patent nonsense. Music that does not accompany words presents no image whatsoever to me; I experience it in a nonvisual, nonverbal, yet thoroughly intellectual and at the same time intensely emotional way. I love to grasp a piece's form as it reveals itself and, simultaneously, to experience and absorb whatever it is communicating to me. But I cannot say what that "whatever" is.

The lack of verbal and visual connections in my perception of non-vocal music may be the result of my having had little contact with opera during my formative years. I came to "classical" music first through my own efforts at the piano keyboard and then by listening to enormous quantities of live and recorded orchestral, chamber, and solo performances. Even my love of German lieder, which began in my mid-teens (first Brahms, then Schubert, then the others), had little to do with the texts, at first, although I made the effort required of a non-German-speaking youngster to understand them; it was generated, rather, by the direct emotional communication of the musical settings—and this despite the fact that I already loved literature almost as much as I loved music. To me, music resisted and resists verbal description.

Certain pieces—they are usually in duple meter and begin on a single-note upbeat in a quick tempo, such as the first movements of Mozart's String Quartet in G Major, K. 387, and String Quintet in G minor, K. 516, or of Beethoven's String Quartet in C minor, op. 18, no. 4, or of Brahms's Fourth Symphony—do seem to me to recount stories in a ballad-like way. Those upbeats, all of which lead immediately into chorded downbeats, pull me into a dramatic narrative. But the narrative is wordless and imageless; it speaks through purely musical structures and progressions and creates what I think of as purely musical emotions. I am capable of saying that the opening of the Mozart quartet seems to glow, that that of the quintet seems anguished, and so on, but I cannot normally proceed beyond short descriptive epithets or state-of-being adjectives of this sort—and even these undeveloped characterizations will no doubt contrast with those that many other attentive listeners might hazard. Similarly, I admit that the climax of the *Symphonie fantastique*'s first movement seems to me to represent a male orgasm as clearly as the climax of the Liebestod from *Tristan und Isolde* seems to represent a female orgasm (although in the latter case Wagner's story line and text set the listener up to grasp the meaning), and that Chopin's Prelude No. 13 in F-sharp Major seems just as manifestly and intensely erotic as the climaxes of the Berlioz and Wagner pieces, although in a much subtler, more radiant, more caressing, more protractedly sensual way. But in these examples, too, I can suggest only states of being rather than specific verbal associations or visual depictions. I always feel that the music I love is telling me something, and the instrumental music that I love most—music by Bach, Mozart, Beethoven, Schubert, Chopin, Schumann, Brahms, Bartók, Stravinsky—is music in which a great deal of telling is telescoped into concentrated time spans. But precious little of my perception of the telling that goes on in music can be expressed verbally, despite the fact that, as a writer, I am deeply and continually concerned with verbal expression.

In recent years, the English conductor Sir Roger Norrington has been speaking out in favor of the sort of approach to music of which Fourestier was an exponent. "In the earlier part of this [the twentieth] century, music went through an abstract patch," Norrington said in an interview, "and it was thought that all music was abstract and mustn't tell a story, that it's cheap to think that music is telling a story. But in 1804, when the ["Eroica"] symphony was written, and for many years later during the nineteenth century, it was not immoral for music to tell a story; it was essential."

I certainly don't believe that making use of such stories is "immoral," but neither can I believe that it is or ever was "essential"—that thinking of starry nights, hand-holding lovers, or any other image, be it vague or definite, silly or sophisticated, would necessarily aid anyone's musical perceptions. Wagner, whose attitudes toward musical performance were typical for his day, liked to develop descriptive stories, or "programs," for pieces of instrumental music, yet there is a telling passage on this subject in one of the diaries kept by his second wife, Cosima. Richard was sitting at the piano one evening in 1879, playing "the return to the tremolo and the opening" (technically, the retransition to the recapitulation) of the first movement of Beethoven's Ninth Symphony and describing it as " 'the cauldron, the daemonic one which has been seething throughout.' " Cosima—who was also Liszt's daughter—intervened:

> I admit to R[ichard] that in this work I feel no need for a program, and I even put his [program for it], based on Faust, right out of my mind. R. says everyone conjures up his own images for it—but in my case not even that happens, and I can compare what goes on inside me only with the springing up of mysterious seeds and buds, the spirit being just a guide to the enchanted ground where this magical act of creation is taking place, its role merely that of a myrmidon, bereft of all power.

In other words, the music itself communicated to her something very direct but nonverbal and nonvisual. And in this respect, Cosima Wagner's thinking was more modern than that of her husband.

I am profoundly interested in the historical and biographical background behind the music and composers I love, but I do not want either to build stories onto compositions or to perceive compositions as having been built on stories. However inadequate and fluid my perceptions are, for me they are sufficient and complete at any given encounter with a piece. Extraneous elements would fragment, divert, or dilute my concentration rather than unify, focus, or strengthen it. Saul Bellow, a master of words, wrote that through music, "the logically unanswerable was, in a different form, answerable. Sounds without determinate meaning became more and more pertinent, the greater the music." Bellow would probably have agreed—as I agree—with the German conductor Wilhelm Furtwängler's observation: "It is in the very nature of music that the clarity of the language it uses is different from the clarity of words: but the language is none the less definite for all that." And Furtwängler may have been familiar with Felix Mendelssohn's statement on this subject—a statement written only fifteen years after Beethoven's death: "The thoughts which are expressed to me by music that I love are not too indefinite to be put into words, but on the contrary, too definite. And so I find in every effort to express such thoughts, that something is right but at the same time, that something is lacking in all of them." Even Wagner, who was not given to admitting his own fallibility, confessed toward the end of his life that although he had attempted to describe the Ninth Symphony at length, "what this [first] movement is cannot be expressed in words."

In his essay "Is Music Unspeakable?" the Franco-American cultural historian Jacques Barzun tells the story of a composer who goes to the piano and plays, for some guests, a piece he has just written. Afterward, one of his listeners asks him what the piece's meaning is; the composer responds by returning to the piano and playing the piece a second time. "The composer's answer was entirely right," says Barzun. "The meaning is inside any work of art and it cannot be decanted into a proposition." Or, as Stravinsky put it, "Music means itself." But Barzun goes on to point out, "If music merely tickled the ear, it would still be agreeable, but it would remain a trifling pastime. We know it is much more, and it is plain that the composer can use sounds to set off a particular stirring within us. But the stirring is nameless, so that if it does not accompany the words of a text and yet we want to refer to it, we have to make up some analogy." The analogy chosen will vary from one listener to an-other, regardless of whether the listener is a professional musician (or musicologist or critic) or a music lover who does not pretend to have in-side information. But what most musicians, including this book's author, hear and feel and imagine in outstanding pieces of music is—music.

Yet we know that composers of "pure" instrumental music may have mental pictures, verbal texts, reminiscences of people or places or situa-tions, or any of countless other ideas or images consciously or uncon-sciously in mind while they are planning or writing their works. Many composers attempt to communicate identifiable ideas, images, and/or stories through given instrumental pieces; the myriad examples range from Vivaldi's *The Four Seasons* to the tone poems of Richard Strauss and Debussy, from Berlioz's *Harold in Italy* to Gershwin's *An American in Paris* and beyond. But it is highly unlikely that a person hearing these works for the first time without knowing their titles and/or "programs" would be likely to grasp the ideas or visualize the images that the com-poser intended to express or depict, no matter how musically sensitive the listener in question might be and notwithstanding such "special ef-fects" as the terrifying drumrolls in Strauss's *Till Eulenspiegel* or the honk-ing car horns in the Gershwin piece. For that matter, if one were to play wordless, instrumental arrangements of "O patria mia," "Dich, teure Halle," or "Près des remparts de Séville" for ten people who had never heard *Aida, Tannhäuser,* or *Carmen,* one would probably receive ten dif-ferent opinions as to what the subjects of those arias might be.

Think for a moment of the striking example of the introduction to *The Creation,* in which Haydn makes a semi-cacophonic orchestral "Representation of Chaos" lead into a tremendously affirmative choral-orchestral outburst in C Major on the final word of the phrase, "und es ward Licht" ("and there was light"). Barzun points out that although "the words of Haydn's oratorio are one analogy for the burst of C Major . . . other events would go with the music just as well—say, the escape of a prisoner unjustly condemned; or Dante's first sight of Beatrice; or a wan-derer in the desert reaching an oasis; or even Archimedes leaping out of his bath and shouting 'Eureka!' because he has found the solution to his problem. Viscerally, these correspond."

An example of how far afield instrumentalists may stray when they invent stories to explain the music they perform is pianist Mitsuko

Uchida's description, in an interview, of one of Schubert's last works, the Sonata in B-flat Major, D. 960: "In the first movement you are basically dying," she said, "and in the slow movement you are already dead. In the scherzo, the daughters of the Erlkönig are dancing around, and in the last movement the gate closes in front of your nose: Bang!"—and so on. Inventing stories of this sort may help some performers to sort out their interpretive ideas, but such tales are gross simplifications of whatever stories—if any—composers may have had in mind when they wrote their music.

And Beethoven? Most of us who listen attentively to his music believe that we can distinguish among the playful, serious, self-assertive, angry, tragic, joyful, meditative, consolatory, and other characteristics in his works, and we know that he often had specific emotions or even situations in mind at certain points in those works—not only in compositions that he prefaced with verbal hints (the second movement of the "Eroica" Symphony, for instance, or all five movements of the "Pastoral" Symphony, or the third movement of the String Quartet in A minor, op. 132), but in parts of virtually all of his instrumental works. Yet when he composed major works with verbal texts—*Fidelio,* the *Missa Solemnis,* and the Ninth Symphony's finale are the most obvious and significant examples—he undertook a much more ambitious project than the expression, through sound, of emotions or soul states, however powerful the emotions or however complicated the soul states. He aimed to contribute directly and specifically to the course of human development.

For instance, *Fidelio,* Beethoven's only opera, cost him extraordinary effort and was particularly dear to him because he believed that a parable that described clear-cut choices between good and evil was the best sort of story to set to music, for the edification of large numbers of people. As a result, although the music that he wrote for *Fidelio* is highly dramatic, the work is not a drama in any traditional sense, whatever Beethoven may have believed it to be. Despite its engaging musical character sketches of the good-hearted but fearful jailer, his romantically misguided daughter, her thwarted suitor, and the demonic prison governor, *Fidelio* is essentially a musical-theatrical representation of spiritual progress, of the triumph of virtue over baseness, and of mankind's struggle to move forward from ignorance, bondage, obscurity, and turmoil toward wisdom, freedom, illumination, and peace. "Gott! welch dunkel hier!" ("God! What darkness here!") are the first words sung by Florestan, the opera's victim-hero, and they are charged with the most evident of subtexts. Florestan's subsequent hallucinatory vision of hope as he languishes in his underground prison cell is nothing other than imagined light, or perhaps a glimmer of real light from the torch carried by his heroic wife, who is about to arrive and save him. "Ist nicht mein Grab mir erhellet?"—"Is it not true that my tomb is being illuminated for me?" he wonders.

The *Missa Solemnis,* too, is a study in the contrasts and conflicts between wishes and reality: peace versus strife, acceptance versus rejection, hope versus despair, lightness versus density, assonance versus dissonance, and, once again, illumination versus obscurity. And so, in part, is the Ninth Symphony, which is a secular companion piece to the *Missa:* Beethoven completed them within a year of each other. J.W.N. Sullivan, in his classic 1927 study, *Beethoven: His Spiritual Development,* refers to the "intolerable yearning" that forced the composer to try, in the Ninth

Beethoven in 1818.
(Pencil drawing by August von Kloeber.)

Symphony's finale, to "make himself one with the whole human family, considered as the children of a Heavenly Father." According to Sullivan, this "solution is a natural one, and is apparently as 'lofty' as could be desired, but it is nevertheless felt as an inadequate culmination of the spiritual process portrayed in the first three movements." Sullivan believed that this presumed inadequacy was not the result of the introduction of human voices, as some of the movement's other critics have suggested, but rather of an inherently defective goal. "We feel that the spirit which has climbed up the heights of those three movements should now, like Moses on Sinai, be granted a vision of God Himself," rather than mere joy on earth. Such a vision is revealed in the *Missa Solemnis,* Sullivan says, but not in the Ninth, whose vocal-instrumental finale is "the one instance of [Beethoven's] failure, in a major work, to rise to the height of his great argument."

Sullivan's evaluation of the symphony is that of a thinker who has read Schiller's diffuse, almost dithyrambic ode and Beethoven's excerpted, reorganized version of it; found them wanting in comparison with the timeless, otherworldly aspirations of the Roman Catholic Mass's unalterable text, as it had been established by Pope Pius V in 1570; and automatically put the symphony's music in the same category as the words it sets. He seems not to have noticed that the music of the Ninth's finale first transforms the words, then leaves them in a trail of dust. In the *Missa,* Beethoven had to limit his interference with the text to rudely thrusting into the background the parts of it that he evidently didn't like. In the Agnus Dei, however, his settings of the three words "Dona nobis pacem" ("Grant us peace") are at times sweetly dream-like—as if to say, "We know that we're asking for something impossible, something that will never happen, but we can't help wishing it would anyway"—and at other times ferociously demanding, even raging: "Where is this long-promised peace of yours, God? Are you or are you not going to grant it to us? How much longer are we going to have to put up with the horrible mess you've made for us? GRANT US PEACE, damn it!" In 1796, Haydn had briefly used martial trumpets and drums in setting the same words in his Mass in C Major—the *Missa in tempore belli* (Mass in time of war)—but he was referring to real, physical war: The French army had invaded Austria, and the work was a prayer for victory first, peace later.

Beethoven, on the contrary, used the sounds of war as a symbol of spiritual strife.

Alfred Einstein, a pioneering musicologist in the first half of the twentieth century, described the *Missa* as "a tremendous and intensely subjective disputation between man and God," which proceeds from "awe, entreaty and unquestioning faith" to "perturbation and unrest." I do detect, in Beethoven's setting, the disputation, awe, and entreaty, not to mention the dramatic recounting of the death and resurrection of Christ as symbols of human suffering and hope, but at no point do I perceive any hint of "unquestioning" faith. I would almost connect the violent protest in Beethoven's setting of the *Dona nobis pacem* with Woody Allen's facetious complaint about God "reneging on every promise." In their way, the German composer's interpretations of this allegedly heaven-inspired and heaven-directed text are barely more respectful than the American writer-director's ironic observation. If I were a believer, I would consider Beethoven's treatment of the *Dona nobis pacem* as blasphemous as Allen's joke.

The *Missa,* through the Roman Catholic liturgy and sometimes at cross-purposes with it, restates and goes beyond *Fidelio*'s tale of struggle for illumination and peace; the Ninth Symphony does likewise, purely through music during its first three movements and through a mixture of music and humanistic poetry in the finale. "In its freedom and recklessness of expression and means the Ninth Symphony forms an antithesis to the Mass and a complement," said Alfred Einstein. It "throws a bridge over abysses of despair, distraction, and fond yearnings to the goal of mankind reconciled in brotherly love and certainty of God's fatherly goodness." Nowhere is Beethoven's search for transcendence—what I have already described as his yearning to exist in an ideal Elsewhere and as a member of an ideal Humanity—more unmistakably evident than in these works.

The music of the Ninth Symphony's finale does to Schiller's poem what the music of the *Missa Solemnis* does to the Latin Mass: It comments on the text, creates fantasies around it, focuses on certain details, eliminates others, and forces listeners to confront a brave new emotional, spiritual sound universe in which multiple galaxies of mind and "soul" coalesce. Indeed, the *Missa* and the Ninth are two sides of the same coin.

Or, more precisely, both works are both sides of similar coins: Each of them attempts to comprise the entire, blackness-surrounded essence of human existence, but from a unique angle. In the *Missa*, Beethoven turns the Nicene Creed and other ancient pieces of ecclesiastical doctrine into a humanistic, nondenominational "plea for inner and outer peace." (The words are his, written in the original manuscript at the first appearance of the words "Dona nobis pacem.") In the finale of the Ninth, on the contrary, Beethoven gathers up his—and humanity's—all-too-earthly struggles, places them in an ideal world of pure spirit—"over the canopy of the stars," as the text states—and resolves them, ideally. And he seems to tell us that *this is how it shall be.* Never mind the when and the how: *This is how it shall be,* because to believe otherwise, he implies, is to negate the very possibility that either we ourselves or a Supreme Force, if there is one, can give any purpose to human life.

What does music communicate?

But let's take a step backward. Although Beethoven was one of the greatest masters at depicting rapidly shifting emotions in music, he was by no means one of the first. At least as early as the fourteenth century, in the works of the French composer Guillaume de Machaut, emotional fluctuations, both obvious and subtle, were a key element in "cultivated" music. Beethoven's immediate predecessors—eighteenth-century composers of vocal-instrumental music—particularly concerned themselves with such contrasts, and the attempt to move from darkness to light, from spiritual confusion to comprehension, seems to have been as much a preoccupation for them as it became for him. In Bach, the emotion generally emerges over relatively substantial time spans, as, for instance, in the almost unbearably beautiful, suffering plea expressed throughout the opening Kyrie of the Mass in B minor, or in the slowly surfacing, hard-to-achieve, but eventually triumphal hopefulness that seems to be expressed by the Mass's final "Dona nobis pacem." In Haydn and Mozart, as in Beethoven, the contrasts usually take place over shorter stretches, between one theme and another or even within a single phrase. One of the best-known examples of the long-night's-journey-into-day problem that Beethoven later took up at a more abstract level is the plaintive but mysterious request made by the fable-like hero of Mozart's *The Magic Flute,* in the opera's first-act finale. In the despairing key of A minor, Tamino asks, "O ew'ge Nacht! wann wirst du schwinden?—wann wird das Licht mein Auge finden?" ("O eternal night! when will you fade?—when will the light find my eye?") Less than a minute later, after mystical voices have told Tamino that his beloved Pamina "still lives," the delighted young man sings a happy little ditty in sunny C Major. And at the end of the opera, when the "good" Sarastro has eliminated the "bad" Queen of the Night, the former proclaims, "Die Strahlen der Sonne vertreiben die Nacht!" ("The sun's rays banish the night!")

Yet there was a difference, maybe even a line of demarcation, between the approach and intentionality of Beethoven and that of his predecessors. This was partly because Bach, Haydn, and Mozart worked almost entirely on commission: They composed for specific patrons—individuals or organizations—and usually for specific occasions. Music publication, as we have seen, was a relative rarity before and during Bach's day; it became more common during the second half of the eighteenth century, when Haydn and Mozart flourished, but even then it was considered an "extra"—a desirable extra, to be sure, that allowed works to circulate widely and that might bring in a bit of income beyond what composers and performers were paid by their patrons, but not one that raised serious thoughts of artistic immortality. As professional musicians, Bach, Haydn, and Mozart were aware of and admired some of the music by composers of the past, but they knew that few members of the general public were interested in works written a generation or two—let alone centuries—earlier. Musical fashions changed: This was a fact of life. Those three masters would no doubt have been overjoyed to know that millions of people in the twenty-first century would listen to and love their music and that today's musicians would be debating more hotly than ever questions of how eighteenth-century and older music ought to be performed, but they would also have been puzzled, perhaps even shocked, and certainly frightened by such foreknowledge. They wrote for their contemporaries and did not expect their music to endure for hundreds of years.

To a considerable degree, they and their predecessors indirectly owe their posthumous lives to Beethoven, whose belief in writing for posterity gradually became central to his creative impulse and who thus, largely inadvertently, helped to create the reverent attitudes toward artistic genius that have come to symbolize the Romantic era for later generations. Composers before Beethoven certainly understood the concepts of self-expression and originality, as musicologist Robert L. Marshall pointed out in a friendly exchange of opinions with Charles Rosen in *The New York Review of Books*. Marshall quoted from a letter written by the twenty-one-year-old Mozart: "I cannot write in verse, for I am no poet. I cannot arrange the parts of speech with such art as to produce effects of light and shade, for I am no painter. Even by signs and gestures I cannot express my thoughts and feelings, for I am no dancer. But I can do so by means of sounds, for I am a musician." And, Marshall said, "Mozart was quick to report from Vienna in 1784 about a work in progress—his never-finished opera *L'oca del Cairo:* 'I guarantee that in all the operas which are to be performed until mine is finished, not a single idea will resemble one of mine.' " Rosen agreed with Marshall that "Mozart's concern with originality" is "underrated" and that the composer was "proud of the originality of his piano concertos, and knew that no one in Vienna had ever heard anything like them." But Rosen made the point that Mozart's intention, in his music, was to express his thoughts and feelings rather than "his personality or his biography. . . . No doubt the music does express his personality and is influenced by his life; but this was not a specific intention of Mozart, as it would be for some later artists."

Beethoven's convictions about the composer as artist rather than artisan and about the arts ranking above nearly everything else in the hierarchy of human endeavors were convictions whose time had come. And the main tool for realizing his goal of reaching out to posterity was the burgeoning music publishing industry. As the bourgeoisie grew, so did its interest in the "finer things in life" that had once been an exclusive province of the aristocracy. Increased demand led to increased supply: From 1795, when the twenty-four-year-old Beethoven published three piano trios as his opus 1, until the end of his life, more than three decades later, the sale of his music to publishers in various countries was one of his major sources of income, thus also one of his most time-consuming concerns. Although he, like his predecessors, wrote works that were commissioned of him, usually for specific occasions, the commissions often served him more as starting impulses than as primary motivators. He wrote for publication, and the great majority of his most significant works and many of the minor ones were, in fact, published during his lifetime; whatever he may or may not have believed about an other-worldly afterlife, he certainly hoped that his compositions would win him a long afterlife here on earth.

The importance of getting into print can hardly be overestimated. Writers since Gutenberg's day had been accustomed to the notion that literature could be so widely disseminated as to become virtually deathless—to such an extent that some authors have felt obliged to disabuse their readers of the notion that this is necessarily the goal of publication. Edith Wharton, for instance, declared in her memoirs—written half a millennium after Gutenberg—that she had "hesitated for some time" before setting out to describe her writings, "since any attempt to analyze work of one's own doing seems to imply that one regards it as likely to be of lasting interest, and I wish at once to repudiate such an assumption." She then explained:

> Every artist works, like the Gobelins weavers, on the wrong side of the tapestry, and if now and then he comes around to the right side, and catches what seems a happy glow of colour, or a firm sweep of design, he must instantly retreat again, if encouraged yet still uncertain; and once the work is done, and he hopes to contemplate it dispassionately, the result of his toil too often presses on his tired eyes with the nightmare weight of a cinema "close-up."

Wharton was not giving up hope that her work would be "of lasting interest"; she simply refused to assume that this would be the case or to let her readers assume that she wrote for distant posterity. And her Gobelins-weavers analogy was not far removed from the attitudes of such twentieth-century composers as Stravinsky and Hindemith, who—tired, perhaps, of the Romantic notion of genius on a pedestal—began to talk again of the musician as craftsman. But Beethoven, who lived when that notion was just beginning to take hold and when music publication, as opposed to literary publication, was only beginning to become a serious business on a massive scale, was of a wholly different mind. Especially in the works composed during his last decade, he was intentionally writing for those who would follow. In the Ninth Symphony, the path that Beethoven wants us to follow—from despair to joy—is a well-thought-out sequence, a progression, not a random series. Beethoven was not a musical manic-depressive. His works do not bounce us back and forth between emotional highs and lows. Whatever, whoever Ludwig van Beethoven may have been in everyday life (and however well we think we know him, our knowledge is rendered ridiculously inadequate by our temporal distance from him and his environment) Ludwig van Beethoven's music is a distillation, not a representation, of his life experience—a distillation that passed through the chastening refinery of his spiritual and compositional processes. And notwithstanding the Ninth Symphony's vast proportions and the exuberant communicativeness of its finale, nowhere else in Beethoven's orchestral music—indeed, nowhere else in the symphonic literature—has the distilling process been adopted with greater severity.

Many scholars have pointed out that although Beethoven was fascinated by philosophy, he described music as an even higher calling. The opinion might easily be dismissed as a musician's prejudice except for the fact that in using the word "philosophy" Beethoven was not referring to the philosophy of language or to any other form of knowledge or wisdom that was not closely and concretely attached to questions of human beings' behavior toward one another. To Beethoven, the word "philosophy" could probably have been defined as ethical guidance; when he said that music was a higher calling than philosophy, he meant that it was potentially more important as a moral force. Artists, he believed, must strive to contribute to humanity's well-being—must help mankind to find the right path. This is why he condemned Mozart's *Don Giovanni* on moral grounds, despite his admiration for the opera's music, and why the Viennese triumph of Rossini's operas, which, by Beethoven's lights, lacked moral fiber, greatly upset him, as did the local public's adoration of vocal and instrumental virtuosity for its own sake. It is true that he had arranged a good deal of folk music and written dance tunes to earn some easy money, produced some musical doggerel to entertain his friends, and cranked out a few potboilers for special occasions—most notably in *Wellington's Victory* and *The Glorious Moment*. It is also true that in most of his works, Beethoven's strong and often boisterous sense of humor puts in a welcome appearance. Nevertheless, he was on the whole opposed to the notion of music as *only* entertainment, and his opposition was based not so much on musical principles as on ethical ones:

"Bad" music was a sign of "the frivolous and sensuous spirit of the times," he is reported to have remarked.

Like many of his predecessors, Beethoven hoped to give basic solace and sometimes to amuse through his work. Central to his existence, however, was the longing to help mankind raise itself up out of the muck of ignorance and pain. "To see or listen to Beethoven's *Fidelio* without taking into account its concern with injustice, heroism and freedom . . . would be so strange that we would normally say that anyone who claimed to be indifferent to its political and moral qualities was simply not responding to the work," wrote the philosopher Michael Tanner in an essay on art and morality. "If such a person said that they were only moved by the music, . . . we would wonder how they could be moved appropriately by the music without acknowledging that it was articulating the dramatic action. Of course one could listen to the music in a purely abstract way, regarding the voices simply as instruments, but that would not be listening to *Fidelio,* but only to an aspect of it."

In Beethoven's last decade, this moral imperative became an ever more pressing desire, bound up as it was with his exceptionally strange and acute personal misery—and with his genius—and it brought Beethoven to levels of abstract expression and of rarefied, distilled emotion that no one else in the history of Western music has reached. This is not to say that Beethoven is "greater than" Bach or Mozart: Furtwängler wisely commented that "to compare Bach with Beethoven is like comparing an oak tree with a lion," and he could easily have extended the analogy to include a comet-like or solar Mozart. Each of these musical giants, and others as well, possessed unique qualities that will probably continue to be a source of intellectual and emotional stimulation—and of pure pleasure—unless and until human beings take a sharp evolutionary turn or are wiped (or wipe themselves) off the face of the earth. Beethoven's uniqueness lay in his ability to make the intimately personal experience that he transformed into sound symbols function in tandem with his strong sense of intentionality vis-à-vis the future and with his intense longing to improve the human condition. Like Bach and Mozart, Beethoven lived, loved, suffered, created, and died, but unlike them, he undertook to suffer and to create for posterity.

Hegel, writing during the same period in which the Ninth Symphony was created, said, "Philosophy has the universal for its object, and, in so far as we think, we are universal ourselves." In this sense, we may think of Beethoven as a philosopher-in-music.

An attempt to describe the indescribable

Can the Ninth Symphony be deciphered? Did Beethoven intend to make us, or at least let us, perceive certain determinable meanings in this work? If he did, can those meanings be grasped today? What *happens* in the Ninth? What *is* the Ninth?

There are no clear answers to these questions, with respect not only to the first three movements, which are purely instrumental, but also to the vocal-instrumental finale, despite the guidance provided by the verbal text. Yet the fact that Beethoven added words to a symphony, for the first time in the history of the form, forces us to accept the idea that he attributed concrete meaning to this work. But to what degree, and of what sort?

Musicians who attempt to perform Beethoven's music conscientiously will carefully analyze its harmony and structure and the ways in which its rhythmic and melodic motives develop. Anyone with reasonably advanced musical training can see and hear what Beethoven accomplished in the Ninth and—since a great deal is known about his working methods—can understand how he accomplished it, from a technical point of view. But no one can know the internal processes that led to that accomplishment or be certain of the specific significance that the composer may—or may not—have attached to any number of details. As early as 1838, only fourteen years after the Ninth's completion, Hector Berlioz cautioned (using the first person plural to mean himself): "To analyze such a composition is a difficult and dangerous task that we have long hesitated to undertake, a bold attempt that we can excuse only by our persevering efforts to view things from the author's perspective, to penetrate his work's intimate meaning, to feel its effect, and to study the impressions that it has so far produced."

Maynard Solomon, one of the most brilliant and controversial Beethoven scholars, has written about "the musical symbolization of the sacred" in the composer's later works, including the Ninth Symphony. Solomon does not claim that Beethoven's late works were "inspired by or written in emulation of the great cosmological ladders of the world's sacred books and myths, or, more specifically, of such images of world-shaping ascents as 'the laborious climb' in Dante's *Purgatorio* or the ascent through the planetary spheres in the *Paradiso*," but he believes that some of these ladders and images can be interpreted as Beethoven's construction of a parallel musical tradition. One may or may not agree with this or any other interpretation. It is no surprise that Berlioz—given his above-expressed reluctance to make off-the-cuff analyses—avoided seeking "personal ideas that the composer might have wished to express in this vast musical poem" and insisted that the work's form is "justified by an intention independent of all philosophical or religious notions"— "a purely musical and poetic intention"—and that it is "equally as reasonable and beautiful for the fervent Christian as for the pantheist and for the atheist."

Berlioz was probably familiar with Benjamin Constant's treatise *De la religion*, in which the French writer and statesman essentially equated true religion with spirituality—a quality natural to all human beings, he said—whereas formal, imposed religion is inimical to the human spirit. "Religion has been disfigured," Constant wrote. "Man has been pursued right to his last place of asylum, to this intimate sanctuary of his existence. Persecution provokes rebellion. . . . There is a principle in us that becomes indignant at every intellectual fetter. This principle can be whipped into a furor; it can be the cause of many a crime; but it is connected to everything that is noble in our nature." Surely Constant's anti-dogmatic, anti-Establishment, nondoctrinaire, informal, open-ended, open-minded, and indeed Romantic approach to spirituality is closely related to Beethoven's beliefs. The fact that the part of his treatise quoted above was first published in 1824 makes his statement all the more interesting for our purposes.

I stated at the very beginning of this book that the Ninth Symphony has been appropriated by exponents of every sort of political and social philosophy, but never have ideologues theorized about it as wildly as in recent times. Lockwood mentions, specifically, the German social philosopher Theodor Adorno, whose Marxist politics and elitist aesthetic ideas were often at war with each other, and who, seeing the Ninth as optimistic, couldn't bear its apparent populism; the musicologist Susan McClary, who "denounced the first movement as an example of 'horrifyingly violent' masculine rage," says Lockwood; and the feminist poet Adrienne Rich, who "reviled the entire work as a 'sexual message' written by a man 'in terror of impotence or infertility, not knowing the difference." Lockwood courageously denounces the for-us-or-against-us dogmas that are implicit or explicit "in the current phase of ascendant 'cultural studies,' in which modern political and social content is read into every work of art or literature," including those of the distant past, and he reminds his readers that "there is no recourse or final court of appeal" against ideologues. (A wise individual once said that the only difference between academic ideologues and political dictators is that the academics don't have armies at their disposal.)

But there is one inescapable fact: For the duration of time in which it is being played and/or listened to, in whole or in part, the Ninth Symphony belongs to each person who participates in performing it or who attempts to listen to it attentively, whether at a live concert, through a recording, by reading the score, or via aural memory. In this sense, it does not differ from even the crudest, most uninteresting piece of music, and indeed it can provide the same sort of superficial enjoyment that a crude or uninteresting work can provide. The philosopher George Santayana's description of music as nothing but "a drowsy reverie interrupted by nervous thrills" seems to support Richard Strauss's contention that for people who lack musical training, listening to music is "a purely sensual, aural feast, unmitigated by any mental activity," and that such people are presumptuous to assume that they understand music "better than, for example, Turkish." But Santayana was merely a lazy listener, or an uninterested one, and Strauss's attack made a bad situation seem even worse than it really is. Many of the psychological subtleties of a powerful piece of music can be communicated to a person who is sensitive to music and accustomed to a given musical language even if that person is musically illiterate. Not to mention the fact that being musically literate or even being a professional musician does not automatically guarantee sensitivity to those subtleties.

Yet there can be no doubt that any attempt to describe the musical discourse in a technically, emotionally, spiritually, and/or intellectually complex work is severely limited without detailed technical references to harmony, rhythm, form, and all of music's other elements. Furtwängler put the matter thus: "The discussion of purely musical forms on the one hand or simple descriptions of the processes of the soul on the other get us nowhere, for what actually matters is that the spiritual should be perceived in terms of the musical and the latter in terms of the spiritual, that both should be considered one and indivisible, so that the very attempt to divide them is a fatal mistake."

And yet, despite all these caveats from myself and others, and notwithstanding Alexander Pope's much-quoted line about fools rushing in where angels fear to tread, I have gone ahead and written a highly personal description of what takes place in the Ninth Symphony. I have done it because I think it could help to alert casual music lovers to the expressive specificity of music in general and of the Ninth Symphony in particular, and perhaps also stimulate those professional musicians who feel wearied by the daily application of their craft to think again about what's behind the notes on the page. And—I admit—I have done it mainly because I felt an internal compulsion to do it, after half a century of familiarity with and love for this symphony and its composer. But precisely because my description is intended for all sorts of listeners, from the most casual to the most accomplished, I must parachute myself and my readers into a fogbound canyon of mainly nontechnical descriptions of musical phenomena. Let's hope that all of us, Beethoven included, will land safely.*

An ominous sound—not quite music, as the term was understood in the early nineteenth century, yet certainly not random noise, either: This description fits the opening of the fourth movement—the celebrated "storm"—of the Sixth ("Pastoral") Symphony, and it fits the beginning of the Ninth Symphony's first movement as well, although in an entirely different way. The "Pastoral"'s storm music is largely onomatopoetic, and Beethoven probably amused himself a good deal in dreaming up his sound effects; so, presumably, had many earlier composers when they attempted to represent extramusical auditory phenomena—chaos, for instance, in the opening of Haydn's *The Creation*. But the invention of the Ninth's opening sonorities cannot have been an amusing process. It must have grown out of Beethoven's confrontation with the bleakest realities

---

* For the convenience of those who read music and have access to a copy of the score, I am inserting bar numbers at appropriate points, but the description is meant to function with or without recourse to printed music.

of existence, such as the fact that we signify virtually nothing in the universe and that in cosmic terms we count no more during our brief lives than we counted before we were born or will count after we die. As early as 1815, he had written, in a note to himself, that "refined music is not to be thought of in these times," and the rawness, hollowness, fragmentariness of the Ninth's opening bars, their grim-gray colors, their amoral brutality or brutal amorality, demonstrate that Beethoven had taken that idea as far as it would go. These bars are Beethoven's rendering in music of the abyss that the circumstances of his life had forced him to look into, and they are meant to force us, too, to look into it.

Apart from the music itself, Beethoven left one hint about this movement's significance to him when he scrawled the word "Verzweiflung"—despair—on one of his sketches for the piece, as if to remind himself not to lose track of the feeling he needed to capture and convey. A cynical commentator might hypothesize that Beethoven was despairing over lack of progress in his work—a dilemma commonly known as writer's block. But unlike us lesser mortals, and unlike most of his great predecessors, including Bach, Haydn, and Mozart, Beethoven did not usually compose major works to deadline, and this was especially true during his last decade. Even the *Missa Solemnis,* as I mentioned earlier, was not completed until three years after the occasion for which it was intended. Most of Beethoven's compositions, including those commissioned of him, were written within whatever time span they required. His despair had nothing to do with creative crises; it was an all-encompassing feeling with which he was only too familiar, a state of being that he wished to communicate fully and uncompromisingly in this movement.

It is relentless, this beginning, and so is most of the rest of the movement. In the *Missa Solemnis,* the Ninth's sister work, the atmosphere created by the opening, ten-minute-long Kyrie is devotional, calmly joyous, confident (excepting the more urgent plea for mercy in the *Christe eleison* segment); Beethoven waits until he is well into the second section—the Gloria—before he begins to probe and interpret the text in ways that are not only brilliant and beautiful but also tough-minded, bold, disconcerting. In the Ninth Symphony, on the contrary, he disconcerts and indeed devastates immediately. No quarter is given.

The word "allegro" in the tempo indication "Allegro ma non troppo e un poco maestoso" (fast but not too much so and somewhat majestic) refers purely to speed, certainly not to the "cheerful" connotation that Italian-speaking people hear in it; on the other hand, the Italian "maestoso," as used here, means much more than its English cognate, "majestic": Beyond pomp and solemnity, its significance includes eternal divinity and the absolute power connected to it. (The word "maestà" is, among other things, the name given to early Renaissance paintings—by Duccio, Cimabue, Giotto, and others—of the Madonna and the Christ child enthroned and flanked by saints.) By the time the first movement of the Ninth Symphony is one minute old, there can be no doubt that the icy, absolute power of God or gods or fate or chance or whatever else might determine the course of a human life is the only aspect of majesty that concerns Beethoven here. He shows us majesty's sweep but not its pomp, its terrifying grandeur but not its grandiosity, and we can do nothing but flail about helplessly, foolishly, as if we had been dropped into a hurricane or hurled to the edge of an erupting volcano's crater. Any attempt to find our bearings, to make sense of what is happening in this maelstrom, is quickly smashed by forces beyond our understanding. The first movement of the Ninth neither beguiles nor coerces us; it befalls us.

David Benjamin Levy, in his excellent book *Beethoven: The Ninth Symphony* (essential reading on the subject for musicians and others who understand the technical language of music), says, "Beethoven realized, far better than his contemporaries or successors, that immensity is better achieved by a process of compression than by expansion." And in this movement, Beethoven compresses human life into a quarter of an hour, reduces it to the barest of essentials, and frames it with nothingness. Listeners must approach this piece of music—probably the most courageous orchestral composition ever written, and the most horrifying one—obliquely, circumspectly, lest it crush them.

On the thorny subject of this movement's tempo—and of courage— I have a story to relate. In 1996, while I was helping Sir Georg Solti to write his memoirs, we discussed many works in considerable detail. When we talked about Beethoven's Ninth, he happened to be studying it for a forthcoming performance with the Chicago Symphony Orchestra at the Proms in London, and he told me that he was determined to use Beethoven's quick metronome indication—quarter note = 88—or something close to it, as the basic tempo for the first movement. He asked what I thought about his plan, and I expressed the opinion that if one exceeded approximately 80 as a basic tempo, one would have to slow down substantially at many points in order to convey the music's full power—at all of the big climaxes, for instance—and in the violins' and violas' thirty-second-note *forte* passages. Otherwise, the result might resemble Sir Roger Norrington's unimaginatively and unconvincingly metronomic recorded interpretation. Solti repeatedly pulled out his electronic metronome and tried to imagine how to take 88 as his point of departure and yet modify the tempo only subtly where he felt the music required greater breadth. I was not in London when he gave the performance in question, but the next time I visited him he had just received a videotape of it and was eager to have a look. I was more than a little surprised to see and hear Solti and the orchestra begin the movement at a fairly deliberate, average tempo well below the one indicated by Beethoven's metronome mark. I asked what had happened, and Sir Georg, who was eighty-four at the time, smiled as sheepishly as a schoolboy who has been caught at some mischief. "I didn't have the courage," he said.

Courage is indeed required here, with respect to questions of tempo and much else besides. The movement begins quietly but not calmly, in an atmosphere of uncertainty. The first and second horns have the difficult task of playing an exposed, open interval very softly and of hanging on to their respective notes for twenty to thirty seconds (depending on the tempo chosen by the conductor) without redrawing breath. The same two notes are played simultaneously in lower registers by the second violins and cellos, which, however, do not cling to the notes as the horns do: They repeat them rapidly, nervously, twelve times in each bar. (At Beethoven's quick metronome indication—quarter note = 88—a bar lasts about 1.4 seconds, and not even the slowest conductors make a bar last much more than two seconds—which means that the violins and cellos play their repeated notes approximately six to eight times per second.) We cannot be sure whether we are in a major or a minor key; something vaguely menacing seems to be moving toward us, but we don't know what it is. The first violins give two quick two-note glimmers that are echoed by the violas and double basses (bars 2–5). A clarinet and then an oboe enter softly (bars 5, 9). A crescendo begins (11)—but this is no ordinary crescendo: It is rapidly increasing voltage being applied to our nerve endings. One flute intervenes, another follows (11, 13); the strings become more insistent, louder; most of the other winds join in (14, 15).

The atmosphere is terribly tense. And then, with the first entry of the trumpets and timpani (16–17), there is a violent, pitiless explosion. We know, now, that we are in a dark, minor key, and we are being buffeted about like motes of dust in a gale-force wind.

"Did you grasp that?" Beethoven seems to ask us. Because, as if to drive his opening statement home, he brings it to an abrupt conclusion and then repeats it, in a different key and with various instrumental and other modifications, but essentially as before. This time, however, the terrible outburst is extended and accumulates even more power than it possessed the first time around. And then, unexpectedly, within less than two seconds, the volume level tapers off drastically, the violent tones evaporate (73), and we are allowed to savor a major-key passage that Beethoven has marked "dolce"—sweet (74). What is it? Respite mixed with longing? Maybe. But after only ten or twelve seconds the sweetness is left to the wind instruments alone while the strings play a nervous, staccato accompaniment (80 and following) that makes us wonder what is coming next. The orchestra soon begins to fulminate again (92–107), although this time in a major key. A tug-of-war between major and minor, between relaxation with an undercurrent of tension and tension with a veneer of relaxation, follows, and is succeeded in turn by a renewed series of outbursts closely related to those that occurred near the opening of the movement, but now in a major key, thus not as dark as before. These *fortissimo* chords and unisons and octaves first ascend, then descend (150–58), giving a feeling of finality, like the last sentence of a chapter in a book. Beethoven has now completed what musicians refer to as the exposition—in other words, he has finished providing us with the thematic material that will form the basis of the rest of the movement— and he has prepared us to enter the development, in which that material will be torn apart, reassembled in new combinations, and variously transformed.

After having made an abrupt, four-note-long transition from *fortissimo* to *pianissimo* (158–60), Beethoven begins the development by presenting an altered version of the movement's ominously quiet, hollow opening. He takes about 50 percent longer than he did the first time to reach a full orchestral outburst, and this outburst is less overwhelming, more ambiguous, than the initial one. A few nervous bars for the woodwinds follow (192–97) and are succeeded in turn by a much more thoroughly permutated version of the opening and of the outburst; the nervous woodwind bars then recur in a different key (210–15), and this time they lead into the development's heart—a combination of several of the thematic elements that appeared in the exposition. This highly unorthodox *fugato* (a passage in the style of a fugue, in which a subject, or theme, is repeated at different points on the musical scale) and its aftermath last approximately two whole minutes—a long time, in Beethovenian musical terms, and more or less one-seventh of this entire, vast movement; within this space, a succession of rapidly moving sixteenth notes entwined with a driving eighth-note accompaniment creates an undertow of anguish. There is no getting off lightly here: Beethoven has us in his grip and won't let go. Not only in the loud, stern passages, but also, and more startlingly, in the soft, tense ones, those driving sixteenth notes wear away at us, take hold of our psyches, and prepare us for what will surely be a cataclysm greater than anything that has gone before.

And so it is. With a hurtling, elementally forceful ten-second buildup (295–300), the development comes to an end and the recapitulation— an altered repetition of the exposition—begins. But Beethoven now dispenses with the movement's ominously quiet, hollow opening, which he redeployed at the beginning of the development, and simply engulfs us in wave after wave of overpowering sound. Although we are, to our aural astonishment, in D Major rather than D minor, it would be hard not to concur with Levy's statement that "never before had a major chord sounded so apocalyptic!" What I described, in the symphony's first bars, as "two-note glimmers" in the first violin, viola, and double-bass parts are now transformed into glancing, too-close-for-comfort thunderclaps and lightning bolts played by the full orchestra at full volume. (If I could talk to Beethoven, one of the musical details I would question him about is why he used a triple *forte*—*fff*, very rare in his music—at climactic moments in the *Leonore* Overture No. 3 and the Seventh and Eighth symphonies but not at this or any other point in the Ninth, which seems to cry out for even more volume than the earlier pieces.) These tremendous blasts of sound are, in a sense, the musical embodiment of the bulging-eyed, swollen-cheeked angels sounding the trumpets of doom in Michelangelo's *Last Judgment;* or, to put it differently, they create an art-beyond-art moment, a moment in which beauty is set aside in favor of a statement meant to stun us and to curdle our blood.

The earthquake lasts approximately one minute before it tapers off into a reprise of the dolce segment of the exposition (339 et seq.), and for well over two minutes the description that I used for the rest of the exposition applies here as well: We hear sweetness tempered by nervousness, occasional fulminations, a tug-of-war between relaxation with an undercurrent of tension and tension with a veneer of relaxation, and the series of ascending and then descending *fortissimo* chords, octaves, and unisons that bring this chapter, too, to a close.

The chapter, yes; the story, no. Not yet. Because the movement continues for at least three minutes more, in a section that is technically called a "coda"—literally, a tail. One could almost describe this coda as a case of the tail wagging the dog, except that the cheery connotations of the word "wagging" could hardly be less appropriate. In these 121 extra but organically essential bars, Beethoven continues his excursion into the abyss, penetrating into even deeper areas of dread than those he drew us into during the movement's earlier portions. He begins by redeveloping the two-note-glimmer motif from the movement's opening, but he sets it now over a syncopated, anxious bass line played by the cellos and double basses (pizzicato) and by the clarinets (427 et seq.). The passage begins quietly but crescendos into a reprise of another of the exposition's explosive motifs (453–62); it then drops again to *piano,* crescendos into a repetition of the same explosive material, but suddenly pulls up short with what may be a protesting, fist-shaking gesture. This lasts only a few seconds (463–68) and is followed by a brief, gentle dialogue among the wind instruments—first the horns, then, in rapid succession, the first oboe, first bassoon, and first flute. But the gentleness lasts only eight bars (469–76), after which the winds' dialogue is transformed into something much more ominous: Beethoven brings back, from the development, those rapidly moving sixteenth notes entwined with a driving, eighth-note accompaniment in the strings—the relentless undercurrent of anguish described earlier. The passage is abbreviated here and ends not with a bang but a whimper—a plaintive, thinned-out and slowed-down restatement of the same motif (505–12).

And then begins the movement's real ending. Surely the fourteen-bar passage (513–26) that initiates it—*pianissimo* at the start, with repetitive and largely chromatic accompanying figures in the strings and bassoons and a dirge-like transformation of the glimmering motif in the other winds and the timpani—is the direst, most hope-abandoned moment in the entire orchestral literature. The conductor Arturo Toscanini wrote in his score, at the beginning of this passage, the following lines from the third canto of the *Inferno* in Dante's *Divine Comedy*—the inscription over the gate to hell: "Per me si va nella città dolente, / Per me si va nell'eterno dolore, / Per me si va tra la perduta gente." (Through me one enters the sorrowing city, / Through me one enters eternal sorrow, / Through me one goes among the lost people.)

By the end of this passage, we have passed through the gate and have entered hell itself. The movement's remaining thirty seconds (431–47) pulverize us unforgivingly. The full orchestra once again plays at full force—Beethoven's dynamic markings are "loud," "louder," "very loud," "always very loud," "reinforced," and again "very loud"—and when, after the last, horrific notes have been summoned from the orchestra's bowels and hurled at us, reducing us to rubble, we find a huge fermata* over the rests. This is nothing more than an instruction to the musicians who are performing the symphony to avoid jumping immediately into the second movement, but there is no harm in thinking of it also as an incitement to performers and listeners alike: Now listen to the sound of Nothing.

And then the silence ends. No sooner have we returned to Earth, after having traversed the lunar landscape that is the Ninth Symphony's first movement, than a series of glancing rhythms jolts us into a different mental and emotional dimension. As the second movement begins, we find ourselves again, or still, in the key of D minor, which could be a harbinger of continuing bleakness. But one doesn't have to know that Beethoven wrote the words "Molto vivace" (very lively) at the top of this movement, or that the movement is technically classified as a "scherzo," to become aware immediately that an extreme change has taken place.

With respect to communicative content, this movement is more closely related to the first movements of the Third ("Eroica") and Fifth symphonies than to the counterpart scherzo movements in those works. Like the second movement of No. 9, the first movements of Nos. 3 and

---

* American musicians call this symbol (⌢) a hold; in other English-speaking countries it is often referred to as a pause. To avoid confusion, we generally resort to the Italian term "fermata," although the Italians call the symbol a *corona* (crown); in modern Italian, a *fermata* is a bus stop!

5 also begin with brusque, startling orchestral outbursts that seem to presage contests of wills. But what differences there are among them! The Allegro con brio of the "Eroica," which was completed almost exactly twenty years before the Ninth, is fundamentally a show of strength: Its two abrupt opening chords—a two-second-long synthesis of the traditional Classical symphony's introduction—are like two feet being planted firmly on the ground; Beethoven, in his early thirties, flexes his muscles and glories in his control over the compositional elements that he is shaping. The movement's dark moments are exactly that—passing conflicts to be dealt with in short order.

The Fifth Symphony was finished only four years after the Third, but from an emotional point of view the Fifth's first movement (also marked "Allegro con brio") is a much more complicated piece than its counterpart in the "Eroica." The opening of the "Eroica"'s Allegro, in all its glorious luminosity, may be described as intense-positive, in which case the angst-ridden opening Allegro of the Fifth would have to be described as intense-negative. Self-assurance and control have given way to agitation and uncertainty, which we perceive instantaneously in the downward turn of the harsh, ultrafamous four-note opening motif and its repetitions and permutations; here, moments of light only occasionally penetrate the darkness. Man shaking his fist at inescapable fate is the interpretation that Beethoven himself was reported (albeit unreliably) to have attached to this piece.

And then comes the scherzo of the Ninth—the only one of Beethoven's symphonies in which a scherzo movement is placed second in sequence, rather than third. His decision to opt for such an arrangement must have had much more to do with what he seems to be trying to communicate in this symphony than with aesthetic questions, let alone purely musical ones. Feet are anything but firmly planted here, yet there is no angst, either. We are beyond all that now, hors de combat. Or rather, the combat has become symbolic: It is something that human nature requires of us even though we recognize its futility. The strings begin, quickly and *fortissimo,* BUM-pa-dum (silence), BUM-pa-dum (silence)—then timpani, BUM-pa-dum—followed immediately by most of the orchestra: *BUM-pa-dum!* About four seconds, in all, including the two bars of silence that follow the full orchestral interjection. (An aside for musicians: The timpani are tuned not to the first D and second

A below middle C, as musicians of the day would have expected, but rather to the first and second Fs below middle C. On first hearing the work, Beethoven's contemporary colleagues might have thought that these Fs would prove useful later in the movement, when Beethoven would surely spend a lot of time in F Major—the relative major of D minor; but in fact he spends virtually no time in F Major. He used the Fs because he was seeking an unusual, suspended-in-air effect—an effect he achieved by having the timpani play octaves on the mediant tone of the D minor scale, rather than on the steadier and more predictable tonic and dominant.)

The initial outbursts are followed at once (bar 9) by the quiet start of a rapid, contrapuntal principal theme. Take a moment to imagine how this theme—a succession of quarter notes that move mainly stepwise up and down fragments of the scale—would sound if it were in D Major rather than D minor: rather banal, even pat. But in the minor key, the note sequence becomes hypnotically stealthy, sinuous, ambiguous. It begins with only the second violins and first oboe, but during the following twenty seconds Beethoven gradually adds more and more instruments while insisting that everyone play as softly as possible; then, over a stretch of not more than six or seven seconds, he calls for a massive crescendo that leads to a *fortissimo* passage involving most of the orchestra. This segues into a few quiet bars (enlivened by the BUM-pa-dum figure in the accompanying parts) that function as a transition to the bold, almost brazen, second theme, in the broad-daylight key of C Major.

If the opening theme seems to protest, hesitantly, against the doom that the first movement has declared to be inescapable, the second theme (beginning at bar 63) is more self-assured—and apparently happy in its self-assurance. But it is short-winded and quickly dissolves into a brief but deeply emotional phrase (117–26) played by the strings and half echoed by the winds. This, in turn, becomes a self-mocking cat-and-mouse game between the same two sections of the orchestra (127–38).

The entire first part of the movement lasts a little over a minute and a half and is repeated, minus the first eight BUM-pa-dum bars; the repetition is followed by a development section in which the principal motifs are elaborated in ways that are partly serious, partly playful, and sometimes both, as in the mysterious three-bar groups ("ritmo di tre battute," Beethoven calls the segment, 177–233) punctuated by boisterous solo timpani interjections. Roughly ten seconds of menace (248–67) are followed by about fifteen seconds of fury (268–95): This is all there is of real anger à la midperiod Beethoven. The furious bit dissolves, and the dissolution initiates a recapitulation at the end of which the entire development and recapitulation are repeated.

The repetition is followed by another transition, this time into an elegiac section (Presto), technically called a trio; its main elements are closely related to the brief, emotional phrase (bars 117–26) heard in the exposition—a phrase that here takes on deeper beauty and consolatory mellowness. This legato melody (see, for example, bars 422–38) alternates with a lilting, staccato passage shared mainly by the strings and the first oboe, except that the oboe's version of it soon ceases to be staccato. Hearing it in its smoothed-out form makes listeners realize that this melody is essentially an upside-down version of the legato melody. It is also, as Levy points out, a musette—a form meant to evoke the sound of "a small rustic bagpipe," thus it would have suggested "the world of nature" to listeners of Beethoven's day. Levy also refers to the "studied naïveté" of these tunes, but the word "studied" implies a touch of cold calculation that probably ought not to be attributed to Beethoven's music in general and certainly not to the case in point. The composer must have relished bringing these melodies to life as he relished his walks in the country, and they are as refreshing as the cool water of a stream.

What comes after the repetition of the bulk of the trio is a sort of coda (491–530) in which legato and staccato blend into a stunning, wordless, organ-like paean; the religious nature of this segment is underlined by the entrance of three trombones (traditionally considered "solemn," rite-related instruments), the first two of which have not yet been heard at all in the symphony—whereas the third (bass trombone) played earlier in the trio for about twenty seconds, to add support to the bass line. This hymn leads into a reprise of the entire scherzo. But when the reprise is over, a passage that seems to be turning into a repetition of the trio ends abruptly after only six or seven seconds, and then, in two seconds' worth of rushed repetitions of the notes A and D for full orchestra (minus trombones and timpani), Beethoven thrusts aside everything he has done so far and brings the whole movement to a sudden close.

Despite the Ninth Symphony's proportions—much more substantial than those of any previous work in the genre—its psychological shifts have taken place, so far, within spans calculated in seconds or, at most, a minute or so. Composers born and raised in the eighteenth century never clobber and reclobber listeners with the "states of being" that they wish to create or describe; they make each point as strongly as possible and then move on to the next one. Not until the works of some of the late Romantics and post-Romantics two, three, and four generations after Beethoven did emotional overkill become a frequent feature in music. This is not to belittle the achievements of those later masters, but merely to point out the differences between them and their predecessors. When a late Romantic or post-Romantic master dwells at length on a single psychological state, the results can be extremely powerful. But after Beethoven and after the works of some members of the first generation and a half of his successors (I am thinking specifically, in this case, of Schubert, Mendelssohn, Chopin, and Schumann), and with the exception, at times, of the "Romantic Classicist" Brahms, one must leap to the mature works of Schoenberg, Bartók, and Stravinsky to find comparable degrees of concision and compression in psychological content.

Even the sublimely lyrical third movement of the Ninth Symphony, which is much more slowly paced than either of the first two movements, rarely proceeds in any given direction for more than a minute and a half before changing course—in performances that stay within shouting distance of Beethoven's tempo markings. The extraordinary inner tranquillity of the opening bars is reminiscent of the opening of the *Missa Solemnis's* Sanctus, except that the Sanctus's devotional feeling is absent here. In devotion there is always at least a hint of submission, but there is no element of submission in the Ninth's slow movement. What we have here is acceptance in its purest form. "When the hurly-burly's done, / When the battle's lost and won": How doubly and triply true Shakespeare's witches' phrase rings here! If the Ninth Symphony's first movement is hurly-burly of the most horrific sort and the second a half-serious, half-playful battle, the third tells us that we have both lost and won—that, as aware human beings, we have no choice but to wade through the horror and anguish and then die, but that we are able, from time to time, to see beyond and soar above these facts and to understand just enough to be able to appreciate the beauty of being mortal. After all, if anguish and death did not exist, art would not exist, nor would sensitivity to beauty. Or, to put a slightly different twist on an aphorism of Nietzsche's, sensitivity to beauty is one of our strongest defenses; without it, we would perish from truth.

And nothing more beautiful than this movement has ever been written for the symphony orchestra. "It lifts me off the earth, removes me from the field of gravity, makes me weightless," Toscanini wrote. "One becomes all soul. One ought to conduct it on one's knees." The bassoons' and clarinets' opening solo notes, gradually blending with the warm, expanding and contracting sound of the second violins, violas, and cellos, immediately begin to console, to suggest that we put behind us the first movement's hurly-burly and the fact that the second movement's half-hearted battle has inevitably been lost, because—as Beethoven continues to repeat—the battle has also inevitably been won, although not through redemption or resurrection in any orthodox Christian sense. (Beethoven probably believed in neither redemption nor resurrection, although he may have wished for both. Like Goethe, who was fascinated by the Hypsistarians—a fourth-century sect in Asia Minor that tried to follow the least doctrinaire elements of paganism, Judaism, and Christianity—Beethoven tended toward a form of nonconfessional pantheism, and this tendency plus his interest in Eastern religions would certainly have made him open to the idea of death as part of the life cycle.) The maelstrom has disappeared and the subsequent struggle has ended; we still cling to pieces of flotsam, but we are approaching the shore.

Those first two bars—bassoons and clarinets supported by some of the strings—serve as an introduction or, as Levy puts it, "a gently opening curtain that reveals some of the movement's most important motivic and harmonic material." The analogy brings to mind Piero della Francesca's theatrical (to modern eyes) painting *The Madonna of the Birth,* in which angels have pulled aside a curtain in order to show onlookers a very pregnant Mary; in a painting, however, time stands still, whereas music, like theater, exists only in a temporal continuum.

With the entrance of the first violins (bar 3), Beethoven begins to present the first of two long, spun-out themes that will alternate with each other, in various permutations, throughout much of the movement. An apparent contradiction confronts performers here: Beethoven's indication at the top of the page is "Adagio molto e cantabile" (very slow and lyrical), but the first violins are immediately instructed to play mezza voce (half voice). The composer, however, is simply making a distinction by carefully warning the players that "cantabile" does not necessarily mean "full-throated." What he is requesting, in all likelihood, is the firm establishment of a sense of respite and relief after everything that has gone before. A long line, yes, but no soaring—not yet. The soaring will come, but it requires psychological preparation. For now, the strings (minus double basses, here and in several other substantial segments of the movement, in order to lighten the texture) alternate and sometimes overlap with the clarinets, bassoons, and horns in stating a theme that is characterized above all by its basic dynamic mark (*piano*) and its feeling of repose. Short crescendo-diminuendo marks are scattered throughout the passage, but the crescendos are never meant to grow very strong and must always slip back into quietness.

In the last four bars (21–24) of this passage, the strings provide a thrumming accompaniment to the melody—now dominated by the clarinet—and in the last three of those bars the dynamic indications gradually subside from diminuendo to *piano* to *più piano* to *pianissimo.* The piece seems to be evaporating almost before it has begun, but in reality these bars are conveying the listener not only away from the basic key of B-flat Major toward D Major—a brighter key than B-flat, and not as warm—but also toward what will be a slightly quicker tempo (Andante moderato—moving along moderately) and, most surprising, toward a new time signature, as Beethoven shifts from 4/4 to 3/4. The new section (bars 25–42) proposes the second of the two themes that will dominate the movement; this first time around, the theme is stated twice by the second violins and violas, which are joined intermittently by the first oboe. Beethoven has marked the theme "espressivo," but it is only at the restatement (bars 33–40), when the first violins and then the first flute enter with a descant over the melody, that the music begins to hint at soaring. Yet here, too, the dynamic level never goes beyond a crescendo above *piano,* and at two points Beethoven demands a diminuendo so striking that he uses the word "morendo" (dying) to describe it (bars 32 and 40). The second theme ends *pianissimo,* like its predecessor, and the ending is a transition back to the key, tempo, and time-signature of the first theme.

Now, however, Beethoven weaves a variation (bars 43–64) around the opening theme. What was already beautiful but not quite ripe suddenly begins to blossom, and the original melodic line, made up mainly of slowly stated half notes and quarter notes, becomes a series of sixteenth notes—not quickly articulated but constantly unfolding, starting to flow. Capable orchestras and conductors maintain the sense of repose that was established at the beginning of the movement while simultaneously allowing more air to fill their lungs, metaphorically speaking (thus not only for the wind players!). This variation, like the original statement of the theme, ends with four bars of thrumming in the strings beneath the clarinets' melodic line, which again diminishes almost to the point of disappearing.

And again there is a transition, this time to a variation (bars 65–82) on the second theme, which, however, is now in G Major rather than D Major. Instead of second violins and violas, the first flute, first oboe, and first bassoon now carry the melodic line, but the first violins again add a descant—of a very different sort—in the second half of the variation, over an accompaniment characterized mainly by gentle pizzicatos in the second violins and violas. Here, too, Beethoven uses the word "morendo" at the points parallel to those at which he used it in the original statement of the theme, and the variation ends with a transition to the first theme's second variation, in E-flat Major.

This variation (bars 83–98) seems at first to resemble the original theme much more closely than did the first variation: slow, sweet half notes and quarter notes again emanate from the winds, with an occasional calm pizzicato interjection from the strings. But then there is some stepwise eighth-note movement in the wind parts, and we hear a melodic fragment that reminds us of something—we're not sure just what it is. Ah, but of course! Beethoven meant this fragment to be a subliminal prefiguration of something that will be heard in a little while, but we who have heard the finale's "Ode to Joy" theme thousands of times grab the minuscule hint, consciously or subconsciously. The prefiguration ends with an almost self-deprecating little up-and-down scale for the fourth horn—who, by the way, has been working quite hard throughout this variation with no help from his or her three colleagues. Suddenly, those calm pizzicatos make a big crescendo, accompanied by increasing numbers of crescendoing wind instruments, until—behold!—the most beautiful transition in the entire symphony has taken place almost before we know it.

It has brought us back to B-flat Major (bar 99), the main key; the crescendo drops immediately to a *piano* and the basic tempo is essentially unaltered, but the entire orchestra (minus the trumpets—and there are no trombones at all in this movement) is now involved, the time signature has changed to 12/8, and the whole soundscape has taken on a different aspect. A sense of tremendous breadth and great beauty overwhelms the listener, and the first violins—who must play like gods here lest they destroy Beethoven's vision—soar and will continue to soar through most of the rest of the movement. Beethoven has brought off a musical miracle: He uses the 12/8 meter to maintain a steady, four-to-the-bar rhythmic underpinning while giving an almost vertiginous, waltz-like feeling to the six sixteenth notes or three eighth notes that are grouped within each of the four main beats. What is more, this section is simultaneously the first theme's third variation and the second theme's second variation, because elements from both subjects are combined within it. Once again, Beethoven maintains a subdued volume level and even sets the word "dolce" at the beginning of the section; for the first minute and a half the dynamics vary from *pianissimo* to short crescendos above *piano,* but since the full orchestra is now involved, the overall impression is that all the earlier restraints have been lifted. If the previous quietness was that of a convalescent, of someone who is relearning to face life, this new quietness is the strong, conscious quietness that emanates from recuperated wholeness, from regained perspective.

As if to demonstrate this newfound or newly reawakened awareness and power, Beethoven pulls us up short and breaks into a brief, emphatic declaration (bars 120–23) that seems a cross between a military fanfare and a shouted "Credo!" Maybe it is a proclamation of self-sufficiency and generosity, of the sort that Walt Whitman would deliver only a few decades later in "Song of Myself": "I celebrate myself, and sing myself, / And what I assume you shall assume, / For every atom belonging to me as good belongs to you." Or maybe it isn't. Whatever it may or may not signify, it lasts not more than ten seconds before a pair of diminuendos marked "espressivo" leads back to what seems to be a reprise of the lyrical, dolce soaring of the first violins. After only two bars, however, the power begins to surge upward again, and Beethoven brings us—more gradually than before—to a repetition of the emphatic fanfare-cum-Credo. This time, the outburst is followed by the movement's darkest, most somber passage (133–36): deep, slow-moving, organ-like B-flat minor and E-flat minor chords punctuated by grim, dirge-like, repeated short notes played by the second violins. The passage is brief—about fifteen seconds—and ends with a transition back to the weaving, soaring music that preceded it, although the soaring begins an octave lower than before—in third gear rather than fifth—and quickly gentles down again, gliding into a sort of coda (beginning at bar 139).

The movement's remaining minute and a half is characterized by a series of brief, intense, alternating buildups and drops that are lyrical at even the most emotionally powerful points; in the last few bars, the timpanist must at times play both drums gently but simultaneously—a technique previously uncalled for in the symphonic repertoire. The final bar disappears on a soft pizzicato chord in the strings and four delicate, repeated, *pianissimo* chords in the winds and timpani. Beethoven seems, here, to have "come to the end of what is necessary"—to borrow a phrase from John Updike. A life could end beautifully as this movement diminishes tranquilly into nonexistence. Beethoven is at peace; the world is at peace.

But not for long.

The third movement is the only one of the four that does not end with a fermata over the final rests. Does this mean that Beethoven wanted the orchestra to launch into the finale after only the briefest of pauses—the duration of an eighth note, or less than a second? Some conductors have had their orchestras attack the fourth movement almost immediately after the close of the third, for dramatic effect, but there is a technical reason why this cannot have been Beethoven's intention. The first and second horns and both trumpets are pitched in B-flat in the third movement and in D in the fourth, and the third and fourth horns are pitched in E-flat in the third movement and in B-flat at the opening of the fourth. In Beethoven's day, horns and trumpets did not have valves; they could not switch automatically from one fundamental pitch to another. In order to change the fundamental pitch, a player had to remove one piece of tubing, called a crook, from the instrument, and insert a longer or shorter one, as each case required. This process in itself would have taken even the most deft of players at least ten or fifteen seconds to bring off, and additional time was needed to blow some warm air into the instrument, to try to bring the newly inserted, cold piece of metal more or less up to the temperature of the rest of the instrument—otherwise bad intonation was guaranteed. We can safely assume that Beethoven expected a break of at least half a minute and probably longer between the end of the Adagio and the beginning of the finale.

The problem still exists for horn and trumpet players in orchestras that make use of period instruments (unless each musician keeps a second instrument at hand), whereas an instantaneous switch is possible for players who use modern instruments. But regardless of whether the break lasts five seconds or five minutes, and regardless of whether one is hearing the Ninth Symphony for the first time or the thousandth time, the contrast between the marvelously peaceful conclusion of the third movement and the jagged, dissonant, blaring opening blast of the fourth never fails to jar. After all that has happened so far, after having proceeded, during roughly three-quarters of an hour, from terror and despair to anger and then to acceptance, why are we now being shaken out of our seats by fifteen wind instruments plus timpani blowing and hammering at bust-a-gut volume in what German musicians call the *Schreckensakkord*—the terror chord (B-flat, D-flat, F, and A natural)—with which the finale begins? Haven't we passed beyond that phase? Can't we be allowed to sit back and enjoy something joyful, or at least pleasant?

Perhaps someday an intrepid scholar will unearth a heretofore unknown document that will prove that Beethoven had a good laugh at his listeners' expense when he realized how their teeth would be set on edge and their hair would stand on end at the unleashing of the *Schreckensakkord*. Yet his original intention was probably not to shock in any sense, but rather to remind—to remind us of what this work is, and of what we are in the universal scheme (or nonscheme) of things.

The terror chord, and the six seconds of rapid-fire notes in the winds (mainly eighth notes) and timpani (sixteenths) that follow it, certainly grab listeners' attention immediately, and our attention is held by the lower strings' gruff reply to this attack. This is the first part of a dialogue in which cellos and double basses comment on brief declarations made by other segments of the orchestra; under this first "comment" Beethoven wrote a phrase in not very good French, with one German spelling and two Italian words thrown in: "Selon le caractère d'un Recitativ mais, in tempo." This translates roughly as "In keeping with the character of a recitative but in tempo." This is self-contradictory because, as Beethoven well knew, one of the salient characteristics of a recitative is, precisely, its nonadherence to a single tempo, especially if the basic tempo is extremely fast, as it is here (Presto). Most conductors have interpreted Beethoven's statement as meaning "Give these passages the expressive freedom of a recitative but don't let the tempo drag." After having heard a few "authenticist" conductors' attempts to have their musicians slam-bang through the recitatives strictly in tempo—in other words, as if the recitatives were not recitatives—I cast my vote in favor of the majority interpretation. This is not a vote against the "authenticists" in general but merely against the outcome of this specific experiment. Furthermore, thanks to a series of remarks that Schindler wrote in one of the conversation books, we know—from Beethoven's implicit responses to his interlocutor—that a strict tempo is wrong here.

> [Schindler:] how many double basses should play the Recitative?
>
> could this be possible? All of them!
>
> there would be no difficulty to play it strictly in time, but to play it singing [that is, in a vocal manner] will require great pains in the rehearsals.
>
> if old Krams were still alive, there would be no need to worry about it, because he led 12 Basses who had to do what he wanted.
>
> so really just so, as if words were placed below [the notes]?
>
> if necessary, I will put words below, so that they learn to sing

As its name indicates, a recitative has to do with recitation, with the rhythms of speech. Musical recitatives are almost always free-form settings of vocal texts. Prior to writing the bulk of the Ninth Symphony, Beethoven had already used vocal-style recitatives in instrumental music, most notably—in open or disguised form—in some of his last piano sonatas, and he would use them again in several of the late string quartets. In each case, he seemed to be trying to say something specific and at the same time tempting listeners to ask, "What could the missing words be?" But there are none, and there must be none. Furtwängler may have exaggerated when he claimed that "the musician in [Beethoven] felt inhibited, not inspired, by a text," but there can be little doubt that pure musical abstraction was Beethoven's greatest strength and that he is nearly always conveying something that can be expressed only through music, not through words.

Yet in the example at hand—the ninety-one bars of the finale that precede the first statement of the "Joy" theme—there can be just as little doubt that Beethoven was leading listeners in specific directions and was coming as close to rendering instrumental music verbal as anyone has ever done. His plan seems fairly clear. The first blast, including the terror chord, is meant, as I suggested above, to remind us of what this work is and of what we are (not much!) in the universal scheme of things; the recitative response, although emphatically stated, nevertheless seems to be meant to have a calming effect, but it is interrupted by a second blast, similar to the first (here, the *Schreckensakkord* consists of D, F-sharp, A, C, and E-flat), which is, in turn, followed by a slightly mellower response from the cellos and basses. The orchestra rebuts with two brusque *forte* chords, but then begins, abruptly, to play a mysterious version of the opening of the symphony's first movement, as if to say, "What are we to do now? Go back to this?"

Equally brusquely, the cellos and basses interrupt to say that this theme will no longer do: We've already been through that cataclysm, and survived; it's time for something less punishing. When this brief recitative fragment tapers off, the orchestra offers an eight-second reminder of the scherzo's main theme. Still imperiously but a little more gently, the recitative reenters, casting off the second suggestion just as it cast off the first. "All right, then, would you like something gentler?" ask the wind instruments as they present the first two bars of the third movement's main theme. The cellos and basses now take up the recitative very quietly but are nonetheless insistent in reiterating that what is needed is not a summary of what we have already heard, but rather something completely different—something that will take us into a new dimension. (One thinks of Heine's poem "Die alten, bösen Lieder": "The old, nasty songs, / The bad, evil dreams, / Let us bury them now, / Fetch a large coffin." Music lovers know this text from Schumann's setting of it in his *Dichterliebe* cycle, which dates from 1840, but the young Heine wrote it in 1822 or 1823, precisely when Beethoven was working on the Ninth Symphony.)

"Hm, then perhaps this?"—and the winds begin to sing ("sweetly," Beethoven commands) hints of the new theme.

"Yes, that's it!" reply the cellos and basses, whose cry is punctuated by happy outbursts from the winds and timpani. And then, suddenly, we are hearing the first statement, hushed but complete, of the "Joy" theme (bars 92–115), played by—who else?—the cellos and basses.

Musicologist Elaine Sisman has written that this echoing of the first three movements' main themes is "elicited by a 'rememberer,' the agent of memory, who is, uniquely, inside the piece," and she argues persuasively that "the cello/bass recitative voice . . . needs to recollect past ideas in order to find the source of a subject [that is, a musical theme] that can be used." As soon as the cellos and basses have presented the first complete statement of the "Joy" theme, the violas and bassoons add their voices, and during the following twenty-four bars the theme takes on some ornamentation. Then the violins enter (140), blending greater glow and density into the texture, and in the last eight bars of this segment all who are playing begin to intensify their sound until the entire orchestra bursts into a full-throated restatement of the theme (164–87). To this, Beethoven adds a little coda that includes an upward-striving, excitement-stimulating harmonic sequence (192–98) from which Wagner was to learn a great deal not many years later. There is a brief pulling-back in instrumentation, volume, and tempo, but then another jubilant outburst leads to . . .

Just a moment—what's this? Something we are not meant to expect at all: a renewed blast of the *Schreckensakkord* and the rapid-fire, menacing bars that follow it! Beethoven wants his listeners to be thrown into total confusion, to lose their sense of direction, and to wonder why, after having found the "right" theme, the orchestra seems to be shooting at random into the crowd. But then the bass soloist stands and sings the first words ever meant to be sung in a symphony—words written by Beethoven himself: "O friends, not *these** sounds! Let us rather sing more agreeably, and more joyfully." The music that accompanies the first part of this declaration (in the original: "O Freunde, nicht diese Töne!") is in part a repetition of the cellos' and double basses' initial, protesting recitative, but it is followed by an increasingly warm, gentling intervention by the string section, which provides a comforting background to the words "Let us rather intone more agreeably" ("Sondern lasst uns angenehmere anstimmen"). The orchestra shouts four happy chords, and the solo bass takes a deep breath and sings his final words in a melismatic, twenty-six-note, eleven- or twelve-second-long outpouring: "and more joyfully!" ("und freudenvollere!")—a technical feat so risky that many singers make a caesura, in order to catch their breaths, before the last seven notes.

We ought to take a deep breath—symbolically—with the singer, because we have, in a sense, "made it." We have survived the first movement's brutality and despair, participated in the second's harsh struggle, and been purified by the third's glowing acceptance of life as it is. What Beethoven wants us to experience now is all-embracing joy. For this is the moment in the work in which Beethoven most unequivocally declares his aim of helping to liberate mankind through art.

Little wonder that volumes have been written about the Ninth's finale: The mere fact that this was the first symphonic movement to function as a setting of a preexisting verbal text—a text, moreover, that the composer manipulated to suit his own purposes—is in itself enough to make musicologists and cultural historians salivate profusely. And the terrain for research and theorizing looks even richer when we realize that Beethoven had wanted to set this particular text to music for over thirty years; that Schiller, like Beethoven, had believed that humanity needed to achieve freedom through the experience of art before it could achieve political freedom; that as far back as 1794–95, Beethoven had created a version of what would become the "Ode to Joy" theme in a song with the unlikely title of *Gegenliebe* (*Requited Love*); that in 1808 he had reused the *Gegenliebe* theme in his Fantasy for Piano, Chorus, and Orchestra

---

* The italics are mine, not Beethoven's. The words "diese Töne" (these sounds) may refer in part to the terror chord and subsequent "sounds" that the orchestra has just finished unleashing for the third time, but they mean, above all, the thematic material that has been quoted from the three previous movements.

(the so-called Choral Fantasy); and that the Choral Fantasy's text—which, it seems, was virtually dictated by Beethoven to the poet Christoph Kuffner—bears a relationship to the text of the "Ode to Joy," as, for instance, in the stanza "Peace and joy float amicably / like the play of the waves. / Anything rough and hostile that intrudes / will become part of the elation." Soaring above all of these facts, however, is the overwhelming, incontrovertible sensation that even in the non-text-based segments of the symphony's finale Beethoven all but screams the word "MEANING!" at us.

After shouts of "Freude" ("Joy") from the solo bass and the bass section in the chorus—the first choral entry in the work—the solo bass sings the first of those verses of Friedrich von Schiller's "Ode to Joy" that Beethoven chose to insert into the symphony:

Freude, schöner Götterfunken,	Joy, beautiful divine spark,
Tochter aus Elysium,	Daughter of Elysium,
Wir betreten feuertrunken,	We enter, drunk with fire,
Himmlische, dein Heiligtum.	Thy heavenly sanctuary.
Deine Zauber binden wieder,	Thy magic reunites
Was die Mode streng geteilt;	What habit brusquely separates;
Alle Menschen werden Brüder,	All men become brothers
Wo dein sanfter Flügel weilt.	Wherever thy gentle wings tarry.

At the beginning of this solo passage, Beethoven wrote the indication "angenehm" (agreeably or pleasantly), and the orchestral accompaniment is cheerful—and minimal: one oboe, one clarinet, and strings playing soft pizzicati. But when the whole, four-part chorus (sopranos, altos, tenors, and basses) enters to repeat the last four lines, most of the rest of the winds join in, the string players take up their bows again, and everyone is given a *forte* indication.

The second verse's setting is a variant of the first's; it is sung by all four solo voices (soprano, alto, tenor, and bass), again with a light orchestral accompaniment (one flute, one bassoon, two horns, and cellos).

Wem der grosse Wurf gelungen,	He who has had the good fortune
Eines Freundes Freund zu sein,	To be a friend's friend,
Wer ein holdes Weib errungen,	He who has found a beloved woman,

Mische seinen Jubel ein!	Let him add his jubilation [to ours]!
Ja, wer auch nur eine Seele	Yea, he who can call his own
Sein nennt auf dem Erdenrund!	Even a single soul on this whole earth!
Und wer's nie gekonnt, der stehle	And he who cannot—he must steal away
Weinend sich aus diesem Bund!	Weeping from this gathering!

As in the first verse, here, too, the chorus reiterates in bolder tones the last four text lines, with strong orchestral accompaniment.

Beethoven follows the same pattern for the third verse, but trilling strings and quicksilver winds begin to make the temperature rise:

Freude trinken alle Wesen	All creatures drink joy
An den Brüsten der Natur;	At Nature's breast;
Alle Guten, alle Bösen	All the good, all the bad
Folgen ihrer Rosenspur.	Follow her rose-bedecked trail.
Küsse gab sie uns und Reben,	She gave us kisses and grapevines,
Einen Freund, geprüft im Tod;	[And] a friend true unto death;
Wollust ward dem Wurm gegeben,	Pleasure is given [even] to the worm,
Und der Cherub steht vor Gott.	And the cherub stands before God.

Again, the chorus exuberantly repeats the last four lines, but whereas in each of the first two verses the choral part is eight bars long, followed by a four-bar orchestral mini-postlude, here Beethoven eschews the postlude and extends the variation itself by ten bars, with the chorus singing full force to the end. In addition, after nearly a hundred bars of sitting solidly in D Major, we are suddenly airlifted into a different key. At first it feels like A Major, but then comes the passage's final explosion on the repetition of the words "vor Gott" (before God), with a tremendous, long-held F-Major *fortissimo* chord on the word "Gott"—and we're not at all sure which key we've landed in.

This midmovement climax, toward which Beethoven has been building since the first complete statement of the "Joy" theme nearly six minutes ago, is so powerful and resplendent that a receptive person listening to the work for the first time would be likely to wonder what could possibly follow it. Two feasible solutions were available to the composer:

either something much bigger—almost impossible to imagine, under the circumstances—or something much smaller, something so lightweight that it cannot be compared to the heaven-rending depiction in sound of cherubs standing before the Lord that the listener has just experienced. Beethoven opted for the latter response. No sooner has the hall stopped reverberating from the grandiose cry of "Gott" than we hear what would sound like a mistake were it not being made by four different instruments at exactly the same time: low, lower, and lowest B-flats played softly by the two bassoons and contrabassoon, respectively, together with a dull thud on the bass drum. (Upon hearing these B-flats, musicians will understand that the huge F-Major "Gott" chord was simply the dominant of B-flat. We finally know which key we're in.) And less than two seconds later they do it again, and then again and again and again and again, now at intervals of less than a second. For the seventh, eighth, ninth, and tenth repetitions, the four instruments are joined by two horns, also playing B-flats, and two clarinets playing Ds. When this group welcomes a piccolo, a triangle, and cymbals into its midst, all in martial rhythm, we realize that what we are hearing is a village band approaching from the distance, playing a syncopated, fragmented variation on the "Joy" theme, in the form of what was known in Beethoven's day as a Turkish march. A few more winds enter, *sempre pianissimo;* there are four extremely soft punctuating phrases by the strings, and the trumpet quietly hints at military bugle calls. After about half a minute of this lighthearted introduction (in 6/8 time, and with the indication "Allegro assai vivace," fast and very lively), the solo tenor enters, brightly singing an embellished version of the variation's fragmented melody:

Froh, wie seine Sonnen fliegen	Happily, like suns flying
Durch des Himmels prächt'gen Plan,	Across the sky's splendid plane,
Laufet, Brüder, eure Bahn,	Run your course joyfully, brothers,
Freudig, wie ein Held zum Siegen.	Like a hero [going] toward victory.

As the tenor begins a difficult final passage and prepares to soar up to a high B-flat, the male voices in the chorus enter to provide weight and support, and the orchestra's contribution grows in size, volume, and outright heart-on-sleeve joyousness. Musicologist Robert Hatten has pointed out that in this variation Beethoven does not merely lighten the musical atmosphere by introducing what sounded, to Europeans in 1824, like popular music; he "transcends the humble comic origins of the Turkish march" and endows it with "universality" by showing that not only heroes but also common people are included among "all men" who someday "will be brothers."

This variation's thunderously festive ending leads without a break into an extended orchestral variation on the variation—a splendid, hundred-bar-long riff (beginning at bar 431), during which joyful and serious moments alternate but the energy level of the strings, woodwinds, and horns never subsides. At the end of this section the orchestra quiets down to a whisper. Two horns, playing a syncopated rhythm, seem to be warning us that something different is on its way, while two oboes and two bassoons, accompanied only by the note B in the strings, quietly intimate the three opening chords of the "Joy" theme and repeat them somberly in the minor. Then a brief crescendo leads into a huge, sonorous reentry of the theme, shouted by the entire chorus (repeating the first verse of the text), woodwinds, and horns, all of which fit together with the variation-on-the-variation music played vigorously by strings, trumpets, and timpani. But when this segment comes to an exceptionally brusque halt (bar 594), and after a pause of a few seconds, the male voices in the chorus, accompanied by cellos, double basses, and the third trombone (this is the first use of a trombone in the finale), enter with what sounds like a very different theme but is, in fact, only a wildly divergent variant of the "Joy" theme:

Seid umschlungen, Millionen!	Be embraced, you millions!
Diesen Kuss der ganzen Welt!	By this kiss for the whole world!

Beethoven's tempo indication is "Andante maestoso," and the prevailing tone is at first solemn, even liturgical. It becomes glorious and full of awe, however, when the same words are repeated by the chorus's female voices, accompanied by woodwinds, all three trombones, and all of the strings. The pattern is essentially repeated in the setting of the next two lines of verse:

Brüder! überm Sternenzelt	Brothers, a loving Father must live
Muß ein lieber Vater wohnen.	Above the canopy of stars.

At the beginning of his setting of the following highly unorthodox yet in some sense deeply religious verse, Beethoven provides a highly unorthodox yet deeply religious indication, not just of tempo but of "tone": "Adagio ma non troppo ma divoto" (slow but not too much so but devout, or with devoutness); "divoto" is also a precise translation of the German indication "Mit Andacht" that Beethoven wrote at the beginning of the *Missa Solemnis*'s Sanctus.

Ihr stürtzt nieder, Millionen?	Do you bow down, you millions?
Ahnest du den Schöpfer, Welt?	Dost thou fear the Creator, world?
Such' ihn überm Sternenzelt!	Seek him above the canopy of stars!
Über Sternen muß er wohnen.	He must dwell above stars.

Here, flutes, clarinets, bassoons, violas, and cellos accompany the chorus, with firm interjections by the three trombones on the syllables "Welt?" and "zelt!" All of these instruments plus the oboes strongly declaim the first statement of the final line. Then, suddenly, the violins and double basses join the rest of the strings in a mysterious *pianissimo* chord. With the entry of woodwinds first, then the chorus—sopranos and altos, followed by tenors and basses accompanied by horns and trombones—a shimmering, mystical, mesmerizing repetition of the final line begins: "He must dwell above the stars."

As soon as the hypnotic final phrase has faded away, Beethoven launches into an unusual and exuberant new variation, labeled "Allegro energico e sempre ben marcato" (energetically fast and always well accentuated), in which a quick, syncopated version of the "Joy" theme ("Freude, schöner Götterfunken," and so on) is thrust together with and juxtaposed against its most recent, more slowly paced variant ("Seid umschlungen, Millionen!" and so on). This is an exceptionally difficult passage for the chorus, especially for the sopranos, who have a series of loud high As, including one that they are asked to hold on to for eight and a half bars in 6/4 time. Those chorus members who survive this exertion without having to be carried from the stage on stretchers must immediately drop their voices down to *piano* and convey the nervous, confused feeling that Beethoven asks for in repeating the "Ihr stürtzt nieder, Millionen?" verse. The first four words are sung by the basses, the next five ("Ahnest du den Schöpfer, Welt?") by the tenors, and the following four

("Such' ihn überm Sternenzelt!") first by the altos and then, in a crescendo, by everyone. And the section ends with warm but emphatic exclamations of "Brüder!" and a swirling, ascending, but softer and softer restatement of the phrase "He must dwell above stars" (bars 745–62).

After the briefest of pauses, off goes a brisk Allegro ma non tanto, which means, roughly, "fast, but don't overdo it"; yet, the section must be quite quick-paced for a variety of reasons: The nature of the music demands it, the time signature is *alla breve* (2/2—by implication, twice as fast as 4/4), and the soloists—who have now been sitting onstage for an hour without a great deal to do—will be heading toward vocal disaster if too slow a tempo is taken. This is the second-to-last section of the symphony and the second-to-last variation on the "Joy" theme; the text is that of the first verse ("Freude, schöner Götterfunken," and so on). At the start (763–81), quicksilver but quiet strings and woodwinds alternate with somewhat more tranquil solo voices, but then a buildup begins, with the chorus entering (795) to support and then take over from the soloists. The conductor must pull the tempo back substantially when the chorus sings, "All men become brothers, / Wherever thy gentle wings settle," then bring it back to its original pace, and then pull it back again for the soloists' elaborate, terrifyingly difficult but highly moving repetition of the same lines. Beethoven would have failed a composition exam in his own day or in ours for his handling of the vocal lines in this segment: The tenor is forced to cross over both the alto and the bass lines at various moments, and each of the singers has such long, florid passages that the only alternative to breathing in the middle of individual words would be learning to breathe through the ears. The composer knew that he was demanding the impossible but went ahead and demanded it all the same. And sensitive, accomplished singers manage to find solutions to the problems, although a sense of strain is always evident in this passage.

The Allegro ma non tanto ends on unresolved, long whole notes for the solo singers, clarinets, and bassoons and a questioning interval for the strings. Again, there is the briefest of pauses, and then the finale's last, breathtaking variation begins. "Poco allegro, stringendo il tempo, sempre più Allegro" (somewhat fast, quickening the tempo, getting faster and faster) Beethoven writes at the start, to help the string players understand how to bring off the initially tentative but increasingly heated

Beethoven's handwritten dedication of the Ninth Symphony, to King Frederick William of Prussia.

opening bars (843–50), which end with a crescendo that includes the winds. And then the orchestra, followed by the chorus, explodes into the final Presto. At first, the text is entirely that of the "Seid umschlungen" and "Brüder!" verses, but Beethoven soon returns to the opening verse, which he marks, this time, with exclamation points: "Freude, schöner Götterfunken! / Tochter aus Elysium!" A tremendous buildup culminates in a majestically slowed-down reiteration of the word "Götterfunken!"—divine spark!—and then the orchestra transforms itself into a comet and hurls itself, prestissimo, to the furthest reaches of the human imagination.

PART FOUR

To Begin Anew

Coping with the G-word

Universal History, the history of what man has accomplished in this world, is at bottom the History of the Great Men who have worked here. They were the leaders of men, these great ones; the modellers, patterns, and in a wide sense creators, of whatsoever the general mass of men contrived to do or to attain; all things that we see standing accomplished in the world are properly the outer material result, the practical realization and embodiment, of Thoughts that dwelt in the Great Men sent into the world.

—THOMAS CARLYLE

Even if we were to change the term "Great Men" to "Great Men and Women," Thomas Carlyle's statement, which dates from May 1840, would appall us today: His apparently smug use of that pumped-up adjective "great" makes us fidget. In the twentieth century, Philippe Braudel and other historians forced people to recognize the fact that "Universal History" is really an agglomeration of micro-histories, each of them shaped by economic and social conditions under which certain individuals emerge and, for better or for worse, take control, to the extent that control is possible. We have learned to mistrust, even despise, these "great" personages, because we know that the realization of their ideals often entails bloodshed on a massive scale and the destruction of large swaths of civilization. Most of these great ones eventually become victims of their own egos and are succeeded by other great ones whose trajectories seem almost to imitate those of their predecessors. When Carlyle said that such heroes were "sent into the world," he presumably attributed their presence among us to a prime mover, in which case they could more often be considered a severe form of punishment visited upon humanity by a cruel creator than a boon to our species.

But Carlyle, who was born in Scotland in 1795, grew up during the Napoleonic period, when the notion of the self-made, heroic man of destiny stood in open contrast to the belief in monarchy by divine right; what today seems an antediluvian attitude would have been interpreted in a wholly different light during the Romantic era. We are, or ought to be, sick of "great" political leaders, regardless of whether they inherited their positions, won them in elections, or simply grabbed them. But Carlyle and his contemporaries saw "great men" as counterfoils to rulers who inherited power without necessarily having any gift for using it.

Besides, political affairs constituted only one of the elements of civilization that great individuals could shape, according to Carlyle. In the six lectures that were published together in book form under the title *On Heroes, Hero-Worship, and the Heroic in History,* Carlyle dealt with "The Hero as Divinity" (Odin), "The Hero as Prophet" (Muhammad), "The Hero as Poet" (Dante, Shakespeare), "The Hero as Priest" (Martin Luther, John Knox), "The Hero as Man of Letters" (Samuel Johnson, Jean-Jacques Rousseau, Robert Burns), and, finally, "The Hero as King" (Oliver Cromwell, Napoleon). In the areas of intellectual and artistic achievement, at least, we can follow Carlyle's line of reasoning, because we can see that certain scientists, inventors, medical researchers, thinkers, and practitioners of the various arts have stood out among their colleagues and contemporaries and have influenced the history of civilization in profound ways. This fact in no way belittles the thousands upon thousands of people in each field without whose work no advances could ever be made; but no more can we deny the fact that a Newton, an Edison, a Pasteur, a Plato, or a Shakespeare stood out among his contemporaries, thanks to his genius or good fortune or extreme determination, or any combination thereof. If greatness exists, its very nature makes it a rarity. And if it is true, as the dictionaries tell us, that Romanticism was an artistic movement or tendency that emphasized inspiration, subjectivity, and the primacy of the individual, then it follows that the notion of the great, heroic, brilliant individual was Romanticism's cornerstone.

Beethoven was one of Romanticism's first and most significant exemplars—a symbol of greatness, heroism, and genius for generations to come. Many thousands of musicians over the last two centuries have become familiar with music by Beethoven's competent and frequently admirable contemporaries—Luigi Cherubini, let's say, or Jan Ladislav Dussek, Jean François Le Sueur, Antonín Reicha, Johann Nepomuk Hummel, Gaspare Spontini, John Field, or Ludwig Spohr—and have played and enjoyed some of their compositions. But the hundreds of thousands of musicians and the millions of music lovers who, over the past two centuries, have considered Beethoven's music more gripping than that of his contemporary colleagues have not simply been duped or taken in by the legend of the great, suffering genius. Nor should we all be accused of antidemocratic tendencies for hazarding the opinion that we listen to much more of Beethoven's music today than we listen to music by Cherubini and the others because, on the whole, his was more inventive, attractive, and profound than that of his contemporaries. In fact, let's be really daring and state unequivocally that we listen to Beethoven's music because so much of it is *great*.

Beethoven himself certainly believed in the concept of the great man, and to expect otherwise of him would be to assume that he owned a forward-moving time machine. Although he obliterated the dedication to General Bonaparte that he had written on the title page of his "Eroica" Symphony when he learned that the general had become Emperor Napoleon, he rededicated the work "to celebrate the memory of a great Man," and in his own field he praised Handel, Haydn, and Mozart. "Art and science," he wrote, "can raise men to the level of gods." But he was not a purveyor of the Romantic cult of genius—an accusation that has been leveled at him in recent decades by some moralizing and politically more-than-correct academics. He was a man of his time whose work was so extraordinary that it has endured.

Beethoven's brand of Romanticism was born of Enlightenment ideas and ideals and had little connection to some of the murkier or more self-indulgent aspects of the Romantic movement (let's call it a movement, for the sake of convenience) in its subsequent manifestations. Unfortunately, as one of Romanticism's iconic figures, he was often analyzed—and almost as often misinterpreted—by people with no great knowledge of music. Baudelaire, for instance, considered Beethoven a pioneer of the diabolic aspect of Romanticism and made some odd comparisons between the composer and various literary figures. The French poet and critic wrote, in 1861:

> Beethoven began to stir up the worlds of melancholy and of incurable despair that had gathered like clouds in man's internal sky. Maturin in the novel, Byron in poetry, Poe in poetry and in the analytical [that is, psychological] novel . . . ; they projected splendid, dazzling rays onto the latent Lucifer ensconced in every human heart. I mean that modern art is essentially demonic in tendency. And it seems that this infernal side of man, which man takes pleasure in explaining to himself, is growing day by day, as if the Devil were having fun by fattening it up through artificial processes, following the example of goose fatteners, patiently stuffing the human species in his poultry yards in order to prepare more succulent food for himself.

This is not only a misreading of Beethoven; it is also a misreading of Byron, whose diabolic side was patently a put-on, and of the Irish writer Charles Robert Maturin, who died in the year of the Ninth Symphony's premiere and whose darkest intention, in his popular Gothic novel *Melmoth the Wanderer,* was probably nothing more diabolical than to make readers' spines tingle. (Poe's case is more complicated, but the issues that his works raise are distant from this book's various themes.) Yet this interpretation of Beethoven—the only one by Baudelaire that I have come across—brings into high relief the importance that even nonmusical nineteenth-century artist-intellectuals attached to the composer's name. When Baudelaire referred to the "worlds of melancholy and of incurable despair" that Beethoven had "begun to stir up," he must have had in mind works like the "Pathétique," "Moonlight," and "Appassionata" piano sonatas, which provide substantial relief from darkness only in their middle movements. If he was referring to the first movements of the Fifth and Ninth symphonies, he missed the point completely: In both, he may have mistaken for "incurable despair" these works' elemental power and their waiting-to-be-resolved drama. Beethoven conquers despair through strength in the Fifth Symphony, through acceptance and joy in the Ninth.

In short, Beethoven may be seen, today, as a proto-Romantic, or even as The Proto-Romantic par excellence, but he was also much more than that. "The personal ideals of the romantics' favorite rebel, creator and hero, Beethoven, are not simple to define," wrote musician and cultural historian Conrad Donakowski in the 1970s. "That he was a humanist of the eighteenth century who proclaimed his Promethean independence in his life and music is common knowledge. That he believed music to be an exact though unilateral manifestation of the truth is also evident. That he became a humble man believing in the redemptive value of suffering is equally clear from his writings and music." This far transcends the trite image of the disheveled, tempest-tossed, lawless Romantic genius.

But what matters in trying to figure out how Beethoven in general and the Ninth Symphony in particular influenced the Romantic-era composers who followed him is not so much who he really was or what he really intended to communicate as it is how they *perceived* him and his art.*

The hardest possible act to follow

In the broadest sense, Beethoven's achievements influenced everything that has occurred in Western music since his lifetime and much that has taken place in the other arts as well. Every composer born during the first half of the nineteenth century was influenced in some way, major or minor, positive or negative (or both), by Beethoven's music, and the products of that influence were reacted to, in turn, by subsequent generations of composers, and so on down to the present. As for practitioners of the other arts, let Honoré de Balzac speak for them. "Beethoven is the only man who has made me experience jealousy," he wrote. "There is in this man a divine force. . . . What we writers depict is finite, determined; what Beethoven gives us is infinite." Balzac would no doubt have been pleased to know that after his death he would occasionally be compared

---

* Since Beethoven's influence on Romantic and post-Romantic composers extends even to some born in the 1860s and '70s (Gustav Mahler, Richard Strauss, and the young Arnold Schoenberg, for instance), I have limited myself to those born before May 7, 1824—the date of the Ninth Symphony's premiere. Thus Anton Bruckner, whose symphonies demonstrate what may be called a "Ninth Symphony Obsession," but who left few if any documented comments on the subject, misses by a few months, and Johannes Brahms misses by nine years to the day; he was born on May 7, 1833.

with Beethoven. The well-known American cultural critic James Gib-
bons Huneker, for instance, in remarking on "the influence of Balzac on
the world of fiction," wrote: "No one . . . has escaped or can escape
Balzac. He is like Beethoven in his influence on modern composers."

Among musicians, there must have been a few who quickly sensed the
Ninth Symphony's significance. One member of the audience at the premiere was a down-at-the-heel, little-known twenty-seven-year-old Viennese composer named Franz Schubert (1797–1828), who, within the
previous three months, had completed his mysterious, tragic string quartets in A minor and D minor and his alternately lighthearted and night-
marish Octet in F Major. But these works interested virtually no one
until years after their composer's death, when Robert Schumann and
other musicians discovered them and brought them to the world's attention. In the spring of 1824, Schubert, suffering from the effects of secondary syphilis, was too overwhelmed with private pain, physical and
psychological, to be thinking much about the ideals of global brotherhood that Beethoven was proclaiming in his new symphony. "I feel that
I am the most unfortunate, the most miserable being in the world," he
wrote to a friend on March 31. "Think of a man whose health will never
be right again, and who from despair over the fact makes it worse instead
of better, think of a man, I say, whose splendid hopes have come to
naught, to whom the happiness of love and friendship offers nothing but
the most acute pain, whose enthusiasm (at least, the inspiring kind) for
the Beautiful threatens to disappear, and ask yourself whether he isn't a
miserable, unfortunate fellow."

And yet Schubert—who, like Beethoven, was creating powerful,
universalizing expressions of the most intimate human anguish and
longing—had been looking forward to the Ninth's premiere, as he wrote
in a passage, quoted in part 1, from the same letter, in which he described
the program of the upcoming concert. One can hardly help wondering
what he thought upon hearing the first movement of the Ninth, which
corresponds in several ways to the first movement of his own newest string
quartet, known today by the nickname "Death and the Maiden." Both are
in D minor, both have turbulent main themes offset by lyrical second
themes—moments of respite in the midst of extended outbursts of
despair—and both communicate inconsolable horror at human destiny.

Unfortunately, Schubert's impressions of the Ninth are not known.

Although he lived nearly his whole life within walking distance of Beethoven, he revered him to such an extent that he seems to have made no serious attempt to get to know him. Schindler describes a single significant encounter between the two composers, but the story is probably apocryphal; in all likelihood, their only meeting took place about a week before Beethoven's death, when Schubert went with some friends they had in common to pay his respects to the weakened, bedridden, and nearly unconscious master. Schubert was an honorary pallbearer at Beethoven's funeral, and only a few days before his own death—less than twenty months after Beethoven's—the young man asked to hear Beethoven's String Quartet in C-sharp minor, op. 131, which was written even later than the Ninth and is even more complex; his wish is believed to have been granted.

John Reed, one of Schubert's biographers, felt that this sense of awe may actually have inhibited the younger man's musical development, and he quotes a statement by Schubert's friend Joseph von Spaun, who claimed that Schubert had told him: "Secretly, in my heart of hearts, I still hope to be able to make something of myself, but who can do anything after Beethoven?" But that conversation may have taken place as early as 1815, when Schubert was only eighteen. Peripheral resemblances have been found between the Ninth Symphony's "Joy" theme and the beginning of the development section in the finale of Schubert's "Great" C Major Symphony, and between Beethoven's setting of the words "laufet, Brüder, eure Bahn" in the Ninth and Schubert's setting of the line "So sprachst du, Liebchen, heut' zu mir" in the song *Mit dem grünen Lautenbande,* but these connections seem far-fetched and are probably coincidental.*

"Beethoven's titanic figure loomed large over Schubert's life," says Peter Clive in his biographical dictionary *Schubert and His World,* but the younger man was too original to have wanted, let alone attempted, to imitate the older one's stylistic characteristics. The Ninth Symphony's influence might have been felt in various ways in Schubert's later works

---

* I experimented with mentioning specific examples of the Ninth Symphony's influence on later music, but the process proved to be too cumbersome. It would have required extensive use of technical vocabulary and references to musical themes that readers would have had to call up from their memories, look up in scores, or try to locate in recordings. Thus I had to decide to avoid such references—with a few exceptions—in the remainder of this chapter.

had he lived to Beethoven's relatively ripe old age of fifty-six, but when typhoid fever (or some other ailment—historians are not certain) finished off his already ravaged body, Schubert was still a quarter century short of that mark.

Other musicians did record their impressions of Beethoven's last symphonic masterpiece during the early years of its existence. Hector Berlioz (1803–1869) had first heard Beethoven's music (an overture—we don't know which one) at a concert given during a prize ceremony at the Paris Conservatoire toward the end of 1827, eight months after Beethoven's death. Two months later, the exceptionally high-minded, twenty-four-year-old Frenchman, who has since come to embody the Romantic personality in music, wrote to his sister Nanci: "It is when one has heard the sublime instrumental compositions of the eagle Beethoven that one sees the rightness of the poet's exclamation: 'O divine music, language, powerless and feeble, retreats before your magic.' " * In January 1829, Berlioz wrote to a friend, "Now that I've heard that frightening giant Beethoven, I know what point the art of music is at, it's a matter of taking it from that point and pushing it further—not further, that's impossible, it has reached the limits of the art, but just as far along another path. Much that is new must be done, I feel this with extreme energy; and I'll do it, I'm sure, if I live." (Although he probably did not know it, in this statement Berlioz came remarkably close to echoing the words, quoted in part 1, of Franz Grillparzer's funeral oration for Beethoven, to the effect that the composer's successors would have to "begin anew, for he who went before left off only where art leaves off.") Two months later, after having heard a performance of Beethoven's string quartets op. 131 and op. 135, Berlioz wrote to Nanci that the German master had "climbed so high that one begins to lose one's breath."

Berlioz was by nature a rebel and a radical; he had been sent to Paris from the provinces by his father, a doctor, to study medicine, but, consumed with a passion for music, he had enrolled at the capital's celebrated conservatory, where he studied composition with Reicha and Le Sueur, gifted but conservative contemporaries of Beethoven. Beethoven's

---

* I have retranslated into English Berlioz's defective French version of lines from Thomas Moore's poem "On Music." Moore's original version reads: "Music, oh, how faint, how weak, / Language fades before thy spell!"

musical radicalism held overwhelming artistic and spiritual appeal for Berlioz, who suddenly found himself worshipping at a new altar. It is no exaggeration to say that Beethoven transformed Berlioz's life. David Cairns, the French composer's most comprehensive biographer, has written: "Berlioz believes in Beethoven, is willing to go where he leads and, as in an Orphic initiation, to follow him into strange and at first forbidding regions of the spirit. . . . It is an act of faith on his part; he trusts the composer whose symphonies have revealed to him a new world of music of unparalleled grandeur, intensity and scope." Given the uneasy and often downright hostile relationship between German and French cultures—a negative relationship that had been exacerbated in Berlioz's youth by the Germanic states' participation in the defeat of Napoleonic France—the young composer's immediate, instinctive conviction that Beethoven and no one else had shown the way toward music's future is all the more extraordinary. And that conviction quickly became a battle flag for the young composer.

In 1829 Berlioz first studied the score of the Ninth Symphony, which had not yet been performed in France, and he became on the spot one of the first musicians in the world to grasp its importance. "We have read

Hector Berlioz. *(Photo by P. Petit, circa 1860.)*

the score attentively," he wrote in one of a series of polemical articles in
Le Correspondant, intended to defend Beethoven against his adversaries,
"and without flattering ourselves that we understand it in its entirety and
in all its aspects we have no hesitation in regarding it as the culmination
of its author's genius." Cultural historian Jacques Barzun has pointed out
that in the last of these articles Berlioz "calmly asserted that the Ninth
Symphony, which he had read but which no one in Paris had heard, so
far from showing a great man struggling with dementia, was on the contrary a starting point for the music of the present."

By 1834, Berlioz had heard all of Beethoven's symphonies, including
the Ninth, and was publishing heavily ironic attacks on French audiences for their negative attitude toward his musical hero: "There are half
a dozen young people who, under the pretext of claiming that this
Beethoven fellow is the greatest musician in Europe (which isn't possible,
since he's never managed to be played at the Opéra-Comique), would
like to put an end to private conversations [during performances of
Beethoven's music], and they tell everyone that the talkers are uncouth
tradesmen." Four years later, however, perceptions were beginning to
change. Berlioz, writing in the *Gazette Musicale,* now divided the Ninth's
Parisian listeners into five categories:

> Certain critics regard [the work] as a *monstrous folly;* others see nothing
> in it but the *last glimmers of an expiring genius;* some more prudent peo-
> ple declare that at present they don't understand it at all but do not de-
> spair of appreciating it, at least to some extent, later on; most artists
> consider it to be an extraordinary conception of which some parts nev-
> ertheless are still inexplicable or apparently aimless. A small number of
> musicians, naturally inclined to examine carefully everything that is
> meant to expand art's domain, and who have given mature reflection to
> the choral symphony's overall form after having read and listened to it
> many times, affirm that this work seems to them the most magnificent
> expression of Beethoven's genius: this opinion . . . is the one that we
> share.

Berlioz then begins to describe the symphony in some detail; his description is part musical analysis ("This Allegro maestoso written in
D minor begins however on the *A* chord minus the third, that is to say,

on the held notes *A* and *E*, arranged in fifths, arpeggiated above and below by the first violins, violas, and double basses") and part emotional, pictorial narrative ("The peroration contains expressions that move the whole soul; it would be difficult to hear anything more deeply tragic than this song by the wind instruments, beneath which the string instruments' chromatic tremolo phrase swells and rises little by little, rumbling like the sea as a storm approaches"). His verbal interpretation of the work goes on for well over two thousand words, and he follows it with a complete French translation of the parts of Schiller's "Ode to Joy" that Beethoven used in the symphony's finale. "If the audience at the Conservatoire . . . had a translation of this sort in its hands," Berlioz says, "it would most certainly follow the composer's ideas better." But, he notes, "it is nevertheless clear that this audience, which was so cold at first toward this colossal score, is beginning to come under its influence. After two or three more performances, it will feel all of its beauties." * As if this weren't tribute enough, Berlioz concludes his remarks on the Ninth by conjecturing that "when Beethoven, upon completing this work, looked over the majestic dimensions of the monument that he had erected, he must have said to himself: 'Let death come now, my task has been completed.' "

For Berlioz, the example of Beethoven's existence and the expressive power of the Ninth Symphony in particular represented confirmation of his own choices in life and of his emancipation from the musical conservatism of his teachers. Surely it is no coincidence that the full unleashing of his amazing originality took place within a few months of his first encounters with the score of the Ninth, or that not much more than a year later he produced the *Symphonie fantastique,* as new and astonishing a work as the Ninth, albeit in a very different way. The influence may be indirect, but it is nonetheless concrete. And the Ninth influenced Berlioz in more direct ways, too: Echoes of the recitative in Beethoven's finale can be heard in Berlioz's *Roi Lear* Overture (1831), and his entire Dramatic Symphony *Roméo et Juliette* (1838–39) and Dramatic Legend *La Damnation de Faust* (completed in 1846) make ample use of solo and choral voices.

---

* More than forty years later, however, Georges Bizet lamented the fact that Parisian audiences continued to show no understanding of the Ninth.

From the 1830s onward, Berlioz developed a reputation as one of the finest conductors of his day, and he is now regarded as having been an authentic pioneer in the art and craft of conducting. Generous as he was, he must have felt that he was paying back at least a small part of his great debt to Beethoven when, in the late winter and spring of 1852—at the time of the twenty-fifth anniversary of Beethoven's death—he conducted the Ninth Symphony with the New Philharmonic Society at London's Exeter Hall. According to *The Times*'s well-known critic James William Davison, that performance stirred up "an excitement almost unparalleled within the walls of a concert room." Another observer, writing in *The Illustrated London News,* described the event as "the greatest victory ever yet attained in the development of Beethoven's intentions. . . . We heard on Wednesday night professors of no little note, whose sneers and scoffs at the Ninth Symphony years back we had not forgotten, make avowal that it was incomparably the grandest emanation of Beethoven's genius. . . . Well did Berlioz earn the ovation bestowed by the moved thousands who filled the hall on this memorable occasion, one to be treasured for ever in our musical annals." Berlioz was to have conducted the Ninth in Saint Petersburg during his highly successful 1867–68 season in the imperial capital, but a dearth of competent singers caused him at first to decide to perform only the first three movements and then to cancel the entire performance.

By then, however, Berlioz was sixty-four years old, twice widowed, devastated by the death of his only son, abandoned by many of his friends, and considered too radical by one sector of the musical world and passé by another; he died the following year. "My contempt for the folly and baseness of mankind, my hatred of its atrocious cruelty, have never been so intense," he had written in 1861. He seemed almost to be echoing Beethoven, who, toward the end of his own life, had declared: "Our age needs powerful minds to castigate these petty, deceitful, miserable wretches of human hearts—however much my heart refuses to give pain to anyone." We remember Berlioz above all else for his marvelously imaginative music—as well we should—but we should honor him also as the first major figure in European music who grasped and publicly defended the difficult, groundbreaking works of Beethoven's last creative phase.

Berlioz's understanding of "late Beethoven" was remarkably prescient, but other musicians of the day had at least an inkling of what their celebrated contemporary was trying to do. Giacomo Meyerbeer, for instance, wrote in his diary in March 1831, in Paris, that "a performance of Beethoven's giant symphony with chorus, outstandingly played at a Conservatoire Concert (and which I heard for the first time)" had been "among the main events" in his life during that month.

Meyerbeer, a German Jew (his name was originally Jakob Liebmann Meyer Beer) born in 1791, a dozen years before Berlioz, was one of the most popular opera composers of the nineteenth century and, during his Paris years, a pioneer of the French grand opera style and a successor to Rossini, his most important musical forebear—although the prodigious Rossini was a year younger than Meyerbeer. Meyerbeer's *Les Huguenots*, *L'Africaine*, *Robert le diable*, *Le Prophète*, *L'Étoile du nord*, and *Dinorah* are rarely heard today, but in their day and until the end of the nineteenth century some or all of them were in the repertoire of every self-respecting opera ensemble.

Earlier, when Meyerbeer was twenty-three, he may have had direct contact with Beethoven in Vienna: He is said to have played timpani or bass drum (accounts vary) under the composer's direction in a performance of Beethoven's potboiling "Battle" Symphony. According to testimony in Alexander Wheelock Thayer's *Life of Beethoven*, Beethoven had said that the young man " 'did not strike [the drum] properly and was always too late. Therefore, I really had to give him a dressing down. Ha! Ha! Ha! This may have upset him. Nothing will come of him. He does not have the courage to strike at the right moment.' " So much for Beethoven's statement about his heart refusing to give pain to anyone!

Meyerbeer presumably had no trouble understanding and enjoying the works of Beethoven's early and middle years, but his attitudes toward the late-period works varied. Although he was two decades younger than Beethoven, the musical language of the older composer's last years was far more complex than that of his younger colleague. Meyerbeer attended performances of the Ninth Symphony on about half a dozen occasions, in Paris and Berlin, but he did not set down any of his concrete reactions to them. When, near the end of his life, he heard the celebrated pianist and conductor Hans von Bülow play the relatively late Piano Sonata No. 29 in A Major, op. 101—"which I had never heard before"—

he described it as "a gifted, glorious work, particularly the first elegiac movement and the third or fourth, which is a fugue." (Only a few years earlier, the same sonata, played by Anton Rubinstein, had provoked a very different reaction in the Russian writer Ivan Sergeyevich Turgenev, who loved Beethoven but "was unable to understand" op. 101.) Yet nearly thirty years after Beethoven's death—and after the young Berlioz had been bowled over by a performance of Beethoven's very late String Quartet in C-sharp minor, op. 131—Meyerbeer wrote that although that work's scherzo had delighted him (it was, he said, "a masterpiece of invention, humor, and beautiful control"), the other movements had not: "The introduction (*adagio*), the *allegro* and the *andante,* which together form an unbroken movement, still remain incomprehensible to me. I cannot find the leading thread, or grasp the organic structuring."

Meyerbeer was a composer of music for grand spectacles—music meant to please the audiences of his day. Nothing wrong with that! But Beethoven's late works were meant to please everyone and no one, at all times. Parts of them could be enjoyed purely viscerally, but any attempt to grasp them more fully and more profoundly required listeners to be on Beethoven's wavelength, or a similar one, and a willingness to make the effort to meet him halfway. Meyerbeer's musical imagination was too limited for that—or else he was born a little too early. Perhaps, if he had been born a dozen years later, like Berlioz, he would have developed a slightly more modern perspective, as was the case with Felix Mendelssohn.

The Hamburg-born Mendelssohn, who was nearly two decades younger than Meyerbeer and six years younger than Berlioz, admired and certainly was able to grasp Beethoven's music, but he could not wholeheartedly embrace it. He was a Romantic, but a conservative one; Beethoven's challenges to the established order in music and in life were probably a bit much for the well-brought-up Mendelssohn, and the mixture of esteem and puzzlement in his attitude is apparent in a letter to his teacher, Carl Friedrich Zelter—a letter written in Paris in 1832, when Mendelssohn was twenty-three. Although he believed in the sincerity of the admiration for Beethoven that some local musicians expressed (they "really enjoy the great Beethoven symphonies now, and have become quite familiar with them, and it gives them great pleasure to have mastered such things"), he couldn't believe in others' sincerity on the same subject, because these "great squawkers and enthusiasts," as he called them, "disparage the other masters on his account, speak of Haydn as if he were a powdered wig, of Mozart as if he were a simpleton—and such narrow-minded enthusiasm cannot be genuine." The audience, too, he said,

> loves Beethoven uncommonly, because they think one must be a connoisseur in order to love him; very few of them experience any actual joy in it, and I simply cannot stand the denigration of Haydn and Mozart, it drives me mad. Beethoven's symphonies are like exotic plants to them, they don't really have a look at them, but they're a curiosity, and should someone happen to count the filaments and discover that they belong to a well-known family of flowers he leaves it at that and doesn't think anything further of it.

Mendelssohn's Symphony No. 2 in B-flat Major, op. 52—written in 1840 and called the *Lobgesang,* or *Hymn of Praise*—has a choral-orchestral finale and was probably the earliest traditional-style symphony after Beethoven's Ninth to make use of voices.* Despite its low publication number as the second of Mendelssohn's five mature symphonies, chronologically it was the last of them. (The "Scotch," No. 3, was not completed until 1842, but most of it was written in the 1830s.) The *Lobgesang* is a nicely written but not very compelling work—certainly not one of Mendelssohn's best; its long, banal first movement is followed by two shorter, somewhat more interesting ones, and then by a cantata—based on biblical texts—that lasts some forty minutes, a quarter of an hour longer than the Ninth Symphony's finale, and without a trace of Beethoven's startling boldness. The Ninth's influence on it was purely formal. Whether that influence would have grown had Mendelssohn lived to a decent age is, of course, as impossible to determine as it was in Schubert's case, because this amazing genius died in 1847, at the age of thirty-eight.

Frédéric Chopin was part of the extraordinary group of composers—the others were Mendelssohn, Schumann, Liszt, Wagner, and Verdi—

---

* Berlioz's slightly earlier *Roméo et Juliette* is called a "dramatic symphony" but does not follow a traditional symphonic format.

born in the period from 1809 to 1813; all of them were children or adolescents when the Ninth Symphony had its premiere. Various sources indicate that Chopin probably heard the work when it was played by the Paris Conservatoire orchestra (which he described as the "non plus ultra") in 1832, and he heard parts of it two years later, when he visited a music festival in Aachen, Germany, with the pianist, conductor, and composer Ferdinand Hiller—another gifted musician born within that same small clump of years. That Chopin preferred Bach and Mozart to Beethoven is a well-known fact, but he admired Beethoven's orchestral and chamber music. Unfortunately, his thoughts on the Ninth have not come down to us, whereas Robert Schumann, who came into the world less than four months after Chopin, did write and even publish his thoughts on that subject, as on so many others.

At the age of twenty-three, Schumann began a brief essay—"On the D minor Symphony"—with a quotation that he attributes to a friend: "I am the blind man who stands before Strasbourg's cathedral, hears its bells, but cannot find the entrance. Leave me alone, young man, I no longer understand humanity." In other words, I know that the Ninth Symphony is something grandiose, but I can't figure it out. But then, assuming one of the alter ego characters that he had invented for himself in his essays—in this case, the meditative, melancholy personality called Eusebius—Schumann writes: "Who would rebuke the blind man, if he stands before the cathedral and knows not what to say? Just remove his hat, devoutly, when the bells ring on high."

Schumann's livelier alter ego, Florestan, now takes over and says, about Beethoven:

> Yes, just love him, love him well—but do not forget that he achieved poetic freedom by taking the path of many years of study, and honor his never-resting moral force. Do not seek out what is abnormal in him, go back to the foundations of his creativity, do not demonstrate his genius through the last symphony, even though it speaks more boldly and immensely than any tongue before it—you can do this just as well with the first [symphony] or with the slender, Greek one in B-flat Major [No. 4]! Do not rebel against rules that you have not yet thoroughly worked through.

Tucked in amid much more highly colored, metaphoric prose, the essay's final point about Beethoven can be found: "Let us then love that high spirit, who looks down, with indescribable love, upon life, which gave him so little."

Five years later, in a letter to his nineteen-year-old fiancée, the pianist Clara Wieck, in Vienna, Schumann wrote, from Leipzig: "Listen, I have a request. Don't you want to visit our Schubert and Beethoven? Take a few myrtle branches, tie two together for each of them and put them on their graves if you can—then softly say your name and mine—nothing else—you understand."

Finally, in an essay written in 1841, following a performance of the Ninth Symphony, Schumann made fun of the Beethoven fans who built monuments to their hero without really knowing his music or understanding who he was—just as Mendelssohn had castigated Parisian Beethovenians a decade earlier. "Does a great man *have* to have thousands of dwarfs in his train?" Schumann asked. But of the Ninth itself, he wrote: "At last one begins to realize that here a great man has created his greatest work. I do not recall that ever before has it been received so enthusiastically. Saying this we do not mean to praise the work—which is beyond praise—but the audience," for its open-mindedness.

We know a lot—too much, perhaps—about Richard Wagner's life and struggles, about his unsurpassed originality and his monstrous selfishness, about the extraordinary influence he exerted on the course of European music—greater than that of anyone else between Beethoven and Stravinsky—and about the perniciousness of his self-serving racism and nationalism. No major figure in the history of Western culture is more ambiguous, seductive, repulsive, significant, and dangerous than Wagner.

In addition to his thirteen operas and music dramas, of which all but the first three belong to the standard repertoires of major opera houses around the world, Wagner wrote many volumes of prose on a variety of subjects that boil down to one subject: Richard Wagner. Whether he was writing about theater architecture, musicians of the past, or "Judaism in Music" (the title of his most infamous essay), all roads led directly or indirectly to himself. Thus, for instance, in his memoirs Wagner said that in his youth the finale of Beethoven's Ninth "became the mystical lodestar of all my fantastic musical thoughts and aspirations"—in other words, the Ninth was not only great in itself but also, and perhaps above all, a precursor of Wagnerian music drama, a springboard to Wagner's self-realization.

The Ninth's premiere had taken place two weeks before Wagner's eleventh birthday; a few years later—when he was in his mid-teens, not long after Beethoven's death—Wagner observed the celebrated soprano Wilhelmine Schröder-Devrient in the title role of *Fidelio* and then began to delve into the score of the Ninth Symphony. "What first attracted me to it," he wrote,

> was the opinion, prevalent not only among the Leipzig musicians, that this work of Beethoven's had been written in a state approaching in-sanity: it was considered the "non plus ultra" of all that was fantastic and incomprehensible, and this was grounds enough to arouse in me an impassioned desire to investigate this demoniac phenomenon. On first looking through the score, which I obtained only with great diffi-culty, I was struck at once, as if by force of destiny, with the long-sustained perfect fifths with which the first movement begins: these sounds, which played such a spectral role in my earliest impressions of music, came to me as the ghostly fundamental of my own life. This symphony surely held the secret to all secrets; and so I got busy over it by painstakingly copying out the score.

The Ninth is the subject of one of the earliest known Wagner documents—a letter that he wrote to the publisher B. Schott in Mainz in 1830, when he was seventeen years old. "For a long time I have been making Beethoven's magnificent last symphony the object of my deepest studies," the message begins, "and the more I become familiar with the work's high value, the more it grieves me that it is still very much misun-derstood and very much ignored by the majority of the musical public." To try to remedy the situation, he was working on a solo piano arrange-ment of the symphony that he hoped Schott's editors would wish to pub-lish, so that musical amateurs could play through the symphony in their homes. Schott was not interested in the proposal.

Later, after having heard a wretched performance of the symphony in

Leipzig, Wagner began to think that his initial enthusiasm for the work had been misplaced, but during his down-and-out years in Paris, in his late twenties, he changed his mind again on hearing the symphony performed by the orchestra of the Paris Conservatoire under its intrepid conductor, François Habeneck. Wagner later recalled that the "renowned orchestra" had played the work

> with the finish that came from incomparably long study, a performance so perfect and so moving that the conception of this marvelous work which I had dimly formed in the enthusiastic days of my youth, before its execution (in both senses) by the Leipzig orchestra . . . had effaced it, suddenly stood before me bright as day and as palpable to my touch. Where formerly I had seen only mystic constellations and soundless magic spirits, I now found, flowing from innumerable sources, a stream of inexhaustible melody, gripping the heart with ineluctable force.

It was, Wagner added, "the inexpressible effect of the Ninth Symphony, in a performance I had previously not dreamed possible, which revived my former spirit and gave it new life and strength."

Fair enough. But Wagner's take on the Ninth Symphony's historical significance vis-à-vis himself appears in all its contortedly metaphorical glory in his celebrated essay "Das Kunstwerk der Zukunft" ("The Artwork of the Future"), written in 1860:

> Thus the master [Beethoven] forced his way through the most unheard-of possibilities of absolute tonal language—not by hurriedly stealing past them, but by proclaiming them completely, to their last sound, from his heart's fullest depths—until he reached that point at which the navigator begins to sound the sea's depths with his lead; at which he touches solid bottom at ever increasing heights as the strands of the new continent reach toward him from afar; at which he must decide whether to turn about into the fathomless ocean or whether to drop anchor in the new banks. But it was no rude hankering for the sea that had urged the master on to this long voyage; he wished and had to land in the new world, for it was to this end that the voyage had been undertaken. Resolutely he threw out his anchor, and this anchor was

the *word.* This word, however, was not that willful, meaningless word which the fashionable singer chews over and over as the mere gristle of the vocal tone; it was the necessary, all-powerful, all-uniting word in which the whole stream of full heartfelt emotion is poured out; the safe harbor for the restless wanderer; the light lighting the night of endless longing; the word redeemed humanity proclaims from out the fullness of the world's heart; the word which Beethoven set as a crown upon the summit of his creations in tone. This word was—"Joy!" And with this word he called to all mankind: *"Be embraced, ye countless millions! And to all the world this kiss!"* And *this* word will become the language of the *artwork of the future.*

This *last symphony* of Beethoven's is the redemption of music, out of its own element, as a *universal art.* It is the *human* gospel of the art of the future. Beyond it there can be no *progress,* for there can follow on it immediately only the completed artwork of the future, *the universal drama,* to which Beethoven has forged for us the artistic key.

Thus from within itself music accomplished what no one of the other arts was capable of in isolation. Each of these arts, in its barren independence, helped itself only by taking and egoistic borrowing; not one was capable of being *itself* and of weaving from within itself the all-uniting bond.

The conclusion that Wagner seems to want us to reach, if we survive the trek across the blasted heath of his verbiage, is, in essence, that music by itself is good but doesn't involve us completely. What we need is music plus words—not just any "chewed-over" old words (read: Romantic Italian or French opera libretti), but words that communicate Higher Meanings and Higher Feelings—joy, in the case of the Ninth Symphony, or perhaps redemption, which was one of Wagner's fixations: redemption through self-sacrifice or a woman's sacrifice for a man or Christ's sacrifice for humanity, or even through the total sacrifice implicit in universal destruction. Better still, let's add stagecraft to the music and the words, but instead of calling the resulting creations "operas" (heaven forbid!), we'll call them "music dramas." Wagner described the traditional operas of his day as "a chaos of unconnected sensual elements"; he used the term "strumpet" to denigrate Italian opera and "coquette with a cold smile" to demean French opera. Shakespeare and Beethoven were his direct mentors and artistic ancestors—so he apparently believed—but they had to be "redeemed" through the perfect blend of poetry and music that he was in the process of achieving.

Wagner's creative projects jibed perfectly with nineteenth-century notions about progress; his works had to be not only different from those of his predecessors, but also better than theirs—bigger, more complicated technically and content-wise, more taxing for performers and audiences, and, to his way of thinking, more profound, more concerned with abstract ideas. Generally speaking, musicians today do not think that Mozart was greater than Bach, that Beethoven was greater than Mozart, that Verdi was greater than Rossini, or that Puccini was greater than Verdi. They often have preferences or favorites among the composers of the past, but they recognize that each first-rate creator wrote works remarkable enough to be loved by millions of people decades or centuries later. For that matter, Brahms and most of the other masters who were active during Wagner's lifetime did not consider themselves capable of one-upping Mozart or Beethoven; like those earlier masters, they wanted their works to be considered, grasped, and, with luck, appreciated and loved on their own terms rather than "as compared to." Wagner, on the contrary, wanted to be the greatest composer ever, the greatest poet in the German language (he wrote his own libretti, parts of which are awful), and the greatest master of stagecraft in the world. He didn't merely enjoy praise, like most other human beings; he required it, required admiration and adulation. And when he declared that Beethoven, in the Ninth Symphony's finale, "forged . . . the artistic key" that would open the door to "the completed artwork of the future, *the universal drama,*" he left little room for doubt that the only person who knew how to turn that key was none other than Richard Wagner.

A century and a half after the publication of "The Artwork of the Future," we don't know whether to be more amused by Wagner's turgid prose or his blatant self-promotion. But we must not forget that when he wrote those words, the forty-seven-year-old composer had already completed *Der fliegende Holländer* (*The Flying Dutchman*), *Tannhäuser, Lohengrin, Das Rheingold, Die Walküre,* and—most recently—*Tristan und Isolde,* and that during the remaining twenty-three years of his life he would produce *Die Meistersinger, Siegfried, Götterdämmerung,* and *Parsifal.* His achievement is astonishing not only for its quantity and quality but also for its ever-increasing and ever-deepening mastery. *The Flying Dutchman* displays considerable originality and contains much wonderful music, but it is essentially a cross between the pioneering German operas of Carl Maria von Weber and the most formulaic Italian operatic style of the day; *Tristan, Götterdämmerung,* and *Parsifal* exist on an altogether different plane—maybe even in a different dimension. Through much of the latter half of his century, Wagner was not merely an exemplar of musical progressivism; he personified the European artistic avant-garde. As such, he was constantly being attacked on various fronts simultaneously, and his desire to defend himself from present and future foes is easy to understand. His vision of himself as the next great step forward after Beethoven meant that he had to see his predecessor as in some way naïve; thus, in a letter to Franz Liszt, he pinpointed what he felt to

Cosima and Richard
Wagner. *(Photograph
by F. Luckhardt, 1872.)*

be the Ninth Symphony's main weakness—its finale. It was, he said, "the last movement with its chorus which is without doubt the weakest section, it is important only from the point of view of the history of art since it reveals to us, in its very naïve way, the embarrassment felt by a real tone-poet who (after Hell and Purgatory) does not know how finally to represent Paradise." Yet Wagner's identification with Beethoven was so strong that, according to some scholars who have studied the matter thoroughly, it included a belief in metempsychosis—the transmigration of souls.

More specifically, the Ninth Symphony is a recurring theme in the obsessive, worshipful diaries that Wagner's second wife, Cosima, kept throughout the last fourteen years of her second husband's life. (Cosima was Liszt's daughter and the former wife of the pianist and conductor Hans von Bülow, a disciple of Liszt's and Wagner's.) In an early entry, she noted that Richard had played the "Ode to Joy" theme on the piano for herself and their children, and that he had commented: "All wisdom, all art is forgotten in the divine nature of this naïve theme, to which, through his noble bass voice, [Beethoven] imparts the whole force of human feeling. Here the naïve and the emotional are combined." And less than a month before his death, Wagner returned to this notion: Richard "plays the beginning of the 9th!" Cosima wrote. "He compares it to an improvisation and says: 'Such sublime naïveté! How long it takes for one to reach this stage! In the early symphonies he still has scaffolding around him.'"

On another occasion, however, he had told Cosima that "the melody" from the Ninth's first movement (we don't know which melody, but the second theme seems the most likely candidate) "had come into his mind and he had said to himself, 'You have never done anything like that.'" He apparently felt that he was somehow lagging behind his great model.

In May 1872, Cosima wrote that she and her husband had

> talked a lot about the 9th Symphony; what gave B[eethoven] the idea
> of setting Schiller's poem to music? R. believes that he meant from the
> start to write a great symphony of joy in the spirit of the Freemasons
> and to precede it with struggle and mourning, but I have the feeling
> that he wrote the more somber movements first and then, finding, as it
> were, no finale, resorted to words.—But a work such as this remains a

mystery; R. says how remarkable in B. is the hatred of trivialities, the
avoidance of dominants,* for example, and the enormous artistic instinct. Isolated passages are also splendidly orchestrated, such as the
opening of the Adagio. We are, however, more and more convinced
that such compositions as the first movement of this symphony do not
belong in front of an audience, which never achieves the concentration
necessary to grasp such mysteries.

In other words, "we" are good enough for it but "they" are not. Later,
however, Wagner speculated that, after all, a musician might have a
harder time than a layman in understanding the first movement of the
Ninth, because it "in fact has no melody and begins with those fifths—
this tells the true musician nothing, but makes an impression—a ghostly
one—on an imaginative layman to a far greater extent." But he also
thought that it was "curious that this work, not so well proportioned in
its form, should have become so popular."

There are many other references to the Ninth in Cosima's diaries. On
one occasion, Richard tells her that the turbulent beginning of the first
movement's recapitulation "always strikes me as a sort of Macbethian
witches' cauldron in which disasters are being brewed." On another:
"Should one wish to name anything that shows the complete detach-
ment of music, its power, of which up till now nobody has had the slight-
est idea, then he would cite the *fugato* in the first movement of the 9th
Symphony." In the entry for September 26, 1879, Cosima reports, "R.
plays the adagio [of the Ninth], breaking off after the first variation to
exclaim: 'That is an adagio—and what wealth of imaginative feeling in
the variation! There is nothing like it.'" But two years later, in referring
to the fanfare-like passages toward the end of the same movement, Wagner says that he does not like "that rousing of oneself for a sort of triumphal song, a self-mastery which is quite unnecessary, since it is already
there *eo ipso* [by that very act; but Wagner probably means "inherently"]
in the music." Thinking once again about the Adagio, Wagner declares:

---

* Wagner's statement about the "avoidance of dominants" will puzzle anyone who has done a harmonic analysis of the Ninth Symphony. The entire dramatic opening of the first movement, for instance, is built on an unprecedentedly extended contrast of the dominant-tonic relationship.
Cosima may have misheard or misunderstood whatever it was that Richard said on the subject.

"To discover these two themes and to combine them, the one like a dream of Nature, the other like a fair memory, to produce something so divine—only a madman could do that, a person of sound mind could never find such things." Elsewhere, Wagner describes the Ninth's first movement as "wild" and "sorrow-laden" and as "a wonderful piece, though to the shrewd professional musicians of its own time it must have looked like the work of a bungler."

Given the fascination that the Ninth Symphony exerted on Wagner through all the decades of his creative life, the fact that he chose to conduct it at the cornerstone-laying ceremony for his Bayreuth Festival Theater, on May 22, 1872—which was also his fifty-ninth birthday—is no surprise. And when, in 1951, sixty-eight years after Wagner's death, the Bayreuth Festival took place for the first time since the end of World War II, it was reconsecrated with a performance of the Ninth Symphony, as if Beethoven's music and his call for universal brotherhood could somehow have erased from everyone's memory the story of the Wagner family's enthusiastic complicity with the Nazis; or as if it could have hidden the fact that Wagner's racist writings had influenced Hitler, who, like Wagner himself, had considered the festival a shrine not only to Richard Wagner but also to the ideals of Teutonic supremacy. Just as "all great Neptune's ocean" could not wash Macbeth's hands clean, even great Beethoven's Ninth Symphony could not purify Bayreuth's reputation. And yet Wagner's significance in the history of music endures, and must endure. His work can be loved or hated or anything in between, but it cannot be ignored.

Regarded with varying degrees of contempt by Wagner because they were less earth shaking yet more immediately successful than he was, Gioacchino Rossini (1792–1868), Gaetano Donizetti (1797–1848), Vincenzo Bellini (1801–1835), and Giuseppe Verdi (1813–1901)—the four composers who dominated Italian opera throughout most of the nineteenth century—were all born well within Beethoven's lifetime, and all of them were familiar with at least some of his music. They would have heard few if any of Beethoven's orchestral works in Italy, where symphonic music in general was rarely performed before the last quarter of the nineteenth century, but all of them spent substantial periods in Paris in the 1830s and/or 1840s, when, as their contemporaries' writings demonstrate, Beethoven's orchestral works were played excellently—at least by the standards of the day—by the Conservatoire orchestra under Habeneck.

Rossini probably paid a visit to Beethoven in Vienna in 1822, when the Italian composer was the toast of the town, and if third-party accounts of what Rossini supposedly told Wagner many years later are to be believed, on that occasion Beethoven had intimated to his young foreign colleague that Italians should write only comic operas because their grasp of the "science" of composition was inferior to that of the Germans. This seems unlikely; Beethoven must have known that Mozart, who was less than fifteen years his senior, had gone to Italy to perfect his musical training, and Beethoven himself had studied with Antonio Salieri and had declared his admiration for the music of Luigi Cherubini. We know that he was appalled by the success, in Vienna, of "frivolous" Italian operas by Rossini and others, and he certainly did believe that Rossini's music was less profound than his own—but by 1822 he believed that the music of *all* of his living confreres, regardless of their nationalities, was less profound than his own.

According to this same account, Rossini told Wagner that he admired Beethoven and his music and that he pitied him for his deafness and for the squalor in which he lived. But he added: "If Beethoven is a prodigy of humanity, Bach is a miracle of God!" This distinction may have resulted from the fact that Rossini was able to understand Bach's music completely but could not fully grasp the music of Beethoven. About the Ninth Symphony—which was only beginning to gestate in Beethoven's mind at the time of Rossini's presumed visit—I have come across no comment by the younger man, although Rossini lived on for more than forty years after the symphony's premiere and would have had many opportunities to hear it.

Nor, to my knowledge, have any observations on the Ninth turned up in Donizetti's or Bellini's correspondence. The fact that Donizetti was familiar with Beethoven's music is clear, however, from his correspondence, and he esteemed it despite the fact that he did not like hearing his works compared unfavorably with those of the much older German master. In 1840, at the time of the premiere in Paris of his opera *Les Martyrs*—a revised, French-language version of the Italian *Poliuto*—

he wrote to a friend: "I'm waiting now for the *Débats,* a serious journal, in which a fierce enemy of everything that is not by Beethoven, or himself, writes." The *Journal des Débats's* music critic was Hector Berlioz, who did indeed give Donizetti a hard time.

Upon the death of a friend in Bergamo, Italy, his native town, Donizetti wrote to another friend that he would "never forget that through him I got to know all the quartets of *Haydn, Beethoven, Mozart, Reicha, Mayseder,* etc., which were of great use to me for sparing my imagination the effort of making a piece out of only a few ideas." Donizetti had written many quartets as a young man, before Beethoven had written any of his late quartets, but presumably his familiarity with works by the above-named composers had persuaded him that his talent was for other musical genres.

In Vienna a few weeks before he penned the previously quoted letter, Donizetti had written to the same friend, Antonio Dolci, that he was "going out immediately to go to the Imperial Chapel to hear a mass by Beethoven, which is being played especially for me," but he does not say whether the work in question was the *Missa Solemnis* or the earlier Mass in C Major. A few months later, he wrote to a friend in Vienna that he wished to write something for the Austrian empress: "I would like to be *Mozart, Haydn, Beethoven,* to serve her as she deserves. Alas! What I can offer her is not much.—But my good intentions will long remain."

Verdi, who was sixteen years younger than Donizetti and outlived him by more than half a century, had a little more to say about Beethoven than his compatriot had done. Yet his attitude, too, was both admiring and resentful. In 1871, not long after having completed *Aida*— one of the works of his mature years—Verdi gently took a friend to task for praising only melody in music: "There is something more to music than melody, something more than harmony," he wrote. "There is music! You will think that this is a puzzle! This is what I mean: Beethoven was not a melodist; Palestrina was not a melodist! Let's be clear: a melodist according to our meaning of the word." In other words, when outstanding composers have something to say that is worth hearing, it does not matter whether writing beautiful melodies is one of their principal virtues.

A few years later, however, when Verdi was worried about Italian music lovers' growing interest in symphonic music, he declared that in-

Lithograph by J. P. Lyser, after his own drawing of Beethoven.

strumental music is a German art, vocal music an Italian art, and that there should have been a vocal society in Italy

that would have let people hear Palestrina, the best of his contemporaries, Marcello, etc., etc., [which] would have kept alive in us the love of singing, the expression of which is opera. Now everyone tends to orchestrate, to harmonize. The *alpha* and *omega:* Beethoven's Ninth Symphony (sublime in the first three movements, very bad with respect to how the last is crafted). They will never reach the heights of the first movement; [but] they will easily imitate the bad voice writing in the last, and on Beethoven's authority they'll shout: this is how it should be done.

Verdi was already ten and a half when the Ninth had its premiere; indeed, in the last years before his death at the age of eighty-seven (January 27, 1901), he was the only surviving major composer who could remember the year 1824. His slightly older contemporaries Mendelssohn, Chopin, Schumann, Liszt, and Wagner had predeceased him— Mendelssohn by fifty-four years, Liszt by only fifteen—and even Charles Gounod, the composer of *Faust,* who was five years younger than Verdi and who had played through Beethoven symphonies with the painter Ingres at the Villa Medici in Rome in 1840, died eight years before his Italian colleague. Thus it is safe to say that Verdi's final word on Beethoven was the final word of that entire, astonishing generation of musical creators. There were "three colossi" in music, Verdi wrote in 1898—three-quarters of a century after the creation of the Ninth Symphony—in a letter to the French critic Camille Bellaigue: "Palestrina, Bach, Beethoven."

Postlude

1958: Beethoven visits Cleveland, Ohio

During a meeting of music administrators that I attended a few years ago, a young woman—an orchestra executive—surprised me by saying, quietly, "I can't imagine what my life would be without Beethoven." Her words made me begin to think about Beethoven's place in my own life.

When I was eleven and a half and on the verge of adolescence, my parents gave me a box that would determine my future. It was gray and white, made mainly of laminated wood, and I set it on top of the chest of drawers in my bedroom. From that exalted position, it began to confer understanding and solace on me—dim understanding, at first, and only a glimmer of solace, but a hint, at least, that this dying child, this embryonic grown-up, this odd new I, might survive, proceed, and perhaps even learn to assuage from time to time the nameless, incomprehensible ache, or to fill in part of the vast pit of unintelligible sadness that had suddenly and for no apparent reason opened up in the center of life's territory. Maybe, the box said, the ache and the pit would not be adulthood's sole offerings. Maybe something could happen, during the years that stretched forward in an unimaginably long line, to compensate for the ambiguity of existence, something to counterbalance the attractively horrible dreams, strange yearnings, and stranger physical changes that had begun to inhabit me.

The box—a portable, four-speed record player with a single speaker no larger than a grapefruit—seemed to be telling me something important about the world in a language that I felt I had always known, and I sensed that if I gave the box enough of my attention, much that was obscure would be illuminated. I was amazed that there could be such fullness in the midst of such emptiness, such solidity amid such confusion, such immutability amid such an onrush of time. The box didn't soften or sweeten the conflicts within me. On the contrary, it highlighted them and revealed that they were still deeper and more intricate than I had suspected. But it also stated them boldly, filled me with the powerful sensuality of thought, and made me feel that one day I might at least be able to grapple with my problems instead of lying stunned at their feet. The music's ambiguous specificity spoke directly to me and forced me to respond. I "conducted" it, jumped around to it, and imagined that I was explaining it to the girl I was secretly in love with, talking to her about life and about Beethoven, who was my alpha and omega. I spent my best hours familiarizing myself with a newly discovered region: inner life.

Yes: alpha and omega. There was plenty of room for all the in-between letters, too, but my listenings generally began and ended with Beethoven. I had first played some of his easiest piano pieces when I was nine; at that time, Jean Sibelius, the so-called Nordic Beethoven, was still alive; Igor Stravinsky, the most celebrated Beethovenian (insofar as he was a revolutionary) of my grandparents' generation, composed the *Canticum Sacrum* that year; Pierre Boulez, one of several important musical revolutionaries of the generation that was then coming into its own, turned thirty, and the ink was hardly dry on the score of *Le Marteau sans maître,* his most influential work. I hadn't heard of Boulez then, but through my record player I wanted to get to know all of the musicians I *had* heard of, from Bach and Mozart to Bartók and Stravinsky. I loved Tchaikovsky's "1812" Overture, Rimsky-Korsakov's *Sheherazade,* and Leonard Bernstein's jazzy *Fancy Free* ballet, which began with four gun-shot-like drum beats, but Beethoven seemed to speak to me more clearly, more directly, than anyone else, and I often thought about him, about his existence. His music, but also the simplified yet not wholly erroneous published accounts of his life that I devoured, gave me sustenance and courage. Never for a moment did I identify with his genius, and I probably already sensed that my fundamental gregariousness would prevent me from becoming as unbalanced in my human relationships as he had been; yet I was always a crowd shunner, and the idea of the fist-shaking Beethoven making a cry of protest, of nonacceptance, for all to hear, appealed to me overwhelmingly. The "older" Beethoven (younger than I am now)—the Beethoven who sought transcendence—was a discovery I wasn't capable of making at so tender an age. What nourished me then was the heaven-storming "Middle Period" Beethoven. He was my constant companion.

Increasing fluency at the piano keyboard and in score reading was certainly one of my most important roads to Beethoven, as to other composers, when I was in my teens, but just as important was the presence in my life of the Cleveland Orchestra. I was able to attend its rehearsals and concerts under George Szell and other conductors thanks to a family friend who played in the great ensemble's violin section. My main highway to music, however, remained the little gray-and-white box in my bedroom in our house on Cleveland's east side. Among the earliest LPs given to me were Beethoven's Fifth and Seventh symphonies with Erich Kleiber conducting the Concertgebouw Orchestra of Amsterdam and the "Eroica" with Szell and the Cleveland. When an aunt and uncle asked me what I wanted for my twelfth birthday, in June 1958, I opted for the Ninth, and they gave me what, I believe, was the only single-disc version available at the time: Bruno Walter's, with the New York Philharmonic. I must have listened to the whole work once or twice at first, but for weeks thereafter I listened over and over to the scherzo. After that, I familiarized myself with the first movement, then the finale, and only much later the third movement, which was too difficult for even the most enthusiastic twelve-year-old to "feel" profoundly. The slow movements of the Third, Fifth, and Seventh had plenty of "exciting" bits, but in the Ninth's Adagio I had to wait too long for something to "happen"—or, as I would now say, for the sublimity to be interrupted.

At fifteen or sixteen, on first reading *Julius Caesar,* I thought of Beethoven when I came to Cassius's lines "Why, man, he doth bestride the narrow world / Like a Colossus, and we petty men / Walk under his huge legs and peep about / To find ourselves dishonorable graves." I knew that Cassius was speaking ironically and inciting Brutus to rebel against the dictator; nevertheless, those lines, taken out of context and at face value, seemed a magnificent description of Beethoven's standing with respect to most of the rest of us human beings. Again, I was fifteen or, at most, sixteen, when I had an experience that I recollect in nearly Proustian detail, listening for the first time to the String Quartet in C-sharp minor, op. 131. I was sitting in the living room of a friend's home when her father put a recording of it on the hi-fi. I remember everything about those three-quarters of an hour back in 1961 or '62: the room in

which I was sitting and the direction in which I was facing; the single, exposed Bozak speaker vibrating, like an exotic organism, in the unfinished
wooden box that Mr. L. had built to contain it; the quickly dawning realization that the first movement was the most overwhelming piece of
music I had ever heard—a feeling that comes back to me whenever I listen to it, in real sound or mentally, as at this moment; and I remember
(but this memory comes also from countless later listenings) the mysterious, throbbing sound of the first violin's statement of the opening subject in that recording, made by the Budapest Quartet in the early 1950s.

Beethoven turned up everywhere. I was nineteen the first time I took
off in an airplane after dark, and I thought, as I looked at the lights of
New York City below, "Wouldn't Beethoven have been thrilled by a sight
like this?" I was able to project him into the present in a way that I could
not have done, and never would have dreamed of doing, with the other
composers I loved. His physical existence, which had come to an end
nearly a century and a half earlier, colored my own, still fresh and young.
And I know that at the outset of my adult life, when the government of
my native country demanded that I participate in a war that I considered
unjust, cruel, stupid, and tinged with racism, Beethoven and his re-
silient, universalizing music, which seemed to transcend all human tendencies toward disunity but also, simultaneously, toward mindless
obedience—toward following the multitude to do evil—were among the
main influences that made me decide to emigrate rather than do what
was expected of me. That decision altered my life forever, damaging it in
some ways but enriching it in many more.

Half a century has passed since I received the little gray-and-white
box, and I am now several years older than Beethoven lived to be. I still
think of him as my alpha and omega, but in a different sense: as the author of music that transformed my existence at the onset of adulthood
and that continues to enrich it more than any other music as I approach
what are often referred to as life's declining years. His music still gives me
as much sensual and emotional pleasure as it gave me fifty years ago, and
far more intellectual stimulation than it did then. It adds to the fullness
when life feels good, and it lengthens and deepens the perspective when
life seems barely tolerable. It is with me and in me. And I suppose that
this book is a vastly oversized and yet entirely inadequate thank-you note
to Beethoven.

Why 1824?

Several years ago, when I was on the verge of completing a book, a friend encouraged me to choose a year that was important in the history of music and to write a book about that year, with the key musical event or events as the focal point. I liked the idea and began to think about various possibilities. One was 1912, when Stravinsky essentially completed *The Rite of Spring,* Schoenberg wrote *Pierrot Lunaire,* Debussy finished *Images* for orchestra and began work on the ballet *Jeux* and the second book of *Preludes* for piano, Ravel completed *Daphnis et Chloé,* Mahler's Ninth and Sibelius's Fourth symphonies were given their premieres, and Prokofiev burst onto the musical scene with his First Piano Concerto. Another was 1876, the year of the first Bayreuth Festival and the premiere of Brahms's First Symphony. And then there was 1830, when Berlioz's *Symphonie fantastique,* both of Chopin's piano concerti, Donizetti's *Anna Bolena,* and Bellini's *Capuleti e Montecchi* were first heard; Mendelssohn's "Scotch" and "Italian" symphonies were in the works; and the virtuosi Paganini and Liszt were conquering Europe.

In the end, however, 1824 and the Ninth Symphony's premiere attracted me more than any of the other years and events that I had considered. I suppose that the strongest reason for my choice, stronger than my intense interest in the period and its cast of characters, was the desire to talk about Beethoven and his world. Besides, this book is also *my* "ninth symphony"—my ninth published volume, if I include coauthored books. It is not the longest of them, but it is the one that has caused me the most trouble and has forced me to think, more than any of my other books, about what music means to me and what role so-called high culture played, plays, and ought to play in civilization. It has also made me restudy and reconsider Beethoven, a number of his contemporaries, the history of the period, the issue of music and meaning, and—most rewardingly of all, for me—the Ninth Symphony itself. My book is necessarily an extremely modest work in comparison with the one that made me want to write it, but if it stimulates readers to examine or reexamine the works of any of the story's protagonists or the history of the period, it will have served its purpose.

A thousand or five thousand or ten thousand years from now,

Beethoven and our civilization's other outstanding mouthpieces may still have much to communicate to human beings—if any of our descendants are still around—or they may seem remote, cold, obscure. But what matters most in Beethoven's case is his belief that we are all part of an endless continuum, whatever our individual level of awareness may be. In the Ninth Symphony, he used Schiller's words to tell us explicitly what many of his other works, especially his late works, tell us implicitly: that the "divine spark" of joy and the "kiss for the whole world," which originate "above the canopy of stars," must touch and unite us all. The spark is there, he said, and so is the kiss; we need only feel and accept their presence. The goal may prove impossible to achieve, but all the alternatives are doomed to failure.

Acknowledgments

My thanks to the staffs of the British Library, London, and the New York Public Library, for their unfailingly good-natured assistance; to Professor Scott Burnham of Princeton University, who read much of the manuscript and made helpful suggestions; to Eve Wolf, who gave me highly useful criticisms and much-needed encouragement; and to Denise Shannon, my literary agent, for her extraordinary competence and patience.

I owe very special thanks to Susanna Porter, my editor at Random House, who has seen this book through thick and thin over several years and has helped me to find my way with it—no easy task in a work with such diverse and unusual aims. Jillian Quint, her editorial colleague, has also been a careful reader and has helped me with the technological aspects of production, because my technological know-how seems more Paleolithic with every passing year.

Belinda Matthews, my editor at Faber & Faber, has enthusiastically favored this project from its inception and has waited, Penelope-like, during the periods when I was scratching my head over it.

And thanks to the various relatives and friends who have put me up and/or put up with me during my work on this book.

$\mathcal{N}otes$

Prelude

5 **"Beethoven is the quintessential genius"** Tia DeNora, *Beethoven and the Construction of Genius* (Berkeley: University of California Press, 1995).

5 **"if all the music"** Richard Wagner, *My Life*, trans. Andrew Gray and Mary Whittall (Cambridge: Cambridge University Press, 1983), p. 384.

Part One

9 **"If you have something important"** Adolf Glassbrenner, quoted in Frieder Reininghaus, *Schubert und das Wirtshaus: Musik unter Metternich* (Berlin: Oberbaum, 1979), p. 7.

10 **"lying on a disordered bed"** Michael Hamburger, ed., *Beethoven: Letters, Journals and Conversations* (Garden City, N.Y.: Anchor, 1960), p. 198.

10 **"the dreary"** and other quotes in this paragraph, ibid., pp. 207–9.

13 **"The latest news"** Christopher H. Gibbs, *The Life of Schubert* (Cambridge: Cambridge University Press, 2000), p. 117.

13 **"a new grand solemn Mass"** Emerich Kastner, ed., *Ludwig van Beethovens Sämtliche Briefe* (Tutzing, Germany: Hans Schneider, 1975), p. 706; translated by Harvey Sachs.

14 **"not just to create music"** Barry Cooper, *Beethoven and the Creative Process* (Oxford: Clarendon Press, 1990), p. 21.

15 **"a gross monster"** Nicolas Slonimsky, *Lexicon of Musical Invective* (Seattle: University of Washington Press, 1953), p. 42; partially retranslated by Harvey Sachs.

15 **"Grand Musical Academy"** From a photographic reproduction of the original poster; translated by Harvey Sachs.

19 **"what must have been"** Thomas Forrest Kelly, *First Nights: Five Musical Premieres* (New Haven, Conn.: Yale University Press, 2001), p. 143.

19 **the composer had stood** Ibid., p. 136.

20 **"Copy everything exactly"** Emily Anderson, ed., *The Letters of Beethoven* (London: Macmillan, 1961), vol. 3, pp. 1122–23.

20 **"Two women singers"** Ibid., vol. 2, p. 967.

20 **"She vomited"** H. C. Robbins Landon, *Beethoven: His Life, Work and World* (London: Thames and Hudson, 1970), p. 212.

21 **"tyrant over all"** Elliott Forbes, ed., *Thayer's Life of Beethoven* (Princeton, N.J.: Princeton University Press, 1973), p. 970.

21 **"I still see"** Ludwig Nohl, *Mosaik* (1881), quoted in Landon, *Beethoven: His Life,* p. 213.

22 **"Beethoven sat"** Landon, *Beethoven: His Life,* p. 270.

22 **"The whole symphony"** *Allgemeine musikalische Zeitung* 16, April 6, 1864, translated in ibid., pp. 355–56.

24 **"The current musical"** "Musikzustand und musikalisches Leben in Wien," *Cäcilia* 1, no. 2 (1824), pp. 193–200; quoted in David Gramit, *Cultivating Music: The Aspirations, Interests, and Limits of German Musical Culture, 1770–1848* (Berkeley: University of California Press, 2002), p. 159.

24 **"He certainly gave"** Kelly, *First Nights,* p. 112.

24 **"this truly unique Finale"** Ibid., p. 153.

27 **"I ventured in my innocence"** Anton Schindler, *Beethoven as I Knew Him* (New York: W. W. Norton, 1972), p. 232.

28 **"We'll take everything"** Karl-Heinz Köhler and Grita Herte, eds., *Ludwig van Beethovens Konversationshefte* (Leipzig, Germany: Deutscher Verlag für Musik, 1974), vol. 6, p. 151.

28 **"You talk too loud"** Ibid., p. 26.

28 **In 1822, for instance** Alice M. Hanson, *Musical Life in Biedermeier Vienna* (Cambridge: Cambridge University Press, 2009), p. 101.

29 **"Out of the wide circle"** and subsequent quotes, Albrecht, p. 5.

31 **"*the one* man"** Ibid., p. 6.

31 **Viennese beer parlor** *Konversationshefte* 6, p. 112, cited in ibid., p. 8.

32 **"felt by all musicians"** Mary Sue Morrow, *Concert Life in Haydn's Vienna: Aspects of a Developing Musical and Social Institution* (Stuyvesant, N.Y.: Pendragon Press, 1989), pp. 235–36.

33 **"After talks and discussions"** Anderson, *Letters of Beethoven,* vol. 3, p. 1121.

34 **"Sir! As I am told"** Ibid., p. 1120.

35 **"I do not accuse you"** Ibid., pp. 1124–25.

38 **somewhat resembled his grandfather** Ibid., p. 1135.

39 **"Louis van Betthoven [*sic*]"** Revision by Harvey Sachs of translation by Thayer in Forbes, ed., *Thayer's Life of Beethoven,* p. 66.

41 **"after a great deal"** Louis Lockwood, *Beethoven: The Music and the Life* (New York: W. W. Norton, 2003), pp. 3–4.

41 **"With the help"** Ibid., p. 50.

43 **"O ye men"** *Sämtliche Briefe,* translated by Harvey Sachs.

46 **"Who is he"** William H. Gilman, ed., *Selected Writing of Ralph Waldo Emerson* (New York: Signet Classics, 1965), p. 6.

48 **"the new sense of rhythm"** Charles Rosen, *The Classical Style: Haydn, Mozart, Beethoven* (New York: W. W. Norton, 1971), p. 23.

50 **"Do not rob"** Lockwood, *Beethoven,* p. 9.

52 **"the imagination must not pine away"** Saul Bellow, *Humboldt's Gift* (New York: Penguin, 1976), p. 112.

52 **"expressions of homage"** Lockwood, *Beethoven*, p. 400.

52 **"However numerous"** Anderson, *Letters of Beethoven*, vol. 2; translation altered by Harvey Sachs from the original German.

53 **effects of a laxative** Hamburger, *Beethoven*, pp. 202–3.

53 **"Beethoven has been designated"** David B. Dennis, *Beethoven in German Politics, 1870–1989* (New Haven, Conn.: Yale University Press, 1996).

54 **"imputed Sin & Righteousness"** William Blake, *Jerusalem*, in *The Complete Poetry and Selected Prose of John Donne and the Complete Poetry of William Blake* (New York: Random House, 1941), p. 922.

54 **"Your Majesty is not"** Landon, *Beethoven*, p. 211.

55 **"forever enlarged the sphere"** Maynard Solomon, *Late Beethoven: Music, Thought, Imagination* (Berkeley and Los Angeles: University of California Press, 2003), p. 1.

55 **"the condition we call exile"** Joseph Brodsky, "The Condition We Call Exile," *The New York Review of Books,* January 21, 1988, pp. 16–20.

56 **"begin anew"** Forbes, ed., *Thayer's Life of Beethoven*, pp. 1057–58.

56 **"We live 'as if' "** Claire Messud, *The Last Life* (New York: Harcourt Brace, 1999), p. 279.

56 **"He fled the world"** Forbes, ed., *Thayer's Life of Beethoven*, pp. 1057–58.

56 **"Those who flee from love"** Elsa Morante, *Menzogna e sortilegio* (Turin, Italy: Einaudi, 1994), pp. 19–20; translated by Harvey Sachs.

Part Two

65 **"musical hero"** Lockwood, *Beethoven*, p. 335.

65 **"let himself be persuaded"** Ibid., p. 335.

65 **"the best master of ceremonies"** C. de Grunwald, *La Vie de Metternich* (Paris: Calmann-Lévy, 1938), p. 141, quoted in Alan Warwick Palmer, *Metternich: Councillor of Europe* (London: Phoenix, 1997), p. 131.

65 **"held aloof inertia"** H. R. von Srbik, *Metternich, der Staatsmann und der Mensch* (Munich: F. Bruckmann, 1925), vol. 1, p. 187, quoted in Palmer, *Metternich*, pp. 131–32.

65 **"too frightened"** Palmer, *Metternich*, p. 139.

66 **"the most depressed pages"** Ford Madox Ford, *The March of Literature* (Normal, Ill.: Dalkey Archive Press, 1994), p. 780.

67 **"a pure Romantic"** Oliver Strunk, *Source Readings in Music History* (London: Faber and Faber, 1952), p. 777, quoted in Hugh Honour, *Romanticism* (New York: Harper and Row, 1979), p. 24.

68 **"artists were in this period"** Eric Hobsbawm, *The Age of Revolution: 1789–1848* (New York: Vintage Books, 1996), p. 256.

69 **"philosophy may expect attention"** G.W.F. Hegel, *Hegel's Introduction to the Lectures on the History of Philosophy*, trans. T. M. Knox and A. V. Miller (Oxford:

Oxford University Press, 1983), pp. 1–2 (from inaugural lecture at Heidelberg, October 28, 1816).

71 **"a sort of equality"** Lucio Felici and Emanuele Trevi, eds., *Leopardi: Tutte le poesie e tutte le prose* (Rome: Newton and Compton, 1997), pp. 1011–12; translated by Harvey Sachs.

72 **"Europe's civilized nations"** Ibid.

73 **"Some are home-sick"** Samuel Taylor Coleridge, "The Delinquent Travellers," in *Coleridge: Poetical Works,* ed. E. H. Coleridge (London: Oxford University Press, 1967), pp. 443–47.

74 **"wanted to eliminate"** Adam Bunnell, *Before Infallibility: Liberal Catholicism in Biedermeier Vienna* (London: Associated University Presses, 1990), p. 39.

75 **"The princes must"** Walter Consuelo Langsam, *Francis the Good: The Education of an Emperor, 1768–92* (New York: Macmillan, 1949), p. 12, quoted in *Schubert's Vienna,* ed. Raymond Erickson (New Haven, Conn.: Yale University Press, 1997), p. 4.

75 **"In the present conditions"** Donald E. Emerson, *Metternich and the Political Police: Security and Subversion in the Habsburg Monarchy, 1815–1830* (The Hague: Martinns Nijhoff, 1968), pp. 22–23, quoted in Erickson, *Schubert's Vienna,* p. 22.

75 **"several *important people*"** *Saemtliche Briefe,* p. 22; translated by Harvey Sachs.

76 **"Many eras witnessed"** Quoted in Gaia Servadio, *Rossini* (New York: Carroll and Graf, 2003), p. 97.

76 **"another time"** Georg Schünemann, ed., *Konversationshefte* (Berlin: M. Hesse, 1941), vol. 1, p. 328; quoted in Lockwood, *Beethoven,* p. 416.

77 **"And they chatter"** James J. Sheehan, *German History, 1770–1866* (Oxford: Oxford University Press, 1993), p. 446; translated by Harvey Sachs.

78 **"A strong hope"** *American State Papers,* 1, *Foreign Relations,* vol. 5, p. 245.

80 **"the hopeless warriors"** George Gordon Byron, 6th Baron Byron, *Childe Harold's Pilgrimage,* canto 2, in *The Poetical Works of Lord Byron* (London: 1870), p. 18.

81 **"a much injured body"** Leslie A. Marchand, ed., *Byron's Letters and Journals* (Cambridge, Mass.: Belknap Press, 1973), vol. 2, p. 165.

83 **"His house was filled"** Julius Millingen, *Memoirs of the Affairs of Greece* (London: J. Rodwell, 1831), p. 90, quoted in Leslie A. Marchand, *Byron: A Portrait* (New York: Knopf, 1970), p. 431.

84 **"On this day"** Byron, *Poetical Works,* p. 577.

86 **"Youth, Nature"** Marchand, *Byron's Letters and Journals,* vol. 2, pp. 18–19.

86 **"apply modern ideas"** Matthew Arnold, *Heinrich Heine* (Philadelphia: Frederick Leypoldt, 1863), pp. 30–32.

87 **"You are sad"** Alexander S. Pushkin, *The Complete Works of Alexander Pushkin,* vol. 10, *Letters: 1815–1826* (Norfolk: Milner and Co., 1963), p. 161.

89 **"everything breathes"** T. J. Binyon, *Pushkin: A Biography* (London: HarperCollins, 2002), p. 157.

89 **"the Holy Spirit"** Pushkin, *Complete Works,* vol. 10, p. 156.

90 **The deaf English philosopher** Elaine Feinstein, *Pushkin* (New York: Ecco, 2000), p. 100.

90 "He vanished" Stephanie Sandler, *Distant Pleasures: Alexander Pushkin and the Writing of Exile* (Stanford, Calif.: Stanford University Press, 1989), p. 60.

91 **Pushkin considered *Boris*** Feinstein, *Pushkin*, p. 124.

92 "'Tis no easy thing" Alexander S. Pushkin, *Boris Godunov*, trans. A. Hayes (www.fullbooks.com/boris-godunov1.html; trans. originally published in 1918).

92 "Is there any safety" Ibid.

92 "I like not" Ibid.

93 "For many a year" (www.fullbooks.com/boris-godunov2.html; trans originally published in 1918).

93 "The PEOPLE" Ibid., p. 84.

93 "Whether we can take" Sandler, *Distant Pleasures*, p. 107.

93 "I want glory" Alexander Pushkin, "The Desire for Glory," in Sandler, *Distant Pleasures*, p. 16.

96 "j'ai commencé" Eugène Delacroix, *Journal, 1822–1863* (Paris: Plon, 1996), pp. 48–49, translated by Harvey Sachs.

96 **looked more like plague victims** Stendhal [Marie-Henri Beyle], "Salon de 1824" in *Journal de Paris*, reported in J. H. Rubin, "Delacroix and Romanticism," in *The Cambridge Companion to Delacroix*, ed. Beth S. Wright (Cambridge: Cambridge University Press, 2001), p. 32.

96 "vast and terrible" Margaret Drabble, *The Sea Lady* (London: Penguin Fig Tree, 2006), pp. 233–35.

98 "The human spirit" Delacroix, *Journal*, pp. 77–78, translated by Harvey Sachs.

99 "Painting is nothing but" Eugène Delacroix, journal entry, quoted in Wright, *Cambridge Companion to Delacroix*, pp. 1–2.

99 "I must Create a System" Blake, *Jerusalem*, p. 902.

99 "The symphonies of Beethoven" Walter Pach, *Ingres* (New York: Hacker Art Books, 1973), pp. 19, 209.

100 "Nature is nothing but" Charles Baudelaire, "L'Œuvre et la vie d'Eugène Delacroix," in *Œuvres complètes*, ed. Claude Pichois (Paris: Gallimard, 1976), vol. 2, pp. 744–47; translated by Harvey Sachs.

101 "music with learned" John W. Klein, "Stendhal as Music Critic," in *The Musical Quarterly* 29, no. 1 (January 1943), p. 18.

101 "Michelangelo-like" Stendhal, *Vie de Rossini*, quoted in *Stendhal: L'Ame de la musique*, ed. Suzel Esquier (Paris: Editions Stock, 1999), pp. 388, 394; translated by Harvey Sachs.

101 "I am of the opinion" Stendhal, *Racine et Shakespeare: Études sur le romantisme* (Paris: Garnier-Flammarion, 1970), p. 51; translated by Harvey Sachs.

102 **Duke of Wellington** Ibid., p. 135.

102 "over seven months' time" Ibid., p. 144.

102 "the art of presenting" Ibid., p. 71.

103 "France, which had seen" Stendhal [Marie-Henri Beyle], *Paris-Londres: Chroniques* (Paris: Stock, 1997), p. 165; translated by Harvey Sachs.

103 "to avoid the ridicule" Ibid., p. 169; translated by Harvey Sachs.

104 "As I write this" Hugo Bieber, ed., *Heinrich Heine: A Biographical Anthology*,

trans. Moses Hadas (Philadelphia: The Jewish Publication Society of America, 1956), p. 170.

104   **"famous for its sausages"**   Heinrich Heine, *Works of Prose,* trans. E. B. Ashton (New York: L. B. Fischer, 1943), pp. 37–38.

105   **"Heine's eyes must have been"**   Ford, *March of Literature,* pp. 698, 719–20.

106   **"seven closely-printed"**   Arnold, *Heinrich Heine,* p. 21.

106   **"By the sea"**   Heinrich Heine, "Fragen" ("Questions"), from *Nordseebilder (North Sea Pictures),* 1824–1826, translated by Harvey Sachs.

107   **"philosophical-Christian soldiery"**   Philip Kossoff, *Valiant Heart: A Biography of Heinrich Heine* (New York, London: Cornwall Books, 1983), p. 151.

107   **"against the wicked"**   Heinrich Heine, *Selected Works,* trans. and ed. by Helen M. Mustard (New York: Random House, 1973), p. 281.

108   **"If anyone asks you"**   Heinrich Heine, *Works of Prose,* ed. Hermann Kester, trans. E. B. Ashton (New York: L. B. Fischer, 1943), p. 310.

108   **"Paris is the new Jerusalem"**   Antonina Vallentin, *Heine: Poet in Exile,* trans. Harrison Brown (New York: Doubleday, 1956), p. 157.

108   **"Not for themselves"**   Heinrich Heine, "Ludwig Börne: A Memorial," in *The Romantic School and Other Essays,* ed. Jost Hermand and Robert C. Holub (New York: Continuum, 1985), p. 282.

108   **"all men are equal"**   Ibid., pp. 263–64.

109   **"To me, it is"**   Michael Mann, ed., *Heinrich Heine: Zeitungsberichte über Musik und Malerei* (Frankfurt am Main, Germany: Insel-Verlag, 1964), p. 116; translated by Harvey Sachs.

109   **"I am for the autonomy"**   Kossoff, *Valiant Heart,* p. 151.

110   **"great confederation"**   Heinrich Heine, *Memoirs: From His Works, Letters, and Conversations* (London: John Lane, 1920), p. 282.

110   **"I know not"**   Arnold, *Heinrich Heine,* p. 3.

110   **"a refusal to deepen"**   Federico Fellini, *Fare un film* (Turin, Italy: Einaudi, 1980), pp. 155–56; translated by Harvey Sachs.

Part Three

117   **"In the earlier"**   Roger Norrington, "In Search of Beethoven: A Fascinating Look at Contemporary Interpretations of His Music," 2001, http://www.unitel.de/uhilites/150201.htm.

117   **"the return to the tremolo"**   Martin Gregor-Dellin and Dietrich Mack, eds., *Cosima Wagner's Diaries,* trans. Geoffrey Skelton (New York: Harcourt Brace Jovanovich, 1978–83), vol. 2, p. 370.

118   **"the logically unanswerable"**   Bellow, *Humboldt's Gift,* p. 332.

118   **"It is in the very nature"**   Wilhelm Furtwängler, *Concerning Music,* trans. L. J. Lawrence (London: Boosey and Hawkes, 1953), p. 44.

118   **"The thoughts which"**   Felix Mendelssohn to Marc-André Souchay, October 15, 1842, in *Felix Mendelssohn: A Life in Letters,* trans. Craig Tomlinson (New York: Fromm International, 1986), p. 314.

118 **"what this first movement"**   Gregor-Pellin and Mack, *Cosima Wagner's Diaries,* vol. 2, p. 855.

118 **"The composer's answer"**   Michael Murray, ed., *A Jacques Barzun Reader* (New York: HarperCollins, 2002), pp. 325–29.

119 **"the words of Haydn's"**   Ibid., p. 329.

120 **"In the first movement"**   James R. Oestreich, "A Pianist Who Balances Acclaim and Assists," *The New York Times,* May 4, 2008.

121 **"intolerable yearning"**   J.W.N. Sullivan, *Beethoven: His Spiritual Development.*

123 **"a tremendous and intensely"**   Alfred Einstein, *A Short History of Music* (New York: Vintage Books, 1957), p. 147.

123 **"In its freedom"**   Ibid.

126 **"I cannot write in verse"**   "Letters" column, *The New York Review of Books,* December 6, 2007, p. 76.

127 **"hesitated for some time"**   Edith Wharton, "A Backward Glance," in *Edith Wharton: Novellas and Other Writings* (New York: Library of America, 1990), p. 933.

129 **"To see or listen to"**   Michael Tanner, "Art and Morality," *Routledge Encyclopedia of Philosophy,* ed. Edward Craig (London: Routledge, 1998), vol. 1.

129 **"to compare Bach"**   Furtwängler, *Concerning Music,* p. 29.

129 **"Philosophy has the universal"**   Hegel, *Hegel's Introduction to the Lectures,* pp. 55–56.

130 **"To analyze such a composition"**   Hector Berlioz, *Beethoven* (Paris: Editions Corréa, 1941), p. 61; translated by Harvey Sachs.

130 **"the musical symbolization"**   Solomon, *Late Beethoven,* pp. 201–2.

131 **"personal ideas"**   Berlioz, *Beethoven,* pp. 61–62.

131 **"Religion has been disfigured"**   Benjamin Constant, *De la religion considérée dans sa source, ses formes, et ses développements* 1 (Spring 1824), in *Oeuvres* (Paris: Gallimard, 1957), p. 1369; translated by Harvey Sachs.

131 **"denounced the first movement"**   Lockwood, *Beethoven,* p. 420.

132 **"a drowsy reverie"**   Murray, *Jacques Barzun Reader,* p. 336.

132 **"a purely sensual"**   Richard Strauss, *Betrachtungen und Erinnerungen,* ed. Willi Schuh (Zurich: Atlantis-Verlag, 1949), p. 103.

132 **"The discussion of purely"**   Furtwängler, *Concerning Music,* p. 43.

134 **"refined music"**   Quoted in David Gramit, *Cultivating Music* (Berkeley: University of California Press, 2002), p. 62.

135 **"Beethoven realized"**   David Benjamin Levy, *Beethoven: The Ninth Symphony* (New York: Schirmer Books, 1995), p. 49.

138 **"never before"**   Ibid., p. 61.

143 **"a small rustic bagpipe"**   Ibid., p. 71.

145 **"It lifts me"**   Harvey Sachs, ed., *The Letters of Arturo Toscanini* (New York: Alfred A. Knopf, 2002), p. 298.

145 **"a gently opening curtain"**   Levy, *Beethoven,* p. 78.

149 **"come to the end"**   John Updike, "Late Works," *The New Yorker,* August 7, 2006.

151 **"[Schindler:] how many"**   Ludwig van Beethoven, *Konversationshefte* (Leipzig,

Germany: VEB Deutscher Verlag für Musik, 1970), vol. 9, p. 249; translated by Harvey Sachs.

152 **"the musician in [Beethoven]"** Furtwängler, *Concerning Music,* p. 38.

153 **"elicited by a 'rememberer'"** Elaine Sisman, "Memory and Invention at the Threshold of Beethoven's Late Style," in *Beethoven and His World,* ed. Scott Burnham and Michael P. Steinberg (Princeton, N.J.: Princeton University Press, 2000), p. 79.

155 **"Joy, beautiful divine spark"** Translated by Harvey Sachs.

158 **"transcends the humble"** Robert S. Hatten, *Musical Meaning in Beethoven* (Bloomington: Indiana University Press, 1994), pp. 81–82.

Part Four

165 **"Universal History"** Thomas Carlyle, *On Heroes, Hero-Worship, and the Heroic in History* (Teddington, Middlesex: Echo Library, 2007), p. 4.

167 **"Art and science"** Lockwood, *Beethoven,* p. 9.

168 **"Beethoven began to stir"** Charles Baudelaire, "Sur mes contemporains: VII— Théodore de Banville" (1861), in *Œuvres complètes,* ed. Claude Pichois (Paris: Gallimard, 1976), vol. 2, p. 168; translated by Harvey Sachs.

169 **"The personal ideals"** Conrad L. Donakowski, *A Muse for the Masses: Ritual and Music in an Age of Democratic Revolution, 1770–1870* (Chicago: University of Chicago Press, 1977), p. 68.

169 **"Beethoven is the only man"** David Cairns, *Berlioz: The Making of an Artist* (Berkeley: University of California Press, 2000), p. 318.

170 **"the influence of Balzac"** James Gibbon Huneker, "Interesting New French Books," *New York Times Saturday Book Review,* June 16, 1906.

170 **"I feel that I am"** Christopher H. Gibbs, *The Life of Schubert* (Cambridge: Cambridge University Press, 2000), p. 117.

171 **"Secretly, in my heart"** John Reed, *Schubert: The Final Years* (New York: St. Martin's Press, 1972), p. 127.

171 **Peripheral resemblances** Brian Newbould, *Schubert: The Music and the Man* (Berkeley: University of California Press, 1997), p. 380, and Thrasybulos G. Georgiades, *Schubert: Musik und Lyrik* (Göttingen, Germany: Vandenhoeck and Ruprecht, 1967).

171 **"Beethoven's titanic figure"** Peter Clive, *Schubert and His World: A Biographical Dictionary* (Oxford: Clarendon Press, 1997), p. 11.

172 **"It is when one has heard"** Hector Berlioz, *Correspondance générale,* ed. Pierre Citron (Paris: Flammarion, 1972), vol. 2, p. 168; translated by Harvey Sachs.

172 **"Now that I've heard"** Ibid., p. 229.

172 **"climbed so high"** Ibid., p. 244.

173 **"Berlioz believes in Beethoven"** Cairns, *Berlioz: The Making of an Artist,* p. 318.

174 **"calmly asserted"** Jacques Barzun, *Berlioz and His Century* (Chicago: University of Chicago Press, 1982), p. 62.

174 **"There are half a dozen"** Berlioz, *Beethoven,* pp. 76–77.

174 **"Certain critics regard"** Ibid., p. 61.

174 "This Allegro maestoso" Ibid., pp. 63–64.

175 "If the audience" Ibid., p. 72.

176 "an excitement almost unparalleled" David Cairns, *Berlioz: Servitude and Greatness* (Berkeley: University of California Press, 2000), pp. 484–87.

176 "Our age needs" Anderson, *Letters of Beethoven,* vol. 3, p. 1243.

177 "a performance of Beethoven's" Robert I. Letellier, ed. and trans., *The Diaries of Giacomo Meyerbeer* (Madison, N.J.: Fairleigh Dickinson University Press, 1999), vol. 1, p. 414.

177 " 'did not strike' " Quoted in Heinz and Gudrun Becker, eds., *Giacomo Meyerbeer: A Life in Letters,* trans. Mark Violette (London: Christopher Helm, 1983), pp. 30–31.

177 "which I had never" Letellier, *Diaries,* vol. 4, p. 245.

178 "was unable to understand" Leonard Schapiro, *Turgenev: His Life and Times* (New York: Random House, 1978), pp. 125–26.

178 "as masterpiece of invention" Letellier, *Diaries,* vol. 3, p. 398.

178 "really enjoy" Elvers, *Felix Mendelssohn,* p. 178.

180 "I am the blind man" Robert Schumann, "Nach der D moll-Symphonie," in *Gesammelte Schriften über Musik und Musiker Musiker,* vol. 1, pp. 28–30; translated by Harvey Sachs.

180 "Yes, just love him" Ibid.

181 "Listen, I have a request" Eva Weissweiler, ed., *The Complete Correspondence of Clara and Robert Schumann,* trans. Hildegard Fritsch and Ronald L. Crawford (New York: Peter Lang, 1994), vol. 1, p. 95.

181 "Does a great man" Robert Schumann, *On Music and Musicians,* ed. Konrad Wolff, trans. Paul Rosenfeld (New York: McGraw-Hill, 1964), p. 101.

182 "became the mystical lodestar" Wagner, *My Life,* p. 35.

182 "What first attracted me" Ibid., pp. 35–36.

182 "For a long time" Richard Wagner, *Sämtliche Briefe,* ed. G. Strobel and W. Wolf (Leipzig, Germany: VEB Deutscher Verlag für Musik, 1967), vol. 1, p. 117.

183 "renowned orchestra" Wagner, *My Life,* pp. 174–75.

183 "Thus the master" Richard Wagner, "Das Kunstwerk der Zukunft," in *Source Readings in Music History,* ed. Oliver Strunk and Leo Treitler (New York: W. W. Norton, 1998), pp. 1108–9.

187 "the last movement with its chorus" Richard Wagner, *Selected Letters of Richard Wagner,* trans. Stewart Spencer and Barry Millington (New York: W. W. Norton, 1988), p. 343.

187 transmigration of souls Klaus Kropfinger, *Wagner and Beethoven: Richard Wagner's Reception of Beethoven,* trans. Peter Palmer (Cambridge: Cambridge University Press, 1991), pp. 24–25.

187 "All wisdom" Gregor-Dellin and Mack, *Cosima Wagner's Diaries,* vol. 1, p. 86.

187 "plays the beginning" Ibid., vol. 2, p. 994.

187 "the melody" Ibid., vol. 1, p. 450.

187 "talked a lot about" Ibid., p. 491.

188 "in fact has no melody" Ibid., vol. 2, p. 611.

188 "curious that this work" Ibid., p. 470.

188 "always strikes me"   Ibid., vol. 1, p. 450.

188 "Should one wish"   Ibid., vol. 2, p. 173.

188 "R. plays the adagio"   Ibid., p. 370.

188 "that rousing of oneself"   Ibid., p. 762.

189 "To discover these two themes"   Ibid., p. 830.

189 "wild"   Ibid., p. 855.

189 "a wonderful piece"   Ibid., p. 857.

190 "If Beethoven is a prodigy"   Edmond Michotte, "La Visite de Richard Wagner a Rossini," in *Rossini,* ed. Luigi Rognoni (Milan: Guanda, 1956), p. 344; translated by Harvey Sachs.

191 "I'm waiting now"   Guido Zavadini, *Donizetti* (Bergamo, Italy: Instituto Italiano d'arti grafiche, 1948), p. 590; translated by Harvey Sachs.

191 "never forget"   Ibid., p. 602.

191 "going out immediately"   Ibid., p. 590.

191 "I would like to be *Mozart*"   Ibid., p. 640.

191 "There is something more"   Gaetano Cesari and Alessandro Luzio, eds., *I copialettere di Giuseppe Verdi* (Milan: Commissione esecutiva per le onoranze a Giuseppe Verdi nel primo centenario della nascita, 1913), p. 621; translated by Harvey Sachs.

192 "that would have let people"   Ibid., p. 626.

193 "three colossi"   Ibid., p. 415.

Illustration Credits

Index

Page numbers in *italics* refer to illustrations. Works with titles listed alphabetically and not following a composer's name are by Beethoven.

HARVEY SACHS's previous books—of which there are more than fifty editions in fifteen languages—include what have long been the standard biographies of Arturo *Toscanini* and Arthur *Rubinstein;* a history (*Music in Fascist Italy*); two collections of essays on musical subjects (*Virtuoso* and *Reflections on Toscanini*); *The Letters of Arturo Toscanini,* which he compiled, translated, and edited; and, as co-author, the memoirs of Plácido Domingo (*My First Forty Years*) and Sir Georg Solti (*Memoirs*). He has published over six hundred articles in *The New Yorker, The New York Times, The Wall Street Journal, The Times Literary Supplement* (London), *La Stampa,* and dozens of other newspapers and periodicals, and has written for the BBC, PBS, CBC (Canada), RAI (Italy), RSI (Switzerland), and other radio and television networks. He has lectured at more than seventy North American and European universities and cultural institutions and has been a Guggenheim Fellow and a Fellow of the New York Public Library's Cullman Center for Scholars and Writers. Sachs was born and raised in the United States, has lived most of his adult life in Canada and Europe, but now lives in New York. He is a former Artistic Director of the Società del Quartetto di Milano and is currently on the faculty of the Curtis Institute of Music in Philadelphia.

ABOUT THE TYPE

This book was set in Garamond, a typeface originally designed by the Parisian type cutter Claude Garamond (1480–1561). This version of Garamond was modeled on a 1592 specimen sheet from the Egenolff-Berner foundry, which was produced from types assumed to have been brought to Frankfurt by the punch cutter Jacques Sabon (d. 1580).

Claude Garamond's distinguished romans and italics first appeared in *Opera Ciceronis* in 1543–44. The Garamond types are clear, open, and elegant.